To the members of my family to whom I owe everything: my mother Luciana, my father Tullio, and my husband Andrea. They are the ones who taught me to trust that the dots would somehow connect in my future.

Palgrave Macmillan Studies in Banking and Financial Institutions

Series Editor
Philip Molyneux
University of Sharjah
Sharjah, United Arab Emirates

The Palgrave Macmillan Studies in Banking and Financial Institutions series is international in orientation and includes studies of banking systems in particular countries or regions as well as contemporary themes such as Islamic Banking, Financial Exclusion, Mergers and Acquisitions, Risk Management, and IT in Banking. The books focus on research and practice and include up to date and innovative studies that cover issues which impact banking systems globally.

More information about this series at
http://www.palgrave.com/gp/series/14678

Laura Chiaramonte

Bank Liquidity and the Global Financial Crisis

The Causes and Implications of Regulatory Reform

palgrave
macmillan

Laura Chiaramonte
Department of Economics and
Business Administration, Faculty of
Economics
Università Cattolica del Sacro Cuore
Milan, Italy

Palgrave Macmillan Studies in Banking and Financial Institutions
ISSN 2523-336X ISSN 2523-3378 (electronic)
ISBN 978-3-030-06844-8 ISBN 978-3-319-94400-5 (eBook)
https://doi.org/10.1007/978-3-319-94400-5

Cover illustration: Oliver Burston/Alamy Stock Photo
Cover design by Laura de Grasse

Printed on acid-free paper

This Palgrave Macmillan imprint is published by the registered company Springer International Publishing AG part of Springer Nature
The registered company address is: Gewerbestrasse 11, 6330 Cham, Switzerland

Foreword

The subprime crisis, originating in the US real estate financing sector, highlighted the significant interconnections between financial systems and markets and the underlying fragility of many important banking intermediation sectors (investment banking, specialist financing, international financial activity). It also highlighted one of the types of banking crisis less frequent in the financial history and, in some ways, less investigated and known: the liquidity crisis. Traditionally associated with rare events and investigated mainly in its final and most evident manifestation (a bank run), often involving non-primary subjects and cases of embezzlement, falsification or contextual factors deranging normal management dynamics and utterly undermining investor confidence, in this instance the liquidity crisis had very different characteristics. It rapidly became a global phenomenon, sweeping through leading financial systems, starting with the most dynamic and innovative, and had lasting consequences on the functioning of financial mechanisms and markets. The crisis hit institutions of different nature and size, including massive international banks, requiring large-scale public intervention via, among other things, substantial and prolonged liquidity injections into the markets by central banks.

From the point of view of banking management, in a framework of financial innovation and globalization, the crisis revealed the deep and complex relationship between the quality of assets and banking liquidity, as well as the intrinsic risk of banks taking on high levels of leverage and adopting innovative, but potentially unstable business models (such as the Originate To Distribute model, OTD).

From the point of view of the financial markets—in all their ramifications—the crisis sharply highlighted one of the most unpleasant consequences of globalization and computerized transactions: the massively increased sensitivity of operators of all kinds and the spread of unidirectional tendencies that are hard to counteract (a market run) and far more dangerous than 'traditional' bank runs.

In terms of banking and financial supervision, the crisis demonstrated the limited overall effectiveness of the regulatory framework, the limitations of the independence of supervisory authorities, and significant shortcomings in coordination between supervisors at the international level. These negative or limiting aspects also applied to the regulations and restrictions designed to control liquidity risks in banks. Unsurprisingly, later on, after a profound rethinking of the overall approach to banking and financial supervision, for the first time liquidity risk came to occupy a central position, shaping the most recent version of the Basel Accords (Basel III), with the introduction of two coefficients: the Liquidity Coverage Ratio (LCR) and the Net Stable Funding Ratio (NSFR). In addition, principles for the proper supervision and management of liquidity risk were established along with related monitoring tools. In other words, liquidity risk and liquidity crises became the main focus, with a primary role both in banking policies and supervisory action.

Laura Chiaramonte's book explores this crucial function of banking and financial activity in a complete and deep way, in terms of both the size of markets, supervisory and control policies, and the management equilibrium of intermediaries. Specifically, it analyzes the nature and characteristics of 'bank liquidity' phenomenon in multidimensional terms, (i.e. from the point of view of central banks, markets and intermediaries), the causes, implications and consequences of liquidity crises in light of recent experience; the relationship between liquidity crises and bank insolvencies; the role of central banks in the regulation of the interbank market and to support the credit system; and the implications of liquidity risk management in banks.

The work ends with an in-depth analysis of the new Liquidity Regulatory Framework of Basel III, the potential implementation strategies by banks and the consequences of regulation in terms of costs and benefits.

Overall, the book provides a broad, closely argued and up-to-date examination of banking liquidity management that, in the post-globalization world, significantly impacted the overall stability of banking systems, the functioning of financial markets and, ultimately, the development prospects of the economy as a whole. This will be of relevant interest to academics and practitioners who want to understand what happened and the resulting changes and trends in the management and market environment.

University of Verona, Italy Roberto Bottiglia

Roberto Bottiglia is Full Professor in Banking and Finance at the University of Verona—Italy, where he teaches Bank Management. He graduated in Business Administration from the Bocconi University of Milan. Research topics include agricultural credit, financial marketing, IT in banking, the structure of financial systems and banks'strategies, and the crisis of the major banking groups in Europe and the USA.

Contents

About the Author

Laura Chiaramonte is Associate Professor in Banking and Finance at Università Cattolica del Sacro Cuore of Milan, Italy. She gained her Bachelor's in Business Economics and Ph.D. in Business Administration from the University of Verona, Italy. Her main research includes the role of bank credit default swaps (CDSs) in the financial crisis of 2007–2009, the role of cooperative banks in promoting bank stability, the reliability of the Z-score in predicting bank failure, and the role of the Basel III capital and liquidity ratios in reducing bank distress phenomena. Her research has been published in journals, such as *The European Journal of Finance*, *The British Accounting Review*, *European Financial Management*, and *Financial Markets, Institutions and Instruments*.

Acronyms and Abbreviations

ABSs	Asset Backed Securities
AIG	American International Group
ALCO	Asset and Liability COmmittee
ALM	Asset and Liability Management
APP	Asset Purchase Program
ASF	Available Stable Funding
BCBS	Basel Committee on Banking Supervision
BIS	Bank for International Settlements
CBPP	Covered Bonds Purchase Program
CC	Counterbalancing Capacity
CCP	Cash Capital Position
CDOs	Collateralized Debt Obligations
CDSs	Credit Default Swaps
CEBS	Committee of European Banking Supervisors
CFP	Contingency Funding Plan
CLGs	Cumulative Liquidity Gaps
CP	Commercial paper
CPFF	Commercial Paper Funding Facility
CPSS	Committee on Payment and Settlement Systems
DLCR	Dutch Liquidity Coverage Ratio
DNB	Dutch National Bank
DSGE	Dynamic Stochastic General Equilibrium
DVP	Delivery versus Payment
EBA	European Banking Authority
ECAI	External Credit Assessment Institution
ECB	European Central Bank

EFSM	European Financial Stability Mechanism
FED	Federal Reserve
FOMC	Federal Open Market Committee
FSA	Financial Service Authority
FSB	Financial Stability Board
FSF	Financial Stability Forum
FTP	Funds Transfer Pricing
GDP	Gross Domestic Product
GFC	Global Financial Crisis
HQLA	High Quality Liquid Assets
IAS	International Accounting Standards
IFRS	International Financial Reporting Standards
IIF	International Institute of Finance
ILG	Individual Liquidity Guidance
IMF	International Monetary Fund
LB	Liquidity Buffer
LCR	Liquidity Coverage Ratio
LTCM	Long Term Capital Management
LTD	Loan To Deposit ratio
LTROs	Long-Term Refinancing Operations
LTV	Loan-to-value ratio
M&As	Merger and Acquisitions
MBSs	Mortgage Backed Securities
MLG	Marginal Liquidity Gaps
MMFs	Money Market Funds
NSFR	Net Stable Funding Ratio
OBS	Off-balance sheet
ODR	Official Discount Rate
OIS	Overnight Indexed Swap
OMTs	Outright Monetary Transactions
OTC	Over The Counter
OTD	Originate To Distribute
OTH	Originate To Hold
PSEs	Public Sector Entities
PSS	Payment and Settlement Systems
PVP	Payment versus Payment
QIS	Quantitative Impact Studies
Repos	Repurchase agreements
RFQ	Request for quote
RMBS	Residential Mortgage Backed Securities
ROA	Return on assets
ROE	Return on equity

RSF	Required Stable Funding
RTGS	Real Time Gross Settlements
SIFIs	Systemically Important Financial Institutions
SIV	Structured Investment Vehicle
SLR	Structural Liquidity Ratio
SMEs	Small- and Medium-sized Enterprises
SMP	Securities Markets Program
SPV	Special Pourpose Vehicle
SRR	Special Resolution Regime
TLTROs	Targeted Long-Term Refinancing Operations
UK	United Kingdom
US	United States
VRDNs	Variable rate demand notes

List of Figures

List of Tables

CHAPTER 1

Introduction

The Global Financial Crisis (GFC), originated in 2007 from United States (US) subprime mortgage loans, brought to the attention of regulators the issue of bank liquidity and its efficient management in ensuring bank stability. Until then, liquidity risk was underestimated by prudential regulation, since it was thought that illiquidity problems did not jeopardize bank stability and consequently the financial system as a whole. Both with Basel I (1988) and with Basel II (2004) Accords, regulators required banks only to comply with international capital requirements. Liquidity risk was managed by non-harmonized and very different procedures between countries, based on rigid rules that were partly inadequate given the degree of market sophistication.

However, between 2007 and 2009, many banks, particularly large institutions in nodal positions in the network of interbank and interfinancial relations, not only American, but also European banks, through accentuated market integration, suffered liquidity shocks due to the difficulty of finding alternative sources of funding, the lack of creditor confidence and the immediate need to rebuild liquidity reserves. In relation to the latter, their actions further aggravated financial instability and systemic liquidity strains. They sought to obtain liquidity by selling financial assets, with significant decreases in their value, revoking credit positions on both the interbank market and with other financial institutions (wholesale funding). This had two serious effects: on the one hand, the impact of the losses on bank equity (demonstrating the

L. Chiaramonte, *Bank Liquidity and the Global Financial Crisis*,
Palgrave Macmillan Studies in Banking and Financial Institutions,
https://doi.org/10.1007/978-3-319-94400-5_1

connection between liquidity risk and capital equilibrium) and, on the other, the interruption of trading on the interbank market, which ceased to function as a liquidity exchange. In this context, the failure of Lehman Brothers (in September 2008), set off a systemic liquidity crisis throughout 2009, followed by extraordinary and urgent interventions from central banks all over the world aimed at stabilizing and preventing banking crises through significant capital and liquidity injections.

In this context, in 2010, the Basel Committee on Banking Supervision (BCBS) proposed a revision of the regulatory framework at international level to strengthen banks and banking systems. The new regulation, the Basel III Accord, introduced two liquidity indicators for banks: the Liquidity Coverage Ratio (LCR), which came into effect gradually after 2015 and set out to ensure the survival of banks for one month in even acute stress; and the Net Stable Funding Ratio (NSFR), which came into effect in 2018 and aims to avoid structural imbalances in the maturity composition of liabilities and assets over a period of one year.

Although Basel III liquidity rules are geared to ensuring greater banking system stability, they may change the functioning of banks, their profitability, their capacity to lend to the real economy, and so their relationship with the market. In view of this, the aim of this book is to provide a comprehensive understanding of the bank liquidity crisis during the GFC, of the liquidity regulatory reform introduced by Basel III, and its micro and macroeconomic implications.

The book is organised as follow. Chapter 2 provides a discussion of the concept of bank liquidity and its related risk, distinguishing between three different liquidity (risk) types: central bank liquidity (risk), funding and market liquidity (risk). This chapter continues with an analysis of liquidity (risk) interconnections and their impact on financial stability in various scenarios: periods of normality or turbulence, underlining the role of central banks as an immediate, but temporary instrument in managing a liquidity crisis. In light of the strong interlinking of financial and capital equilibrium (underestimated as the GFC of 2007–2009 made clear), the chapter clarifies the linkage between liquidity and solvency, two related but non interchangeable concepts. The difference between the two terms is fundamental because policy actions to address an insolvency or liquidity crisis vary dramatically and assessing the underlying problems of banks is therefore crucial.

This chapter then gives on an overview of the bidirectional relationships of liquidity risk with other risks and the circular pattern of cause-effect. It ends with the description of the factors that over time aggravated the liquidity risk and its management.

Chapter 3 focuses on the banking liquidity crisis of 2007–2009, investigating the origin and causes of the crisis originating with US subprime mortgage loans. It moves on to discuss the emergence of bank liquidity problems during the GFC, analyzing the characteristics of the banks most affected by the liquidity crisis and the type of liquidity problems they faced. It explains how the liquidity crisis turned into a solvency crisis for financial institutions, undermining banking stability. It points to the lessons that can be learned from the GFC, particularly with regard to liquidity risk.

The third chapter ends with an overview of leading studies into the nature of liquidity crises and the policies designed to prevent and manage them, including the importance of the role of central banks and the interbank market in bank liquidity management.

Chapter 4 therefore analyses the link between monetary policy and the management of bank liquidity, firstly focusing on the operating framework of the three main central banks involved in the crisis (the European Central Bank—ECB, the Federal Reserve—FED, and the Bank of England) and the adoption of exceptional instruments put in place to deal with the crisis. Then the chapter reviews the main theoretical contributions related to the role of the interbank market in the transmission of financial crises, examining the functioning of this market during the GFC.

Chapters 5 and 6 shift the focus to bank liquidity regulation. The GFC demonstrated how regulators at the international level had failed to set up homogeneous rules of conduct for banks in terms of liquidity risk management, left to the broad discretion of individual national supervisory authorities. The two chapters examine bank liquidity regulations before and after the GFC. Specifically, Chapter 5 focuses on the Basel I Accord (1988) and the failure of the BCBS to envisage banking liquidity risk. Only in 1992 did the BCBS address the problem of ensuring minimum standards for managing liquidity risk in international banks; however, it limited itself to a report setting out the best practices to measure and manage this risk. The Basel II Accord (2004), and in particular its second pillar, introduced a qualitative supervisory model, but left individual national regulators to consider further measures to monitor and prevent banking illiquidity. The third pillar, relating to disclosure, is also discussed; here, Basel II gave broad discretion to national supervisors in relation to the need to oblige banks to disclose their exposure to, and management of, liquidity risk. Chapter 5 gives ample space to both the aims pursued by liquidity risk management and its main components. It concludes with an analysis of the supervisors' role in liquidity risk management.

Providing a thorough analysis of the new liquidity regulation, Chapter 6 initially focuses on the principles for sound liquidity management and supervision (the so-called Sound Principles) defined by the Basel Committee in September 2008 and then on the content of the Basel III Accord of 2010 (and its subsequent amendments). With reference to the latter, the chapter describes the two minimum liquidity standards for banks, the LCR and NSFR, and then gives an overview of liquidity and monitoring tools designed to strengthen and further promote global consistency in the supervision of liquidity risk.

The seventh chapter reviews the results of the existing empirical studies and analyses the implications of the Basel III liquidity requirements both at the individual bank (microeconomic) level and market (macroeconomic) level. It also looks at the results of Quantitative Impact Studies (QIS) carried out by the BCBS on a representative sample of banks in order to draw some preliminary considerations on the ability of banks to adapt to the new Basel III liquidity ratios and the strategies adopted to comply with the LCR and the NSFR, highlighting the potential differences between the geographical areas considered.

Finally, Chapter 8 concludes the book underlining the importance of keeping the liquidity risk well monitored in the future.

CHAPTER 2

The Concept of Bank Liquidity and Its Risk

2.1 Definition of Bank Liquidity

During the Global Financial Crisis (GFC) which began in the United States (US) in late 2007, albeit with relatively high capital levels, many banks faced difficulties because they had failed to manage liquidity properly. These events highlighted the importance of liquidity in the functioning of the banking sector and spurred regulators and policy makers to pay special attention to liquidity and its risk management in the banking industry (Vento and La Ganga 2009).[1] This interest became urgent during the GFC because the liquidity shortfall in one bank was able to infect and destabilize the entire financial system, since a collapse in confidence in one institution was likely to spread to all others seen as exposed to the same or similar problems. Therefore, studying and understanding liquidity is a very important topic, especially for banks, given that they act as liquidity providers and financial intermediaries in the financial system. However, understanding the term liquidity is an arduous task, fraught with ambiguity due to multiple facets and definitions (Goodhart 2008). Indeed, it has been said that 'liquidity is easier to recognize than define' (Crockett 2008) and is an elusive concept. For example, in the economic literature the notion of liquidity is related to the ability of an economic agent to exchange his or her existing wealth for goods and services or other assets (Williamson 2008). In this definition, two features come to the fore. First, liquidity can be understood as a flow concept

L. Chiaramonte, *Bank Liquidity and the Global Financial Crisis*,
Palgrave Macmillan Studies in Banking and Financial Institutions,
https://doi.org/10.1007/978-3-319-94400-5_2

and not as stock. Second, liquidity is linked to the ability to carry out these flows. Failure to do so would render the financial entity illiquid. Therefore, in this framework, liquidity refers to a set of flows exchanged among agents of the financial system, in particular between banks, the central bank and markets. Consequently, within the financial system three broad types of liquidity exist: central bank liquidity, funding liquidity and market liquidity (Nikolaou 2009).[2] As explained in the following sections, the first is related to the liquidity provided by a central bank, the second to the ability of banks to fund their positions, and the third to the ability to trade in the markets.

2.1.1 Central Bank Liquidity

The ability of the central bank to supply the liquidity needed to the financial system is the first type of liquidity, so-called central bank liquidity. Generally, it is calculated as the flow of monetary base supplied to the financial system from the central bank. Thus, it refers to central bank liquidity operations, which consist in the amount of liquidity provided to the money market through the actions of the central bank, in line with the monetary policy stance. The latter reflects the prevailing value of the operational target, i.e. the control variables of the central bank. In practice, the central bank strategy determines the monetary policy stance, consisting in setting the operational target level (usually the key policy rate). To implement this target, the central bank manages its monetary policy instruments, i.e. open market operations,[3] to influence liquidity in the money markets so the interbank rate stays in line with the operational target rate defined by the prevailing monetary policy stance. Thereby, the central bank, as the monopoly provider of the monetary base, through its open market operations, provides liquidity to the financial system. In practical terms, together with loans to banks and investments in government securities, these operations are shown on the assets side of the central bank's balance sheet against liabilities comprising the sum of autonomous factors (including banknotes in circulation, government deposits, net foreign assets, and other net factors) with the reserves (i.e. the minimum balances that banks must hold in the central bank). Thus, the definition of central bank liquidity refers to its assets side, and particularly to the open market operations used by the central bank to expand or contract the amount of money in the banking system.

To conclude, in the normal course of business, the central bank provides liquidity to the market to smoothen fluctuations, seasonal or otherwise, and functions as the lender of last resort, providing credit to solvent banks when no one else will.

2.1.2 *Funding Liquidity*

The Basel Committee on Banking Supervision (BCBS)[4] defines the second type of liquidity, funding liquidity, as the ability of banks to meet their liabilities, unwind or settle their positions as they fall due (BCBS 2008). The definition used by the International Monetary Fund (IMF) is very similar: funding liquidity consists in the ability of solvent institutions to make agreed-upon payments in a timely fashion (IMF 2008). Drehmann and Nikolaou (2010) are in line with these definitions, given that they argue that funding liquidity is the ability to settle obligations with immediacy, which means that a bank is illiquid if it is unable to settle its obligations on time. For them, funding liquidity is a flow concept. More specifically, they argued that an entity is considered to have sufficient funding liquidity and hence is liquid as long as inflows are larger than, or at least equal to, outflows. Thus, banks (but also firms, investors and traders) are considered liquid if their cash outflows are less than or equal to the cash inflows and stock of money held.

References to funding liquidity have also been made from the point of view of traders (Brunnemeier and Pedersen 2009) or investors (Strahan 2008), where funding liquidity is related to their ability to raise funds (capital or cash) at short notice. However, here, the attention is focused on the funding liquidity of banks, given their importance in distributing liquidity to the financial system (Nikolaou 2009).

Specifically, banks must ensure adequate liquidity at all times. In determining the amount of potential liquidity that banks have to hold to guarantee their day-to-day obligations, they need to do a number of things, including (Sekoni 2015):

- ensure the availability of sufficient cash at customer outlets to meet withdrawals;
- maintain sufficient settlement account balances to meet overnight settlements;
- predict the likelihood of future net withdrawals and cash inflows based on maturing deposits, loan drawdowns, customer transactions and so on.

However, the nature of banking requires investments characterized by assets with different degrees of liquidity (Vento and La Ganga 2009). Consequently, banks are vulnerable to the sudden and unexpected demand for funds by their customers and the inability to honour these requests due to liquidity problems can have serious negative implications for the entire financial system. Therefore, to avoid this kind of scenario, it is useful to consider the different potential sources of funding liquidity for banks, including, on the assets side:

- the asset market, where banks can go to sell their assets;
- the securitization market, where banks can generate liquidity by securitizing existing loans;

and on the liabilities side:

- depositors, who give their money to the bank;
- bondholders, who can buy short and long-term debt instruments issued by the bank;
- the interbank market, where banks exchange liquidity among themselves;
- and finally, funding liquidity directly from the central bank.

All these funding channels work perfectly well in normal times, but in a stress scenario, such as the GFC, they can become blocked, exposing banks to a specific liquidity risk, so-called funding liquidity risk, which is examined in Sect. 2.2.2.

2.1.3 Market Liquidity

Market liquidity, the third type, relates to the ability to trade in the markets. More specifically, it comprises the capacity to trade an asset in the markets at short notice, at low cost and with little impact on its price (Nikolaou 2009). Therefore, a market is considered liquid when it gives investors (including banks) the opportunity to buy and sell a sizeable amount of assets, such as securities, without appreciably affecting the price of the asset.

The fact that any amount of assets can be sold at any time during market hours, rapidly, with minimum loss of value and at competitive prices is determined by the following four criteria (Bank for International

Settlements–BIS 1999): immediacy, breadth (or tightness), depth, and resilience. Immediacy is the time between launching and completing a business transaction in the markets, hence the speed with which trades of a certain size can be carried out. Breadth is the divergence in the price of an asset from mid-market prices and is generally measured by the bid-offer spread. Depth refers to either the volume of trades that can be carried out without affecting current market prices or the amount of orders on the order books of market-makers. Finally, resilience is the speed with which price fluctuations during the execution of a trade return to former levels.

A number of structural market factors ensure the availability of, and increase in, liquidity in the market (David 2007; Caruana and Kodres 2008), such as:

- the symmetrical distribution of information on asset values in the market to potential buyers and sellers, and intermediaries;
- the availability of a large number of assets for trading compared to the number of investors who want to trade;
- the presence of new and highly active market players that attract fresh capital to the markets, increasing their liquidity;
- the introduction of technological advances able to lower trading costs and increase transparency and price competition.

In the banking sector, two types of market liquidity are of paramount importance: the liquidity of the interbank market, where banks can trade liquidity among themselves, and liquidity in the asset market, where assets are traded by financial agents, such as banks. These markets are of fundamental importance for banks, because they are the main sources of funding liquidity from the market. Illiquidity on these markets, such as during the GFC, exposes banks that are over-dependent on the interbank and asset markets to a specific liquidity risk, called market liquidity risk (see Sect. 2.2.3), potentially undermining the stability of individual banks and, in some cases, of the entire financial system.

2.2 Liquidity Risk: Definition and Multidimensionality

Liquidity risk is intrinsic to the banking business. Indeed, as said before, the main role of banks in the financial system is to provide liquidity through intermediation. More specifically, banks mediate between depositors and investors, providing illiquidity loans to the latter, which are funded with liquid deposits from the former. Thus, banks transform short maturities (deposits) into longer maturities (investments) in order to create funding liquidity for investors (Strahan 2008) and to contribute to the efficient allocation of resources in the system. This mechanism is called maturity transformation and means that the balance sheet of a bank is typically characterized by illiquid long-term assets and liquid short-term liabilities. This maturity mismatch can expose banks to liquidity risk and cause bank instability in its role as provider of liquidity on demand to depositors (through deposit transactions), or borrowers (through committed lines of credit). However, a high degree of maturity transformation can lead to liquidity problems for banks principally during periods of stress when the confidence in the banking system tends to decrease. Therefore, since it cannot be avoided, banks need to handle maturity transformation properly. Banks can minimize their exposure to this risk by holding enough liquid assets at any point (Montes-Negret 2009). Nevertheless this is not the optimum strategy because liquid assets generate no returns (cash) or low/lower returns (investments in government securities), given that they are without risk or carry low risk, unlike longer-term (private) assets (such as loans and investments) which are more illiquid and riskier, but yield higher returns. Banks, therefore, always face a trade-off between holding (short-term) low-yield liquid assets to use them as a liquidity cushion, or investing in less liquid but higher return longer-term assets (Strahan 2008). During good times, such trade-offs are often forgotten, but they rear their heads when the business cycle turns or market disruptions make it more difficult and costly to tap several potential sources of funding, including market funding sources (such as interbank lines of credit), or attract or retain deposits. Clearly, there are trade-offs between liquidity risk and bank profitability. Liquidity risk is certainly a major consequential risk, as many failed banks have discovered, but it is equally true that banks cannot afford to maintain enough excess liquidity to survive every conceivable worst case scenario.

Focusing on the peculiarities of bank liquidity risk, it is important to highlight its multidimensional nature. Indeed, it is usually analyzed in the light of (Ruozi and Ferrari 2013):

- the origin of the risk (corporate liquidity risk vs. systemic liquidity risk);
- the timeframe of the risk analysis (short-term liquidity risk vs. structural liquidity risk);

- the economic scenario of the risk (going concern liquidity risk vs. contingency liquidity risk);
- the impact area of the liquidity risk (funding liquidity risk vs. market liquidity risk).

In terms of origin, some factors can accentuate the exposure of a bank to liquidity risk. They include technical factors, relating to some products provided by banks to savers and enterprises that make the time profile of their cash flows less certain and more unpredictable; specific or individual factors relating to an individual bank; and factors of a systemic nature.

Technical factors are products that give counterparties (savers, enterprises, other banks) a high degree of discretion in determining future cash flows. Typical examples are at sight liabilities, which often remain in place for years, but can be withdrawn without notice; the personal guarantees provided by banks, which can be enforced merely at the request of the creditor; and irrevocable credit lines granted to enterprises or special vehicles created ad hoc for securitization purposes. Equally critical are products, such as derivatives contracts traded on the Over The Counter (OTC) markets, which require banks to pay guarantee margins that can increase unexpectedly.

Bank liquidity risk can also increase due to specific factors and events weakening the confidence of customers and operators in a specific bank, prompting them to accelerate the recovery of loans (such as, withdrawing at sight deposits or not renewing forward credit lines). For example, rumours about the honesty of management and truthfulness of the balance sheets, or the decision by one or more rating agencies to revise down the rating of the bank are such events. With reference to the latter, it should not be forgotten that often the funding that banks receive from institutional counterparties contain automatic clauses (so-called triggers), that specify repayment of the credit (or payment of substantial guarantees) as an immediate consequence of a rating downgrade. Hence, all these factors, weakening customers and operators confidence, are likely to increase bank liquidity risk, causing funding difficulties.

The last group of factors rendering a liquidity risk more acute are systemic and can determine funding problems for banks and potential difficulties in selling financial assets. They include events unrelated to the situation of the individual bank, linked to a crisis in financial markets or the economy or in politics, natural catastrophes, acts of terrorism, and so on. A general crises of confidence can lead to a run on a country's banks or to market crises that temporarily render them inoperative, making it impossible to rapidly liquidate listed financial assets or close the gap between the buyer's price (bid) and seller's price (ask), so it becomes disadvantageous to sell securities.

These occurrences, either singly or jointly, create a liquidity risk associated with internal bank factors, so-called corporate liquidity risk, and a risk associated with market or systemic factors beyond the control of the bank, so-called systemic liquidity risk.

Another dimension to consider is the timeframe of the risk analysis. On the one hand, there may be short-term liquidity risk, when problems of short-term liquidity management arise out of the need promptly and economically to fix the imbalances between cash inflows and outflows, re-establishing monetary dynamics; and, on the other hand, there may be a structural liquidity risk, when problems of structural liquidity management are linked to the convenience and opportunity to modify the qualitative-quantitative composition of assets, liabilities, and off-balance sheet items, affecting the future and dynamics of cash flows.

However, these two types of liquidity are strictly interconnected and interact. This was evident in the recent banking crises in various countries and internationally, where liquidity crises caused by structural problems spilled over onto the short-term, which became unmanageable.

For all these reasons, on the one hand, it is important for banks to adopt processes able to separately compute and monitor short-term liquidity management, in order to be able to cope immediately with any payment commitment, whether expected and unexpected, arising from contracts obliging the bank to take monetary action. This ability depends on the availability of adequate liquidity buffers, consisting of cash and other highly liquid unencumbered assets, and on the tools that can be activated to fix temporary imbalances between incoming and outgoing cash flows. On the other hand, banks also have to control the management of structural liquidity, to maintain an adequate balance between monetary inflows and outflows over different time horizons in the medium-long term. Clearly, this structural ability is even more challenging the greater the maturity transformation implemented by the bank. If the weighted average asset maturity is higher than the liability, the cash flows generated by extinguishing assets, over a given period, are lower than the cash flows required to repay the liabilities that expire in the same timeframe. This situation accentuates the potential liquidity risk faced by the bank, given that it is required to maintain a constant credit capability in the market, i.e. the ability to renew liabilities due in order to reconcile the maturity of the liability with that of the asset.

As stated above, the economic scenario is another important dimension of bank liquidity risk. Depending on the economic environment in which the bank finds itself, it faces liquidity risk in normal operations, or going concern liquidity risk, and the risk from stress situations, or contingency liquidity risk, both of which are linked to individual or systemic factors.

In the first case, the risk is linked to situations in which the bank is able to meet its liquidity requirement using its own funding capability. In a going concern scenario, liquidity management and the correct measurement of the related risks, involve simulating future trends in cash inflows and outflows by making assumptions about the evolution of on- and off-balance sheet items that are as neutral as possible.

In the second case, risk refers to stressed conditions that derive from either individual or systemic factors. Given that these crisis situations cannot be faced through the normal funding capability of the bank, recourse to ex-ante formalized extraordinary measures is required, implementing a suitable contingency funding plan (CFP),[5] drawn up prior to the crisis. This document formalizes the intervention strategy, classifies the possible types of liquidity stress, identifies its systemic or specific nature and the balance sheet items most affected, specifies the emergency actions to be taken by management and includes estimates of the back-up liquidity at the disposal of the bank facing a liquidity crisis.

In addition, depending on the possible impact area, bank liquidity risk falls into the following two strictly interconnected categories (The Joint Forum 2006): funding liquidity risk and market liquidity risk. Both are discussed in the following sections, but a brief introduction is necessary.

In its narrow definition, funding liquidity risk is associated solely with the liabilities side of a bank. It consists in the inability of a bank to raise funds to repay its liabilities. In this sense, funding risk is therefore the risk of an increase in the cost of funding. However, it can also be defined in broader and more general terms, taking into account both the liabilities and assets side of a bank. In this case, it refers to the possibility that the bank may not be able to settle its obligations immediately and in a cost-effective way.

By contrast, market liquidity risk is the risk a bank faces when unable to convert a position on given financial assets into money or when it needs to liquidate the asset, taking a price cut, due to insufficient liquidity in the market where it is traded or to temporary malfunctioning of the market itself.

Although logically different, these two risk concepts are strictly related. The need to meet unexpected cash outflows can force a bank to convert substantial amounts of its financial assets into cash. If this leads to losses, the damage arising from the liquidity risk is more severe (Banks 2005). The likelihood of facing both funding liquidity risk and market liquidity risk is greater the larger the maturity mismatch between liabilities (mostly short-term) and assets (mostly long-term).

Apart from funding and the market liquidity risk, few scholars consider a third type of liquidity risk, central bank liquidity risk, i.e. the risk that the central bank is unable to provide liquidity to the financial system (Nikolaou 2009). As described in the next section, this type of risk is almost always considered zero, since the central bank holds the monopoly of liquidity supply and can dispense liquidity at any time and for any amount.

2.2.1 *Central Bank Liquidity Risk*

As stated above, central bank liquidity consists in the ability of the central banks to provide the liquidity financial systems need. Hence, the associated risk is called central bank liquidity risk, largely ignored in the financial literature due to the general belief that central bank liquidity risk does not exist, given that the central bank is always able to supply base money and can never be illiquid (Nikolaou 2009). As the monopoly provider of liquidity (i.e. the originator of the monetary base), the central bank can provide liquidity as and when required in order to balance the supply and demand for liquidity in the banking systems, ensuring there is neither too much nor too little, in line with its policy stance.

A central bank can be considered illiquid in the sole case of zero demand for domestic currency, when the supply of base money by the central bank cannot materialize. Such a scenario may happen in periods of hyperinflation or during an exchange rate crisis, however unlikely, especially in developed industrialized countries. Hence, central bank liquidity risk is not dealt with in the literature.

Finally, in its role as liquidity provider, a central bank can become involved in different types of risks that do not necessarily reflect liquidity risk. They include counterparty credit risk related to collateral value; monetary policy related risk, such as the risk of mistaken signalling; or wider risks to financial stability, i.e. moral hazard in cases of emergency liquidity assistance in crisis periods. Overall, none of these risks affects the central bank's ability to provide liquidity.

2.2.2 Funding Liquidity Risk

Another aspect of bank liquidity is funding liquidity, consisting in the ability of a bank to settle its obligations on time. The risk strictly associated with this type of bank liquidity is funding liquidity risk, considered an endemic risk of the financial system. It is in the nature of a bank to take on funding liquidity risk due to the maturity mismatch of its assets and liabilities. As stated earlier, maturity transformation is one of the main functions of a bank. However, by definition, this creates liquidity and rollover risks (the risk that the depositors do not rollover their deposits) and, therefore, funding liquidity risk.

There is no single definition of funding liquidity risk and two different conceptions. Seen narrowly, it is the inability of a bank to raise the funds required to repay its liabilities, because all the alternative sources of funding previously described in Sect. 2.1.2, such as the interbank market, depositors, etc., are blocked. So, funding liquidity risk is associated only with the bank's liabilities side. However, from a broader point of view, funding liquidity risk refers to the possibility that a bank may not be able to settle its obligations immediately and in a cost-effective way. Therefore, in this broader definition, funding liquidity risk can refer to both liabilities (such as repayments of liabilities), and assets (such as commitments to provide funds or requests to increase existing guarantees).

Regardless of these two definitions, what they have in common is the trigger factor. Funding liquidity risk originates in an endogenous event, such as a firm-specific operational-risk problem or damage to the bank's reputation.

Funding liquidity risk is the most commonly studied configuration of liquidity risk in the financial sector, where most attention has been focused. However, as explained in detail in Chapter 5, there are still no robust shared management methodologies for dealing with it, and countries have handled it in different ways. Banks use three main models to measure this risk.

Briefly, the first is a stock-based approach, which aims to measure the volume of financial assets that can be speedily liquidated or used in refinancing facilities, which bank can use to meet a future liquidity crisis. Essentially, through this approach, the bank vulnerability to liquidity risk can be calculated using simply indicators based on the bank's stock of assets. It provides a static representation of liquidity risk, given its neglect of the dynamics of cash inflows and outflows associated with management as a whole and the precise moment they become manifest.

A more satisfying approximation of reality is provided by dynamic analysis, in which the liquidity situation is assessed on the basis of the cash flows generated or absorbed in a given time period. Hence, mismatch-based approaches (or cash-flow analysis) that identify future cash inflows and outflows, grouping them into homogeneous bundles by maturity date, and checking for a proper balance between the inflows and outflows. Via a series of maturity ladders, this second approach involves splitting the diverse future cash flows to establish the balance between the inflows and outflows in various timeframes. Positive net flow, in a given period, indicates the amount of financial resources which will be added to existing resources and can be reutilized for new activities. Negative net flow indicates a requirement to find the resources that management needs in the given time span to cover the imbalance.

The third approach integrates the two described above, by adding to the expected future net flows the inflows that can be generated by using the stock of financial assets capable of simple and immediate liquidation or usable as collateral in refinancing operations. At one level, liquidity management based on hybrid approaches presupposes the simulation of the balance between cash inflows and outflows over different timeframes, as in the cash flow approach. At another level, the monitoring of the short-term liquidity position requires the measurement of financial assets that can be promptly liquidated or committed to refinancing operations, including all the positions that can be refinanced with the central bank or used as collateral in secured finance operations, valuing them at market prices and applying the haircut required by the supervisory authority or by the bank's internal risk policy. By adding net cash flows and financial assets, it is possible to calculate the liquidity risk of a bank at normal times. At a third level, it is necessary to define operating limits based on the maximum liquidity deficit a bank can tolerate, related to the various operational currencies and within each unit of the banking group. The constant monitoring of these operating limits identifies ex-ante the likely outbreak of a liquidity crisis based on expected cash flows.

In all three models, contractual cash flows are ignored in favour of real cash flows, corrected to include possible alternative scenarios. The several corrections depend on the scenario taken into consideration, normal or stressed. Specifically, in a normal operating environment, the identification of cash flows in diverse timeframes reflects bank expectations based on past experience and is related to a normal, stable market situation. In a turbulent scenario, simulation exercises are carried out to assess the effects on liquidity risk of particular adverse situations. The input for these exercises may be events that have involved the bank itself or competitors (historic approach), statistical simulations based on a hypothesis for the distribution of the risk factors (statistical approach), or subjective estimates formulated by the bank's management (judgement-based approach). These approaches can be used separately to simulate the effect of single risk factors or to build worst case scenarios in which many risk factors act jointly to create strong liquidity stress on the bank or the banking system as a whole (Matz and Neu 2007).

Although the development of stress tests is still at an experimental stage, they are fundamental for the measurement of liquidity risk. The methods are still rather heterogeneous and often based on judgemental approaches both for sensitivity analysis and in relation to scenario testing. Despite limitations due to the arbitrary nature of the data used, these simulations appear to be useful because they enable banks to organize in advance a CFP to be implemented if the hypothetical scenario actually occurs.

Finally, although funding liquidity risk is the most commonly studied configuration of liquidity risk, up to now, few are the works that investigated the peculiarities of funding liquidity risk. In particular, Matz and Neu (2007) find that it can arise at any time, but is most severe in an environment of heightened market liquidity risk. Indeed, as explained below, the two risks are closely interconnected. This is confirmed by Drehmann and Nikolaou (2010), who find that, like market liquidity risk, it is generally low and stable, but undergoes occasional spikes during turbulent times, such as the recent financial turmoil.

2.2.3 *Market Liquidity Risk*

The last type of liquidity is market liquidity, which is the ability of a banking institution operating in the market to raise funds at market prices. When a bank cannot access the market to sell its assets at fair prices and has to accept lower or 'fire-sale' prices, it is experiencing market liquidity risk (Montes-Negret 2009). Thus, market liquidity risk relates to the bank's assets, because it is the risk that a bank cannot easily offset or eliminate a position without significantly affecting the market price of the security, due to inadequate market depth or market disruption.

Therefore, in general, the liquidity of any financial instruments market depends on the following factors: the speed of trading; the implicit cost of the transaction in terms of bid-ask spread; and the ability immediately or quickly to absorb any imbalances between buying and selling proposals without generating significant price changes. In theory, in a perfectly liquid market, it is possible to disinvest in a very short time and at just one price. In practice, the time and cost of disinvesting a position are related to both exogenous and endogenous factors (Bangia et al. 2001). On the one hand, exogenous factors are the result of market liquidity features and involve all potential participants. As stated above, they include the depth, the spread between bid- and ask-prices, the resilience, and the immediacy of the market. The joint operation of these factors determines the time and cost of disinvesting in a given position for any market participant. On the other hand, endogenous factors are specific to some positions. They are related to the amount of exposure and grow with the increase in the position held, involving only some market participants. Both types of factors have to be integrated in the classical metrics of risk evaluation to ensure that the risk exposure of the bank is not underestimated due to both the market liquidity component and the possible risks associated with disinvesting large or small positions in order to deal with any misalignment between cash inflows and outflows.

On the basis of what has been said above, the trigger event of market liquidity risk is a market-wide liquidity problem, so an exogenous event. In addition, it is the systematic, non-diversifiable component of liquidity risk. This has two important consequences. The first relates to common features of liquidity risk across markets. These commonalities are identified theoretically (Brunnemeier and Pedersen 2005, 2009) and recorded at an empirical level in stock, bond and equity markets (Chordia et al. 2005). Moreover, liquidity risk, through more extensive propagation mechanisms, can also be transferred over interbank and assets markets. The second is the fact that market liquidity risk should be priced, i.e. this type of risk is generally considered a cost or premium in the asset pricing literature, positively affecting the price of an asset (Holmström and Tirole 1997; Bangia et al. 1999; Pastor and Stambaugh 2003; Acharya and Pedersen 2005; Chordia et al. 2005) and able to influence market decisions (such as optimum portfolio allocation as in Longstaf 2001) and market practices (including transaction costs as in Jarrow and Subramanian 1997). The larger the premium, the higher the market liquidity risk. In practical terms, starting with the liquidity-based asset pricing model of Holmström and Tirole (1997), asset pricing models typically measure liquidity risk as the covariance (commonality) between a measure of liquidity (innovations) and market returns (Pastor and Staumbaugh 2003; Acharya and Pedersen 2005; Liu 2006). Liquidity risk moves with simultaneous returns, but it is also possible to predict future returns based on current liquidity risk estimates (Chordia et al. 2001; Acharya and Pedersen 2005; Liu 2006). Overall, in the related literature, asset prices reflect the liquidity costs associated with the existence of liquidity risk.

Market liquidity risk, such as funding liquidity risk, is low and stable most of the time. High liquidity risk is rare and episodic. Its episodic nature can derive from downward liquidity spirals, as a consequence of mutually reinforcing funding and market illiquidity (Brunnemeir and Pedersen 2005, 2009) and is rare due to benefits from cooperation in trading (Carlin et al. 2007). With reference to the latter, it is important to add that financial links are established only when the benefits are greater than the costs, i.e. when the likelihood of a financial crisis, and therefore elevated liquidity risk, is low (Brusco and Castiglionesi 2007). This means that crises and financial contagion are rare. In the light of the behaviour of market liquidity risk, it is clear why liquidity varies over time and is persistent in normal periods (Amihud 2002; Chordia et al. 2000, 2001, 2002; Pastor and Staumbaugh 2003).

Another important aspect is the fact that market liquidity risk refers to banks funding themselves in financial markets, potentially creating externalities for others (negative asset price spirals). Therefore, market (systemic) liquidity risk can lead to financial crises, able to undermine financial stability as a whole, disrupting the allocation of resources and, ultimately, affecting the real economy (Hoggarth and Saporta 2001; Ferguson et al. 2007). Hence, given its impact (from a systemic point of view) on financial stability, market liquidity risk immediately alarms policymakers.

Attention to this type of liquidity risk has increased in recent years, due to the significant dependence of banks on markets and wholesale funding. Despite this, until a short time ago, market liquidity risk was completely ignored by bank risk management systems in leading industrialized countries (Matz and Neu 2007). In addition, due to its strict interrelationship with market risks, market liquidity risk is often computed and managed by the risk management unit entrusted with the evaluation of market risks, instead of the unit set up for the measurement and management of liquidity risk (Deutsche Bundesbank and Bafin 2008).

2.3 Liquidity Interconnections in Normal and Turbulent Periods

As described above, in the financial system, three types of liquidity are intensively interconnected: central bank liquidity, funding liquidity, and market liquidity. The linkages between them are complex, strong and dynamic and can have positive or negative effects on financial stability. Specifically, in normal times, i.e. periods of low liquidity risk, the effects are positive. In these periods, a virtuous circle of the three liquidity types fosters the stability of the financial system, whereas, in turbulent periods, with high liquidity risk, the effects on financial stability are negative. The causes of liquidity risk lie in departures from the complete market and symmetric information paradigm, which can lead to moral hazard and adverse selection phenomena.[6] To the extent that such conditions persist, liquidity risk is endemic to the financial system and can prompt a vicious circle between the three liquidity types which can ultimately undermine the financial system.

In order to get a better understanding of the links between the three types of liquidity and their impact on the financial stability, the following pages analyse the interconnections via two alternative scenarios: periods of normality and periods of turbulence. But first, it is necessary to point out that the interdependence of the different types of liquidity is stronger in banking system models where securitization is prevalent, such as the Originate to Distribute (OTD) model.[7]

In smooth financial periods, liquidity circulates in the financial system efficiently and without obstruction and hence liquidity does not matter. In these periods each liquidity type (central bank, market and funding liquidity) performs its role unproblematically. The central bank provides the amount of liquidity that balances supply and demand; markets ensure its redistribution and recycling; and funding needs the efficient allocation of liquidity resources among agents. Indeed, in practice, the amount of liquidity provided by the central bank is received by the banks and, through the various markets, such as the interbank and asset markets, is distributed to the agents in the financial system who need it most, according to their funding liquidity requirements. After redistribution, the central bank measures the new demand for liquidity and supplies it, and the liquidity circle starts again (ECB 2004). Therefore, each liquidity type depends on the other two because each has a unique role in the financial system, relying on the proper functioning of the other two for the system to be liquid overall (Nikolaou 2009). The amount of liquidity provided by the central bank is able to flow without problems to the agents only if the following two conditions are met simultaneously: the market effectively recycles the liquidity; and funding liquidity makes efficient and effective allocations in the system. Market liquidity depends both on the fact that there is enough aggregate liquidity in the financial system and that each counterparty demands liquidity in line with their funding needs. In addition, funding liquidity depends on the availability of funding liquidity sources.[8]

Generally, in normal times, liquidity flows unobstructed and easily through the financial system and banks can choose between the different liquidity options available. When markets are efficient, the price determines the choice of the alternative liquidity providers (Ayuso and Repullo 2003; Ewerhart et al. 2007; Drehmann and Nikolaou 2010). So, banks are able to choose the funding option that is the most cost-efficient.

To conclude, sufficient liquidity in smooth periods reduces the likelihood of a financial crisis, guaranteeing financial stability. However, normal periods do not last forever. Indeed, turbulent periods—however rare and episodic—may occur and are often intense and destabilizing. This is because turbulent times are characterized by the existence of asymmetric information and incomplete markets and these are the sources of liquidity risk in the financial system. Liquidity risk is endogenous to the system. The spread of liquidity risk tends to affect the interactions between the three liquidity types (central bank, funding and market liquidity). Their linkages continue to be strong, but in turbulent periods they act as risk propagation channels, destabilizing the financial system. So, instead of a virtuous circle as in normal times, there is vicious illiquidity spiral in the financial system, which undermines its stability. To understand how, an arbitrary case is presented below in which a bank has high funding liquidity risk which spreads through the system via market liquidity risk. The role of the central bank in this situation is also discussed.

As stated in previous sections, banking is characterized by persistent funding liquidity risk. This risk is endogenous to the traditional function of banks, which includes providing maturity transformation services to the economy by taking on relatively short-term liabilities and transforming them into relatively long-term (not easy to trade) assets. This activity can make banks fragile, by causing instability in their role as providers of liquidity on demand to depositors or borrowers, exposing them to funding liquidity risk. Given this intrinsic bank fragility, in turbulent times, the presence of asymmetric information and incomplete markets can lead to failures in coordination between actors, in particular depositors demanding liquidity from the bank and causing a run on the bank, the most extreme form of funding liquidity risk. Typically, a bank run is when depositors simultaneously decide to withdraw their deposits before maturity. The problem arises when a bank has difficulty in meeting the increased demand for liquidity and, in such a case, even a perfectly sound and solvent bank can fail. Bank runs may be sparked for different reasons. For example, low expectations driving coordination failures are self-fulfilling prophecies (Diamond and Dybvig 1983, 2000). Or inadequate information may fail to reassure fundamental worries and rational concerns associated with departures from the classical economic paradigm. Namely, imperfect information may lead to bank runs. If the soundness of the borrower is uncertain, runs may occur when a commonly observed signal about the borrower increases uncertainty among depositors, because it is optimal to pre-empt withdrawals of others by borrowing first (Morris and Shin 2004). Moreover, bank runs may result from incomplete markets, since aggregate risk cannot be hedged away (Allen and Douglas 1998).

The existence of funding liquidity risk in an individual bank is not a source of concern for regulators and policymakers. However, if funding liquidity risk becomes systemic, in more than one bank, it prompts fundamental worries. In the following pages, the analysis focuses on how funding liquidity risk can spread to market liquidity risk via two propagation channels.

The first channel is the interbank market. Funding liquidity risk is directly linked to interbank market liquidity risk. Specifically, Diamond and Rajan (2001, 2005) argue that banks are linked by a common market for liquidity. Indeed, the failure of an individual bank can decrease the common pool of liquidity that links all banks together, propagating a lack of liquidity to other banks and therefore determining a contagion of failures. Various interlinkages between banks mean that individual illiquidity can lead to market illiquidity. Some examples are balance sheet linkages (Cifuentes et al. 2005), or, more generally, cross-holdings of liabilities across banks (such as deposits, interbank loans and credit exposures or committed credit lines), and highly interconnected bank payment systems (Flannery 1996; Freixas et al. 1999). In addition, they can take the form of information spillovers to the interbank market, leading to a general run on the banks.

Theoretically, all these interlinkages can be propagation channels for a banking crises; in practice, a run on the banks requires the combination of an incomplete set of contingent securities (i.e. it is not possible to hedge against future liquidity outcomes) and information asymmetries about the solvency of the banks (i.e. it is not known if a bank is illiquid or insolvent). Both can determine fears of counterparty credit risk (Allen and Douglas 2000; Drehmann et al. 2007; Brusco and Castiglionesi 2007; Strahan 2008). The presence of incomplete markets and asymmetric information can also lead to moral hazard and adverse selection. Specifically, moral hazard can arise as insolvent banks act illiquidly, free-riding on the common pool of liquidity in the interbank market. These banks can then engage in risk-prone behaviour by under-investing in liquid assets (Bhattacharya and Gale 1987) and gambling for resurrection (Freixas et al. 2004). This then prompts adverse selection in lending, i.e. a situation in which liquidity is given only to insolvent banks, mistakenly deemed to be illiquid, and solvent but illiquid banks receive none. Adverse selection in lending can translate into limited commitments of future cash flows (Hart and Moore 1994; Diamond and Rajan 2001) and uncertainty about future lending due to counterparty credit risk (Flannery 1996). It may also lead to liquidity hoarding, due to concerns about counterparty solvency (Rochet and Vives 2004), or doubts about the bank's own ability to borrow in the future (Freixas et al. 2004; Holmström and Tirole 2001). Thus, some banks are rationed by the system. In this scenario, the few remaining surplus banks, acting as an oligopoly, may seek benefits by strategically under-providing lending in order to exploit the others' failure (Acharya et al. 2012). Such a situation can aggravate interbank market illiquidity, or short-squeeze liquidity-thristy banks. This determines an increase in the cost of obtaining liquidity (Nyborg and Strebulaev 2004).

The second propagation channel from funding liquidity risk to market liquidity risk is asset markets, through the liquidation of assets at 'fire-sale' prices. Specifically, when the interbank market is distressed, banks may seek liquidity by selling assets. However, in turbulent times it is difficult to find someone willing to buy these securities. This pushes asset prices downwards forcing banks to sell them at prices much lower than the original purchase price, leading to capital losses for these banks. The problem has even more serious repercussions if the assets are highly illiquid and subject to steep price declines, as with some securitized products (Montes-Negret 2009).

Up to now, the analysis has focused only on the transmission channels from funding to market liquidity. However, the opposite can also occur; a funding need can arise from market illiquidity, for example when an institution is unable to securitize or syndicate loans. In the case of fire sales, losses may be incurred, placing pressure on earnings and capital. If an institution is unable to securitize or syndicate loans, its balance sheet size increases, resulting in capital pressure. The deterioration in credit quality may also constrain the institution's access to funding markets. The resulting funding liquidity risk in the single bank can be transmitted to its creditors, thereby leading to interbank liquidity risk, which may prompt a new round of asset sales (Cifuentes et al. 2005) and further distress pricing. In this sense, the interaction between funding and market liquidity creates a loop between these two types of liquidity (from market liquidity to funding liquidity and back again) leading to a dangerous downward liquidity spiral in the markets (Brunnemeier and Pedersen 2009).

During the crisis of 2007–2009, the spread of the OTD model, characterized by the widespread use of securitization, tightened the connection between funding liquidity (risk) and market liquidity (risk), leading to more direct contagion channels and faster transmission from asset market to funding liquidity and vice versa. Securitization can have twofold effects. On the one hand, it is an important source of funding for banks. Moreover, by transferring credit risk off their balance sheets, it allows banks to save regulatory capital and enables them to optimize asset management. On the other hand, securitization makes banks more dependent on market funding rather than funding via bank deposits.

Moreover, the interaction between funding and market illiquidity is fundamental to understanding how systemic financial crises play out. The crisis of 2007–2009 exposed the linkages of these two risks and showed that the interaction between the two can have consequences that reach far beyond an individual institution. Since securitization tightened the connection between funding liquidity (risk) and market liquidity (risk), the failure of one bank revealed a systemic problem (insolvency) and threatened the potential crash of the whole banking system, due to its dependence on market liquidity, previously taken for granted. Specifically, as noted by Montes-Negret (2009), the actions of one institution can impact externally (contagion) and its attempts to sell assets can reduce general market liquidity, placing other institutions under liquidity pressure, even though they have suffered no significant first order losses. And the fall in market prices caused by 'fire-sales' can place other institutions under earnings and capital pressures. These institutions will then have liquidity needs of their own, with asset sales to meet their funding needs creating a potential feedback loop to market illiquidity. Institutions that suffer large liquidity shortfalls may seek to close out lending positions, particularly in the interbank market. These actions create direct funding liquidity needs for other market participants.

Finally, the central bank should be in a position to face systemic liquidity risks in its role of guarantor of the entire economy and capacity as the originator of the monetary base. However, it has a short-term stabilization function (Humphrey and Keleher 1984). This means that central bank interventions can provide temporary liquidity injections which aim to break the vicious loop between funding and market liquidity risk, so that downward liquidity spirals fail to further distress markets. Therefore, the role of central bank liquidity in turbulent times is unable to guarantee success. Moreover, its function can be hindered by the very causes of liquidity risk because a central bank cannot distinguish between illiquid and insolvent banks with certainty. By providing liquidity to undeserving banks, it can cause further damage to the system. This happens when it actually damages the funding liquidity of solvent but illiquid banks, the prospects of market liquidity and its own functions (Nikolaou 2009). Hence, a full vicious circle running through central bank liquidity is established in the financial system liquidity. The trade-off between costs and benefits of intervention should be taken into consideration when the central bank has to decide on its liquidity provision strategy. This task is not easy and there are no precise rules.

2.4 The Linkages Between Liquidity and Solvency

Liquidity and solvency have been called the barely distinguishable Castor and Pollux of banking (Goodhart 2008). Since these twins interact in complex ways, especially during crisis periods and in the presence of information asymmetries, it is hard to tell them apart.

Indeed, they are not two utterly distinct. An insolvent bank is generally illiquid, and vice versa, a bank with liquidity problems may subsequently become insolvent, but an illiquid bank is not automatically insolvent although insolvency is unlikely to be far away, since banking is grounded in information and confidence, and it is confidence which, in the end, determines liquidity. In other words, liquidity is very much endogenous, determined by the general condition of a bank, as well as how it is perceived by the public and market participants.

Although illiquidity and insolvency are two related concepts, they are not interchangeable terms. From an accounting point of view, a bank is considered balance sheet insolvent when its total liabilities exceed its total assets (negative net assets) and, therefore, it has no option but to default on some obligations, leading the bank into receivership, intervention or bankruptcy. On the other hand, a bank is illiquid when it has a specific liquidity problem or experiences a liquidity crisis and cannot obtain the funding needed, in a timely form, at market prices, to meet its obligations when due. Therefore, insolvency reflects a structural and stock problem, while illiquidity refers to a temporary cashflow and pricing problem. One major issue for creditors, central banks and supervisors is that it is difficult to know if a bank is illiquid because it is or is not insolvent. Moreover, illiquidity can also rapidly lead to insolvency if the problem is not addressed quickly and effectively, reassuring depositors and other creditors. In the worst case scenario, it can undermine the stability of the individual bank and of the entire banking system.

The difference between the two terms is fundamental not least because policy actions to address an insolvency or liquidity crisis vary dramatically and, therefore, assessing the underlying problems of banks becomes crucial.

Insolvency applies to individual banks or systemic problems. Specifically, during the financial crisis of 2007–2009, the underlying problem of some financial intermediaries heavily invested in subprime mortgages was solvency, which was translated into a liquidity crisis in view of the uncertainty about asset values and counterparty risks, dramatically increasing market liquidity risk. As discussed in Chapter 2, some banks were highly leveraged, often through off-balance sheet special purpose vehicles (SPVs) or structured investment vehicles (SIVs), having securitized products which defaulted, creating not only a structural solvency problem (for the SPVs), but also a liquidity crisis for the bank, as some of these vehicles required additional liquidity support. The large shadow banking system in the form of off-balance sheet vehicles placed extraordinary liquidity demands on banks at the worst possible time. Some of these transactions were financing long-term, low-quality credit with short-term funds, at a time when market liquidity was abundant and continuous refinancing was possible. Once liquidity tightened and even started to freeze, and market liquidity risk skyrocketed, participants started to hoard cash, making even solvent banks illiquid overnight (Roubini 2007). It should be noted that precautionary hoarding increases when the likelihood of liquidity shocks rises and market funds are more difficult to obtain, triggering a liquidity spiral and often cross-bank contagion (Brunnermier 2009). Hence, the concept of liquidity is critical for banking activities in good and, even more so, in bad times, when they face more limited access options (higher market liquidity risk) and become more dependent on central bank liquidity support.

2.5 The Relationships Between Liquidity Risk and Other Typical Bank Risks

Liquidity risk has relations with other typical risks of a bank. Bidirectional relationships exist: from liquidity risk to other risks and vice versa, with circular cause-effects.

Specifically, liquidity risk is directly and indirectly influenced by credit risk. Banks are exposed to counterparty credit risk. If the conditions of one of the counterparties deteriorate and it is unable to cope with its commitments to the bank, the bank may suffer a decrease in cash inflows and consequently may also not be able to make payments due.

The bank's creditworthiness also affects the degree of liquidity. If a bank's creditworthiness deteriorates, it may find some difficulties in raising funds promptly and at a reasonable cost. The deterioration in liquidity risk in turn reflects on the credit granted and credit risk. During the financial crisis of 2007–2009, the tendency of banks to reconstruct their assets by increasing the liquid components impacted on the amount of credit granted to the economy, with consequences, partly deriving from other factors, that turned out to be negative. Thus, the increased credit risk negatively impacted on the profitability of the banks themselves.

Market risks can impact on liquidity risk. The impacts are expressed in terms of asset/market liquidity risk: negative market factors are reflected in the prices of financial assets and lead to more costly solutions for liquidity risk. In turn, the search for interventions for liquidity risk management can cause the deterioration of the factors—rates, financial asset prices—which typically comprise market risks.

Liquidity risk can derive from operational risk. For example, liquidity problems can occur as a result of operational problems with critical participants or service providers. Another cause is failure or delay in the system managing the transactions.

Finally, reputational risk may be both the cause and the effect of liquidity problems. In the banking sector, bank reputation is a key factor in obtaining funding. If the reputation of a bank decreases it has repercussions on both the funding activity and funding costs. Vice versa, when the liquidity problems of a bank are known to the market, they damage the bank's reputation and may change both its rating and its profits.

2.6 The Aggravating Factors of Liquidity Risk

In recent years liquidity risk and its management has become more critical due to several factors. One of them is the globalization of large financial groups which now hold assets and liabilities, including via local subsidiaries in emerging countries, with a large number of counterparties. Hence, it is more difficult to have an updated picture of all the possible future cash flows. Due to financial globalization, there are many more relationships between banks and with other actors in the financial system. This involves not only ordinary credit/debt cross-relationships arising from funding operations, credit and investment activities, and services provided, but also the need to negotiate so that each party can handle financial imbalances and manage liquidity risks.

In addition, technology has sped up the transfer of funds held by banks, not only professional counterparts, but also retail customers, via internet banking.

The spread of a new banking management model, the OTD model, based on the widespread use of securitization and confined to Anglo-Saxon countries, has recently contributed to increasing bank liquidity risk. In these countries, before OTD, under the Originate to Hold (OTH) model banks relied on stable and low-cost core deposits (demand, savings and time deposits) as the primary source of funding to generate a portfolio of (rather illiquid) loans held to maturity.[9] This involved a fundamental risk, as banks are, in general, structurally illiquid. However, as long as liquid assets were sufficient in relation to more volatile liquid liabilities, i.e. liquid assets outweighed liquid liabilities, in normal circumstances banks were fine (liquid). More recently the availability of alternative investments and savings products, provided by a wide range of financial institutions, has reduced the banks' traditional funding base and made it less predictable (i.e. more volatile) and more costly. This required the adoption of the new OTD banking intermediation model, which has led banks to rely more and more on price and credit sensitive market funding, in general, on the liabilities side, increasing the share of wholesale funding in total bank funds, and, on the assets side, reliance on securitization markets. As stated above, in the OTD model, customer loans are not held by banks in their balance sheets until maturity. They are systematically securitized and transferred to other intermediaries or investors. Consequently, banks with the OTD model change not only their revenues, no longer derived from interest on existing loans but from commission on the loans originated and sold, but also change their funding, no longer from funds raised by customers, but principally from the sale of assets. Thus, in the OTD model recourse to the market and related risks, untypically stem from the emergence of an ordinary financial imbalance to manage. In addition, the management of banks based on the OTD model focuses on the aspects involved in the process of structuring the assets to be transferred, rather than the relationship with customers to be funded, along with their credit rating. This involves exposure to different risks, such as credit risk, which occurs over time through the insolvency of debtors whose payments are placed at the service of securitization, and market risk, as a result of the loss of value of financial assets arising from securitization as well as liquidity risk. The latter, in the form of market liquidity risk, during the financial crisis of 2007–2009, affected actors with financial assets in their portfolio, since these were low-value assets, less usable for obtaining liquidity. In addition, the banks that securitized most of their credits were affected by liquidity risk, in this case in the form of funding liquidity risk, due to their difficulty or inability to continue their activity based on the systematic use of the market to acquire the liquid funds needed to finance the renewal of the loan portfolio. This can give rise to systemic risk, all the greater the larger and more widespread are the investments in financial assets derived from the securitization of loans granted with little attention from the banks originators. The financial crisis that began in 2007 is a perfect example.

Liquidity risk also became more critical due to the increased competition from other banks, non-bank financial institutions and securities markets. This put additional pressure on banks' net interest margins and has forced them to optimize liquidity management, resulting in a secular decline in lower-yielding, on balance sheet, liquid assets (Montes-Negret 2009). The search for yield (i.e. rising return on assets–ROA, and return on equity–ROE) by shareholders and bank managers in competitive markets, led banks to increase their leverage and take more risks, including higher liquidity risk, by increasing the illiquid portion of their assets either through more lending or by an over-reliance on the permanence of market liquidity to securitize loans on demand.

Added to this was the concentration of large financial groups giving rise to a small number of institutions controlling a large share of the market (known as Systemically Important Financial Institutions–SIFIs), making the failure of one likely to bring the entire system down.

Finally, during a financial crisis, the weight and pervasiveness of interrelations can be troublesome. More specifically, liquidity risk (and other financial risks) can have a knock-on or domino effect in the financial system. The crisis makes the liquidity risk more severe by intensifying market interconnections and hence the likelihood of contagion across the markets and banking systems.

Notes

1. For more details of liquidity risk management in the banking industry before and after the GFC, see Chapters 5 and 6, respectively.
2. Some studies argue in favour of two (rather than three) types of liquidity, i.e. funding and market liquidity (European Central Bank–ECB 2002; ORACLE 2009). They indicate that the role of the central bank as provider of liquidity during financial crises only cushions their effects, but is unable to guarantee success.
3. Open market operations are used by the central bank to give (or take) liquidity to (or from) a bank or a group of banks in its currency. For more details, see Chapter 4.
4. The BCBS is a committee of banking supervisory authorities established in 1974 by the central bank governors of the Group of Ten countries. It provides a forum for regular cooperation on banking supervisory matters. Its objective is to enhance the understanding of key supervisory issues and improve the quality of banking supervision worldwide.
5. For more details on CFP, see Chapter 5.
6. Adverse selection and moral hazard are both examples of market failure situations, caused due to asymmetric information between buyers and sellers in a market. Adverse selection occurs when there's a lack of symmetric information prior to a deal between a buyer and a seller, whereas moral hazard occurs when there is asymmetric information between two parties and change in behaviour of one party after a deal is struck.
7. The subprime mortgage crisis has brought attention to the OTD model, adopted by a vast majority of Anglo-Saxon banks. Its main characteristic is that the originator of a loan sells most of them to third parties through a securitisation process. For more details, see both Sect. 2.6 and Chapter 3.

8. For example, in normal periods, a bank is liquid as long as it can obtain enough liquidity to satisfy its funding needs directly from the central banks or through the markets (interbank or assets markets).
9. Only Anglo-Saxon countries underwent the change from an Originate To Hold (OTH) credit model, where loans granted to a single bank are kept in its balance sheet until they are extinguished, to an OTD model, in which the bank providing loans does not keep them on its balance sheet until their maturity, but through widespread use of securitization, transfers them to third parties, together with the related credit risk.

References

Acharya, V., & Pedersen, L. H. (2005). Asset Pricing with Liquidity Risk. *Journal of Financial Economics, 77,* 375–410.

Acharya, V., Gromb, D., & Yorulmazer, T. (2012). Imperfect Competition in the Interbank Market for Liquidity. *American Economic Journal: Macroeconomics, 4,* 184–217.

Allen, F., & Douglas, G. (1998). Optimal Financial Crises. *The Journal of Finance, 53,* 1245–1284.

Allen, F., & Douglas, G. (2000). Financial Contagion. *Journal of Political Economy, 108,* 1–31.

Amihud, Y. (2002). Illiquidity and Stock Returns: Cross-Section and Time-Series Effects. *Journal of Financial Markets, 5,* 31–56.

Ayusi, J., & Repullo, R. (2003). A Model of the Open Market Operations of the European Central Bank. *Economic Journal, 113,* 883–902.

Bangia, A., Diebold, F. X., Schuermann, T., & Stroughair, J. D. (1999, June). *Liquidity Risk, with Implications for Traditional Market Risk Measurement and Management* (Working Paper 99). Wharton School.

Bangia, A., Diebold, F. X., Schermann, T., & Stroughair, J. (2001). Modelling Liquidity Risk, with Implications for Traditional Market Risk Measurement and Management. In S. Figlewski & R. Levich (Eds.), *Risk Management: The State of the Art.* Amsterdam: Kluwer Academic.

Bank for International Settlements (BIS). (1999, May). *Market Liquidity: Research Findings and Selected Policy Implications.*

Banks, E. (2005). *Liquidity Risk. Managing Asset and Funding Risk.* Hounmills: Palgrave Macmillan.

Basel Committee on Banking Supervision (BCBS). (2008, February). *Liquidity Risk: Management and Supervisory Challenges.*

Bhattacharya, S., & Gale, D. (1987). Preference Shocks, Liquidity and Central Bank Policy. In W. Barnett & K. Singleton (Eds.), *New Approaches to Monetary Economics* (pp. 69–88). New York: Cambridge University Press.

Brunnermier, M. K. (2009). Deciphering the liquidity and credit crunch 2007–2008. *Journal of Economic Perspectives 23,* 77–100.

Brunnermeier, M. K., & Pedersen, L. H. (2005). Predatory Trading. *The Journal of Finance, 60,* 1825–1863.

Brunnermeier, M. K., & Pedersen, L. H. (2009). Market Liquidity and Funding Liquidity. *Review of Financial Studies, 22,* 2201–2238.

Brusco, S., & Castiglionesi, F. (2007). Liquidity Coinsurance, Moral Hazard, and Financial Contagion. *The Journal of Finance, 62,* 2275–2302.

Carlin, B. I., Lobo, M., & Viswanathan, S. (2007). Episodic Liquidity Crises: Cooperative and Predatory Trading. *The Journal of Finance, 62,* 2235–2274.

Caruana, J., & Kodres, L. (2008, February). Liquidity in Global Market. *Financial Stability Review, 11,* 65–74.

Chordia, T., Sarkar, A., & Subrahmanyam, A. (2005). An Empirical Analysis of Stock and Bond Market Liquidity. *Review of Financial Studies, 18,* 85–129.

Chordia, T., Roll, R., & Subrahmanyam, A. (2000). Commonality in Liquidity. *Journal of Financial Economics, 56,* 3–28.

Chordia, T., Roll, R., & Subrahmanyam, A. (2001). Market Liquidity and Trading Activity. *The Journal of Finance, 56,* 501–530.

Chordia, T., Roll, R., & Subrahmanyam, A. (2002). Order Imbalance, Liquidity, and Market Returns. *Journal of Financial Economics, 65,* 111–130.

Cifuentes, R., Gianluigi, F., & Shin, H. S. (2005). Liquidity Risk and Contagion. *Journal of the European Economic Association, 3,* 556–566.

Crockett, A. (2008). Market Liquidity and Financial Stability. *Financial Stability Review, 11,* 13–17.

David, L. (2007, October 3). 'Liquidity, Liquidity, Liquidity', Remarks by David Longworth, Deputy Governor of the Bank of Canada to the Investment Industry Association of Canada, Toronto.

Deutsche Bundesbank and Bafin. (2008, February). *Liquidity Risk Management Practices at Selected German Credit Institutions.*

Diamond, D., & Dybvig, P. (1983). Bank Runs, Deposit Insurance, and Liquidity. *Journal of Political Economy, 91,* 401–419.

Diamond, D. W., & Dybvig P. H. (2000). 'Bank Runs, Deposit Insurance, and Liquidity', Federal Reserve Bank of Minneapolis. *Quarterly Review, 24,* 14–23.

Diamond, D. W., & Rajan, R. G. (2001). Liquidity Risk, Liquidity Creation, and Financial Fragility: A Theory of Banking. *Journal of Political Economy, 109,* 287–327.

Diamond, D. W., & Rajan, R. G. (2005). Liquidity Shortages and Banking Crises. *The Journal of Finance, 60,* 615–647.

Drehmann, M., & Nikolaou, N. (2008). *Funding Liquidity Risk: Definition and Measurement.* New York: Mimeo.

Drehmann, M., & Nikolaou, K. (2010, July). *Funding Liquidity Risk: Definition and Measurement* (Working Papers 316). Bank for International Settlement (BIS).

Drehmann, M., Elliot, J., & Kapadia, S. (2007). Funding Liquidity Risk: Potential Triggers and Systemic Implications, Mimeo, Bank of England.
European Central Bank (ECB). (2002, May). *Development in Banks' Liquidity Profile and Management.*
European Central Bank (ECB). (2004). *The Monetary Policy of ECB.* Germany: Frankfurt am Main.
Ewerhart, C., Cassola, N., & Valla, N. (2007). *Declining Valuations and Equilibrium Bidding in Central Bank Refinancing Operations* (FINRISK Working Paper 407).
Ferguson, R. W., Hartmann, P., Panetta, F., & Portes, R. (2007, November). *International Financial Stability* (Geneva Reports on the World Economy 9).
Flannery, M. (1996). Financial Crises, Payments System Problems and Discount Window Lending. *Journal of Money, Credit and Banking, 28,* 804–824.
Freixas, X., Giannini, C., Hoggarth, G., & Soussa, F. (1999, November). Lender of Last Resort: A Review of the Literature. *Bank of England Financial Stability Review 7,* 151–167.
Freixas, X., Rochet, J. C., & Parigi, B. M. (2004). The Lender of Last Resort: A Twenty-First Century Approach. *Journal of the European Economic Association, 2,* 1085–1115.
Goodhart, C. (2008). Liquidity Risk Management. *Financial Stability Review, 11,* 39–44.
Hart, O., & Moore, J. (1994). A Theory of Debt Based on the Inalienability of Human Capital. *Quarterly Journal of Economics, 109,* 841–879.
Hoggarth, G., & Saporta, V. (2001). Costs of Banking System Instability: Some Empirical Evidence. *Journal of Banking & Finance, 26,* 825–855.
Holmström, B., & Tirole, J. (1997). Financial Intermediation, Loanable Funds, and the Real Sector. *Quarterly Journal of Economics, 112,* 663–691.
Holmström, B., & Tirole, J. (2001). LAPM: A Liquidity-Based Asset Pricing Model. *The Journal of Finance, 56,* 1837–1867.
Humphrey, T. M., & Keleher, R. E. (1984). The Lender of Last Resort: A Historical Perspective. *CATO Journal, 4,* 275–321.
International Monetary Fund. (IMF, 2008, April). *Global Financial Stability Report.*
Jarrow, R., & Subramanian, A. (1997). Mopping Up Liquidity. *Risk, 10,* 170–173.
Liu, W. (2006). A Liquidity-Augmented Capital Asset Pricing Model. *Journal of Financial Economics, 82,* 631–671.
Longstaf, A. (2001). Optimal Portfolio Choice and the Valuation of Illiquid Securities. *Review of Financial Studies, 14,* 407–431.
Matz, L., & Neu, P. (2007). *Liquidity Risk Management.* Singapore: Wiley.
Montes-Negret, F. (2009, November). *The Heavenly Liquidity Twin. The Increasing Importance of Liquidity Risk.* The World Bank Europe and Central Asia Region Finance and Private Sector Department.

Morris, S., & Shin, H. (2004). Co-ordination Risk and the Price of Debt. *European Economic Review, 48,* 133–153.
Nikolaou, K. (2009, February). *Liquidity (Risk) Concepts: Definitions and Interactions* (Working Paper Series 1009). European Central Bank (Eurosystem).
Nyborg, K. G., & Strebulaev, I. A. (2004). Multiple Unit Auctions and Short Squeezes. *The Review of Financial Studies, 17,* 545–580.
ORACLE. (2009, November). *Liquidity Eisk Management in Financial Services Strategies for Success.* An Oracle White Paper, Oracle Financial Services.
Pastor, L., & Stambaugh, R. F. (2003). Liquidity Risk and Expected Stock Returns. *Journal of Political Economy, 111,* 642–685.
Rochet, J. C., & Vives, X. (2004). Coordination Failures and the Lender of Last Resort: Was Bagehot Right After All? *Journal of the European Economic Association, 2,* 1116–1147.
Roubini, R. (2007). *Worse Than LTCM: Not Just a Liquidity Crisis; Rather a Credit Crisis Crunch.* RGE Monitor.
Ruozi, R., & Ferrari, P. (2013). *Liquidity Risk Management in Banks. Economic and Regulatory Issues.* Heidelberg: Springer.
Sekoni, A. (2015, October). *The Basic Concepts and Feature of Bank Liquidity and Its Risk* (Munich Personal RePEc Archive (MPRA) Paper 67389).
Strahan, P. (2008, February). *Liquidity Production in the 21st Century Banking* (Working Paper 13798). National Bureau of Economic Research (NBER).
The Joint Forum. (2006, May). *The Management of Liquidity Risk in Financial Groups.*
Vento, G. A., & La Ganga, P. (2009). Bank Liquidity Risk Management and Supervision: Which Lessons from Recent Market Turmoil? *Journal of Money, Investment and Banking, 10,* 79–126.
Williamson, S. D. (2008). Liquidity Constraints. In Durlauf, S. N., Blume, L. E. (Eds.), *The New Palgrave Dictionary of Economics* (2nd ed.). Basingstoke: Palgrave Macmillan.

CHAPTER 3

The Bank Liquidity Issues During the Subprime Crisis

3.1 The Subprime Crisis

This chapter investigates the recent banking liquidity crisis. However, first, it is necessary to turn to the GFC, because the liquidity problems of many banks were the final manifestation of the subprime crisis (Ruozi and Ferrari 2013). The latter, although originated from the United States subprime mortgage loans, through intensive market integration, was transmitted in a number of ways and to varying degrees, to major European banks. It was a highly complex phenomenon and is therefore difficult to interpret. Its complexity stems from the many causes underlying the crisis and the numerous markets and actors involved. Prior to the outbreak of the subprime crisis, several strongly interconnected macro and microeconomic elements of fragility, were present in the US.

To understand the origin of the subprime crisis, the following Sects. (3.1.1 and 3.2.2) look first at what led to the GFC and then review the main triggering factors that snowballed the crisis.

3.1.1 The Origin

The GFC was caused by several macro and microeconomic factors[1] in the United States during the favourable phase of the economic cycle before 2007.

L. Chiaramonte, *Bank Liquidity and the Global Financial Crisis*, Palgrave Macmillan Studies in Banking and Financial Institutions,
https://doi.org/10.1007/978-3-319-94400-5_3

The macroeconomic factors included: the expansive [REMOVE RESTRICTIVE] restrictive monetary policy adopted by the Federal Reserve (FED) during the so-called Greenspan period,[2] characterized by enduring low interest rates, especially between 2001 and 2004 (Felton and Reinhart 2008; White 2009); and the continual flow of capital into the US from the major Asian economies, especially China (Lastra and Wood 2010).[3]

The microeconomic factors were principally in Anglo-Saxon countries and relate to the behaviour of the protagonists of the crisis, i.e. major US banking groups, including a mind-boggling increase in processes of financial innovation with the intensive use of innovative securitization techniques in the real estate sector (Litan 2010); and the transition from the OTH to the OTD banking model (ECB 2009a).

As explained below, these two groups of factors are closely inter-related. Specifically, the first determined a favourable macroeconomic environment in the United States until the early months of 2006, with increased demand for credit by fundraisers (i.e. enterprises, householders, private equity funds, hedge funds, etc.). This flow of abundant liquidity in the US financial system profoundly and persistently affected the financing and investment choices of many actors before the outbreak of the GFC. On the one hand, it encouraged lenders, primarily banks, to look for higher and hence riskier returns (Black et al. 2009). Before the subprime crisis, many US banks had intensified[4] the supply of loans to families and enterprises with low credit ratings, i.e. so-called subprime customers (Madalino and Peydrò 2009).[5] For various reasons, they increased the credit supply to problematic parties (Holt 2009) not only to garner higher yields from these riskier loans, but also because of the mistaken conviction by American banks that US house prices would continue to grow for a long time to come, as a consequence, especially, of the long period of low interest rates. Hence, US banks believed that, if subprime borrowers failed to pay their instalments, the insolvencies would be covered by the sale of the houses used as collateral for the subprime mortgage loans. Unfortunately, their confidence was misplaced because US home prices, as described below, had grown rapidly for many years, creating a huge housing bubble in the United States by early 2006, and the bubble was bound to burst (Levitin and Wachter 2012).

On the other hand, the flow of abundant liquidity characterizing the US financial system at the beginning of 2006, influenced many investment decisions. Specifically, easily obtainable funding at a relatively low cost, due to low interest rates, attracted a large number of debtors, bumping up banking indebtedness, with increased investments in consumer spending, especially in the real estate sector (Holt 2009). For the first time, several Americans were able to realize the (American) dream of buying their own home. The immediate consequence was a sharp increase in US house prices and the creation of a massive real estate bubble by 2006 (Baker 2008). The rise in houses prices led borrowers to request larger loans, for longer periods. This caused a dilemma for the US banking system: what could they do to cope with the intense and rapid expansion of credit to householders and enterprises? What could they do to speed up their fundraising? To solve this problem, in the years immediately preceding the crisis, American banks decided to use a funding instrument—securitization—applied for the first time to subprime mortgage loans. Hence, the term 'subprime mortgage securitization' or 'innovative securitization' (the first microeconomic factor). Unlike the securitization technique relating to high-quality loans (so-called classical or traditional securitization), widely used by American banks to raise funds since 1970 (Segoviano et al. 2013), innovative securitization was adopted by US banks only some years before the outbreak of the subprime crisis. Through several financing vehicles described below, they radically innovated traditional securitization with effects that turned out to be perverse.

In order to understand the complexity of innovative securitization, how it differed from the traditional version, and the downside including liquidity problems, some simplification may be needed. As shown in Fig. 3.1, the innovative securitization technique can be divided into three separate, but connected, levels. The first level replicates the functioning of traditional securitization, but with a significant difference relating to the quality of the securitized assets. To raise funds, innovative securitization allowed banks—the so-called originators of the operation—to include poor quality (i.e. the subprime mortgage loans) assets in the securitization process. Originators transferred their assets (included those of poor quality) and the related borrowers, to a Special Purpose Vehicle (SPV) created ad hoc by the bank for this operation. The SPV transformed these assets into negotiable bonds called Asset-Backed Securities (ABSs), where the underlying assets were loans, and Mortgage-Backed Securities (MBSs), where the underlying assets were mortgages, including subprime mortgages. Before placing these originated securities (ABSs and MBSs) with potential investors, the rating agencies assessed them (Ashcraft et al. 2009). On the basis of the rating,

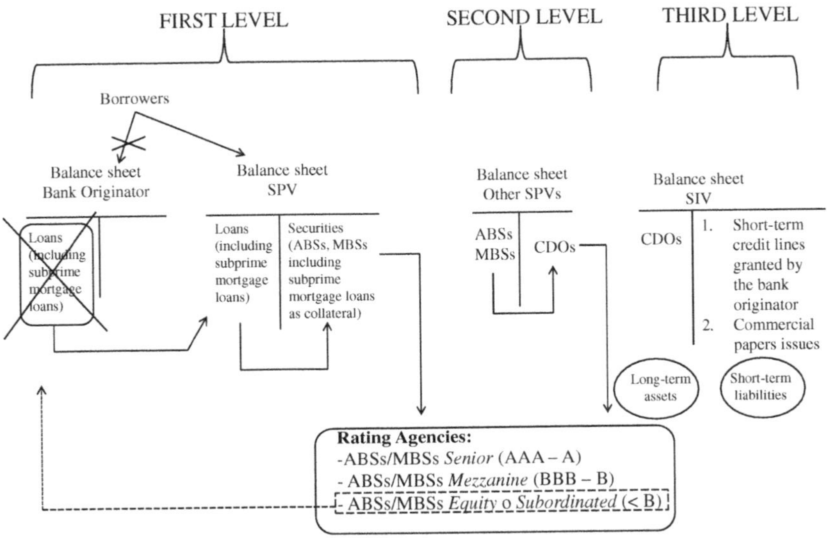

Fig. 3.1 The functioning of the innovative securitization process (simplified) (*Source* Author's elaboration)

they were divided into the following three tranches: senior, mezzanine, and equity or subordinated,[6] characterized by increasing degrees of risk and return. The equity or subordinated tranche was the riskiest and most profitable, and hence was usually underwritten by the bank originator, shown as an asset in its balance sheet. This process meant that the credit risk, initially transferred off the originator's balance sheet, returned to it. This too was different from traditional securitization, where originators cannot purchase the bonds generated by the SPV.

As with traditional securitization, the money raised by the SPV through the sale of ABSs and MBSs was transferred to the bank originator, thus meeting its funding requirement. Finally, the SPV repaid subscribers from interest paid by debtors and borrowers surrendered by the bank originator.

The second level of innovative securitization involved the creation of further SPVs by the bank originator, as potential investors in the ABSs and MBSs generated by the first-level SPV. These additional SPVs in turn securitized the ABSs and MBSs they had bought and which were shown on the asset side of their balance sheets, creating new securities, called Collateralized Debt Obligations (CDOs), shown as liabilities. The underlying assets of these CDOs were ABSs, MBSs (including subprime mortgages as collateral), high yield securities and junk bonds. As with the first level, the CDOs were assessed by rating agencies before placing them with investors. However, the CDOs resulting from the second-level securitization or re-securitization (so-called collateralization), were more opaque than ABSs and MBSs. This problem was only partially solved by rating agencies, due to the conflict of interest between them and bank originators, who paid them for their ratings.

The third level of innovative securitization featured another financial vehicle, also created by the bank originator: the Structured Investment Vehicle (SIV). Like SPVs, SIVs were independent legal entities with a small amount of capital. Their activity consisted in subscribing CDOs that appeared in their balance sheets as medium and long-term assets, funded through both short-term credit lines granted by the bank originator, and by issuing commercial papers (CPs), i.e. short-term securities. In practice, SIVs financed long-term assets with short-term liabilities. Therefore, unlike SPVs, these vehicles were characterized by the existence of a maturity mismatch between liabilities (mostly short-term) and assets (mostly long term). Unfortunately, when the subprime crisis occurred, due to the intense maturity transformation activity, SIVs ran into liquidity problems, specifically by funding liquidity risk. Their mistake was over-reliance on the continuous renewal of the CPs maturities, necessary to pay interest to previous buyers of the CPs. For SIVs it was fundamental to have an efficient CPs market.

Therefore, in view of the functioning of the innovative securitization described above, the following important characteristics of traditional securitization were lacking:

- good quality assets securitized by the bank originator or, overall, any rigorous and transparent assessment of that quality;
- an exactly matching maturity between the assets and liabilities on the SPV balance sheet;
- technical and contractual conditions between the originator and the finance vehicle that ensured separation between the two subjects. The former could not make repurchase commitments for the assets transferred to SPVs, directly finance these vehicles or repurchase their issues placed with third parties.

As said before, a further microeconomic factor, together with the massive use of innovative securitization by US banks, explaining the origin of the subprime crisis, was the adoption of the OTD banking model. As already stated in Chapter 2, in Anglo-Saxon countries, from 1990 onwards, there was a shift from the classic OTH banking model, where banks kept most of the credits granted to customers on their balance sheet until the expiry data of the loans, to the OTD model, where loans were securitized and offered in the form of bonds to a large number of investors. The OTD model was widely used in the US banking sector, partly driving the development of lending activity in the subprime segment. The preference for the OTD banking model was due to the fact that banks used this model as a tool to optimize asset management, multiplying the volume of loans issued at the same level of capital invested, and to save on regulatory capital[7] (ECB 2009a). Through the widespread use of securitization, US banks shifted loans off the balance sheet, releasing regulatory capital to cover other types of risks.

However, the OTD model and innovative securitization—the two microeconomic factors behind the subprime crisis—led to a series of contraindications. Firstly, they increased market interconnections and the effects of contagion between markets and banking systems. Innovative securitization transferred risk between geographic market areas and, as explained below, exposed the entire banking system to liquidity risk (both funding and market liquidity risk). Overall, they facilitated the spread of the liquidity crisis to the banking markets.

Another effect of the two microeconomic factors was the irresponsible behaviour and short-termism of the actors involved. Irresponsibility because the ability to transfer the risks of loans reduced the need for banks engaged in large-scale securitization (i) to properly screen (in advance) by granting only loans with likely repayments and (ii) to properly monitor (ex-post) debt repayment capabilities over time. This increased the moral hazard in US banks with intensive use of the innovative securitization technique. By securitizing their loans, they offset the associated risks. And short-termism through various actors, including institutional investors, maximizing quick profits without due consideration to, or an understanding of, the risks associated with products such as ABSs, MBSs, and CDOs. In addition, rating agencies were affected by short-term behaviour, since their revenues from assessing these securities generated by the securitization mechanism were about double the remuneration from ordinary securities.

As a consequence, both structured products such as ABSs, MBSs and CDOs, and credit derivatives, especially credit default swaps (CDSs)[8] grew exponentially. All these instruments are highly complex, opaque, non-standardized and traded predominantly on OTC markets. In particular, the large-scale use of these products led to genuine pricing difficulties and complicated the lives of rating agencies which found it hard to assess the risk, structurally affected by conflicts of interest (ECB 2009b).

A further problem was the vulnerability of banks to the insolvency of borrowers (primarily with subprime loans), not eliminated or mitigated by the securitization technique. Indeed, risk returned to the banks via various transmission channels, such as the direct possession of the securities resulting from the securitization of subprime mortgage loans, for investment or trading purposes. In addition, originators had to subscribe the equity tranches issued by their SPVs. Another channel comprised credit enhancements, added by issuers (i.e. the originator) to securities arising from securitization for the purpose of making them more attractive to investors. Credit enhancements were dangerous because the risk of loans transferred outside the bank via securitization returned through the back door in the event of the insolvency of the vehicles (SPVs and SIVs).

Finally, both the OTD model and the innovative securitization mechanism created a US shadow banking system characterized by the presence of non-regulated vehicle companies (SPVs and SIVs) closely linked to banks and therefore able to undermine the stability of the entire banking system (National Commission on the causes of the financial and economic crisis in the United States 2011).

3.1.2 *Triggering Factors*

Also deserving of attention are the main events that speeded up the subprime crisis, the so-called 'triggering factors', which occurred in the United States at the end of 2006: the bursting of the US real estate bubble and the adoption of a restrictive monetary policy by the FED (Bernanke 2007). Both factors changed the US macroeconomic scenario, creating conditions that led several banks into difficulties, including one of the most important American investment banks, Lehman Brothers, which failed in September 2008, sparking the global financial crisis (Zingales 2008).

The first triggering factor, the collapse in US house prices, meant it was difficult to extract liquidity from the rapidly falling value of real estate. This was true particularly of debtors who had relied on prices to cope with rising rates. As long as real estate prices grew, debtors who had difficulties in making payments could either sell the house at a good price or access new loans. But when prices began to fall, this was no longer possible, particularly for subprime borrowers. Face with the collapse in house prices, they were obliged to comply with the contracts and could not renegotiate the mortgages on more favourable terms. For increasingly large groups of borrowers, the decline in property prices made it more convenient to give up their home rather than continue to repay the mortgage, which now totalled more than the value of the property.

The second trigger was the gradual increase in interest rates by the FED in order to contain inflationary pressures. The restrictive monetary policy significantly affected the ability, especially of poor quality customers to repay the banks. As shown in Fig. 3.2, the increase in the subprime mortgage payments, typically loans at variable rates, generated an increase in defaults. The failure to make payments created a series of negative effects for banks, including liquidity problems (see Sect. 3.2), undermining their stability. This was perhaps the key factor in the banking liquidity crisis.

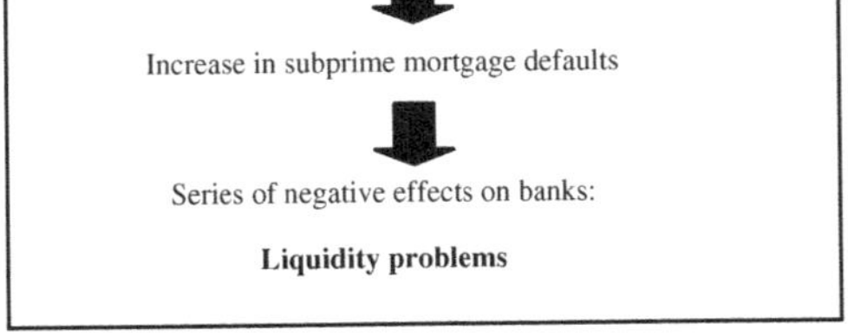

Fig. 3.2 Main effects of the US restrictive monetary policy adopted in 2006 (*Source* Author's elaboration)

3.2 Bank Liquidity Problems During the Subprime Crisis

A liquidity crisis is almost always the result and not the cause of a banking crisis. Indeed, it was only when the GFC was in full swing, that mainly American, but also European banks, due to significant interlinkage between markets, ran into liquidity problems, threatening their stability and consequently the entire financial system.

The following sections focus, firstly, on the main characteristics of the banks most affected by the liquidity crisis and the type of liquidity problems they faced (see Sect. 3.2.1). Secondly, they examine how the liquidity crisis turned into a solvency crisis for financial institutions (Sect. 3.2.2). Finally, they turn to the lessons that can be learnt from the GFC, particularly with regard to liquidity risk (Sect. 3.2.3).

3.2.1 *The Characteristics of the Banks Most Affected by the Liquidity Crisis of 2007–2009*

Before identifying what types of liquidity problems were faced by many banks during the GFC, it is necessary to understand which banks were most affected and why. The analysis focuses mainly on the American banking system, since the subprime crisis began there.

The US banks most affected were those that had adopted aggressive/risky asset-liability management during the boom period, i.e. up to early 2006. This strategy, designed for survival and profit in an increasingly competitive market, meant that several US banks had balance sheets, particularly on the assets side, as shown in Fig. 3.3. On the assets side, the US banks most affected by liquidity problems were those that before the outbreak of the subprime crisis:

- had decided to minimize their liquid assets, especially cash, through a misguided trust in the functioning of both the secondary securities market and the interbank market to raise funds when necessary. They had also decided to minimize cash due to the high cost-opportunity of liquidity holdings. Until 2008, the interest paid on deposits at the FED was zero, whereas, in the same period, Treasury bond yields were relatively high (Anderson 2008);
- had securitized most of their medium and long-term assets, included subprime mortgage loans, generating so-called toxic assets,

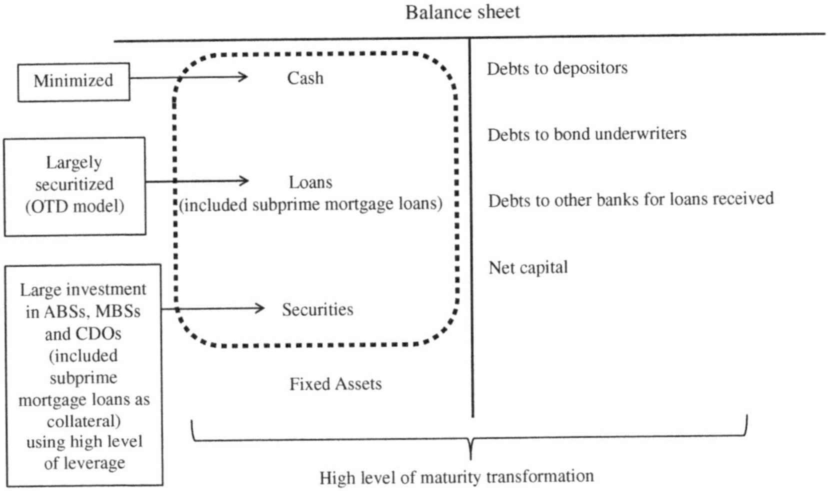

Fig. 3.3 Balance sheet characteristics of the US banks most affected by liquidity problems (*Source* Author's elaboration)

i.e. securities which included subprime mortgage loans as collateral, such as ABSs, MBSs, and CDOs (Dwyer and Tkac 2009; Litan 2010). Their widespread was due to the fact the OTD nature of the United States banking system, being an intermediation model that allows a large use of securitization (ECB 2008);

- with high level of leverage, had invested a large portion of their portfolio in products derived from securitization (such as ABSs, MBSs and CDOs) including subprime mortgages loans as collateral, often in junior tranches, the most risky and profitable. Short-term maximum profits were pursued irrespective of the related risks.

In addition, these US banks were characterized by a high degree of maturity transformation (Goodhard and Perotti 2015), favoured by both the abundant liquidity in the markets and the sharp reversal of bank assets closely linked to the increase in leverage and caused by the spread of the OTD model. These led to a fall in the quality of real estate portfolios, poorly monitored by originators and held for sale, the growing use of short-term funding instruments, mainly commercial paper, the US market for which is based on Money Market Funds (MMFs), and, all in all, ever greater exposure to both credit and liquidity risks.

US banks with a balance sheet structure as shown in Fig. 3.3 were hit by two different types of closely related liquidity problem: market liquidity risk and funding risk.

As stated in Chapter 2, market liquidity risk is the risk that a bank is not able to sell its securities without incurring significant losses due to insufficient market liquidity. The US banks were affected by this first type of liquidity risk when the subprime borrowers stopped making payments as a consequence of the FED's restrictive monetary policy. Thus, US banks no longer received the expected return from ABSs, MBSs and/or CDOs with subprime mortgage loans as collateral. Hence, many banks decided to sell these ABSs, MBSs and CDOs, only to discover that there no buyers. Indeed, the liquidity crisis on the secondary market of ABSs, MBSs and CDOs led to a dramatic fall in the prices of these securities and many US banks were forced to sell at much lower than the purchase prices. Obviously, a large number suffered significant capital losses. And many European banks were affected because of their involvement through both their US subsidiaries and massive subscriptions of toxic assets.

Even the banks that decided not to sell these securities, but to keep them in their portfolios, suffered capital losses because of the drop in fair value, following the mark-to-market rule (Pozen 2009).[9]

For these reasons, from the summer 2007 on, many United States and subsequently European banks began to announce write-downs and losses on portfolio activities linked to subprime mortgage loans. These losses, together with the continued downgrading of toxic assets by the rating agencies, weakened the confidence of customers in the banking system, complicating the fundraising activity of many banks. Hence, US banks with balance sheets as shown in Fig. 3.3 were exposed to funding risk as well as market liquidity risk.

Funding risk consists in the inability of a bank to raise the funds required to repay their debts. Specifically, it occurs when a bank is not able to refinance itself to satisfy both 'standard' demand (from depositors, bond underwriters and from other banks for loans received), but also 'non-standard' demand from the phenomenon of bank runs. Fortunately, the few cases of bank runs were blocked by the prompt intervention of central banks through injections of liquidity, and governments through recapitalization or nationalization. These actions were necessary to avoid a world economic collapse.

Thus, several US banks were also affected by funding risk, because during the crisis years they were unable to raise funds, given that all the traditional channels for funding were blocked. Indeed, focusing on Fig. 3.3, they were unable:

- to use cash, since US banks did not hold much cash before 2007;
- to securitize other assets because the market was completely frozen and refractory to new operations;
- to sell the securities in their portfolio (including ABSs, MBSs, and CDOs), again because of market liquidity risk. In addition, two phenomena, the flight to quality and the flight to liquidity, were increasing the difficulties of selling securities (Dong and Yi 2017);
- to sell real estate assets, often the collateral for the mortgages, because of liquidity crisis in that market and banks would have incurred capital losses;
- to rely on new depositors, because this channel was blocked due to the loss of confidence in the banking system (lack of confidence determined the flight to liquidity);
- to issue new securities and new CPs since no one wanted them in a context of flight to quality and liquidity;
- to use the interbank lending market, also illiquid, to raise funds. Banks did not trust each other with lending given the inability to assess the credit risk of the counterparty (Afonso et al. 2010).

Some European banks were also affected by funding risk as a consequence of the liquidity crisis on the interbank lending market. Northern Rock, a British bank over-dependent on the functioning of the interbank lending market, is a significant example. When the market froze, Northern Rock had serious liquidity problems leading to a bank run (Bruni and Llewellyn 2009).

3.2.2 *The Relationship Between Liquidity and Solvency Problems and Their Impact on Bank Stability*

The banks facing the liquidity issues described above also suffered from solvency problems. This is evident, for example, in the decrease in capital of many banks during the subprime crisis, as a consequence of market liquidity risk or the mark-to-market rule. The decrease in bank capital triggered the bank solvency crisis.

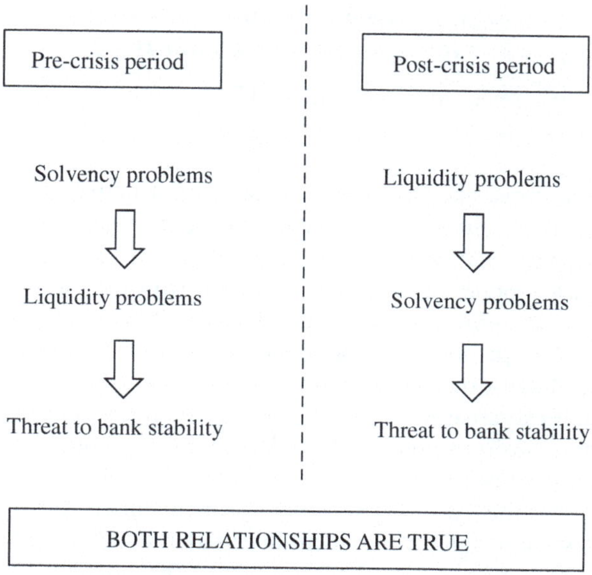

Fig. 3.4 Relationship between liquidity, solvency, and bank stability (*Source* Author's elaboration)

Since liquidity problems partially caused a solvency crisis, affecting the stability of the whole banking system, after the GFC, for the first time, regulators realized that liquidity risk is not necessarily the result of solvency problems in a bank, but can itself impact on bank solvency and stability (see the right side of Fig. 3.4). Before the bank liquidity crisis occurred during the GFC, regulators believed that the liquidity risk was only a consequence of solvency risk (as shown on the left side of Fig. 3.4). Indeed, both the first and the second International Agreement on Bank Capital of 1988 and 2004 (the so-called Basel I and Basel II Accords) established rules for bank capital and not for bank liquidity, given that the BCBS thought that the stability of a bank was given by the proper balancing of capital and risk.

After the GFC it became clear that liquidity and solvency were strongly interdependent, and rules needed to be introduced to contain future liquidity problems as well.[10]

3.2.3 *The Main Lessons from the GFC with Particular Reference to Bank Liquidity*

Several lessons emerged from the GFC. As summarized below, they include general considerations, but also specific lessons related to bank liquidity.

In general terms, like all major political or social crises, the GFC was a profound crisis of values which affected different subjects, such as households, enterprises, national or local authorities, financial intermediaries, financial market operators (National Commission on the Causes of the Financial and Economic Crisis in the United States 2011). Specifically, there were the spread of: exasperated search for profit, uncontrolled innovation, global expansion and personal power. In the banking sector these became excessive leverage, the search for high-yield assets, expansion into new business areas and market segments, entry into predominantly speculative business areas, etc.

Additionally, the GFC highlighted the problem of the responsibility of financial system supervisors, including: federal and public authorities, supervisors of both the banking system and the financial markets, specialist agencies by type of subjects or sector. Overall, all of them failed in their duty to maintain financial stability through careful prevention and control. The severity of the responsibilities is shown by the magnitude of the deficiencies and failures to take action: inertia in the governance of financial innovation, lackadaisical promotion of the dissemination of best practices in the field of accounting, organization, control and transparency; acceptance of totally inadequate credit standards; insensitivity to governance issues and in particular to the implications of the abnormal spread, in the finance industry, of conflicts of interest.

Although financial intermediaries were extensively involved in all aspects of the system, increased tensions originated from two specific areas of financial activity: mortgage lending (housing and commercial property finance, and support for property development) and investment banking (structuring and placing issues, securities trading, activities in the OTC derivatives markets), transformed by the OTD model and real estate securitizations into the so-called 'mortgage machine' that distributed toxic assets all over the world.

Moreover, the crisis gave rise to a dangerous and unstable link between financial intermediaries and markets, where ease of access to globalized markets prompted these intermediaries, including large banks, to push business development to the limit. This facilitated the creation of high leverage, while high liquidity on the market created the illusion of growth based on the systematic renewal of short-term issues. The evidence shows that excess ends up breaking even solid systems, turning into a weakness what had traditionally always been considered the strength of the US financial system: the existence of a widespread and efficient financial market of short-term funds based on the issue of CPs.

The GFC also raised questions about the role of bank mergers, leading to the creation of large financial groups, increasingly involved in international finance (Bottiglia et al. 2010). Many of the actors steeped in the crisis underwent prolonged and intense growth through mergers and acquisitions (M&As), including Citigroup, Bank of America, Wachovia, Washington Mutual and other intermediaries such as US investment banks, where the crisis followed a different path. Equally significant were the cases of banking groups involved in M&As, but which emerged relatively unscathed from the crisis (such as, JPMorgan Chase, Wells Fargo, Bank of New York Mellon, and State Street). Some large mergers were carried out to rescue banks. The consequences of these operations, which significantly redesigned the structure of the US financial system, can only be appreciated in the medium-long term. However, overall, a link between the crisis and M&As seems clear in the upper echelons of the banking system, where extensive and highly complex structures were created in a short period of time under the control of a management that drove M&A growth in a continuous accelerated development logic, under the noses of government and regulatory authorities.

Finally, the abnormal shortcomings in governance and the behaviour of the top management of many large banking groups seem to have played a significant role in the GFC. The first aspect (governance) was shown by a variety of deficiencies in controls and risk management activities as well as the significant link between risky business practices and management remuneration almost exclusively based on short-term profits. The second aspect (managerial shortcomings) came in various shapes and sizes, with a combination of irresponsibility and inability, all the more incomprehensible in view of the complexity of the tasks, the qualifications required and the high level of remuneration offered.

In addition to these lessons, some relate to bank liquidity. In this connection, the crisis of 2007–2009 showed that liquidity risk was underestimated by the Basel Accords both before (Basel I) and during the crisis (Basel II), given that regulators believed it could not threaten bank solvency and stability. Before the GFC, regulators thought that adequate capital ratios guaranteed bank stability, hence Basel I and II established rules only for capital and not liquidity.

In addition, recent episodes have shown that liquidity risk cannot be 'cured' through a higher level of bank capital. An increase in bank capital does not solve liquidity issues. Indeed, the subprime crisis is proof of the vulnerability of well-capitalized banks to liquidity problems.

Finally, as a consequence of the above, regulators realized that bank capital and liquidity are equally important in promoting bank stability. Therefore, they reviewed the Basel II document in 2010 introduced a new international regulatory framework for banks, so-called Basel III. This new accord for the first time, set quantitative liquidity standards for banks, in addition to revised risk-weighted capital buffers introduced in Basel II. The introduction of these liquidity rules, together with higher capital requirements, should reduce future potential bank distress problems and increase the stability of banks.

3.3 Liquidity Crises: Common Features and Some Prevention and Management Policies

The GFC showed the key role of liquidity shortages in determining distress in the banking sector. Policies aimed at preventing and managing these crises have therefore regained the urgency they had lost for some time (Goodhart 2007). We now turn to the nature of liquidity crises and the policies designed to prevent and manage them (Borio 2009).

All liquidity crises have two things in common. The first is related to their dynamics once they materialize. As explained in Chapter 2, market liquidity (crisis) and funding liquidity (crisis) are closely linked. Sometimes, market liquidity is the first to evaporate, leading to funding problems. This was the case during the GFC. From the summer of 2007 on, the difficulties of assessing and trading complex structured products from securitization (ABSs, MBSs and CDOs) and the vehicles (such as SIVs) where these products were placed, caused investors to refuse to renew the commercial paper financing them (Fender et al. 2008). In turn, the problem spread to the interbank market (Borio 2008; Brunnemeier 2009).

At other times, it is funding liquidity that evaporates first, followed by market liquidity issues. One example is the Long Term Capital

Management (LTCM) turmoil of 1998, when nervous counterparties withdrew their funding and asked for higher margins, threatening fire sales that caused some secondary markets to seize up (Committee on the Global Financial System—CGFS 1999).

Not only intermediaries, but also markets, are subject to runs via a similar mechanism. In the case of bank runs, funding liquidity constraints lead to strains on solvency, by precipitating fire sales and generating a credit crunch. The difficulty of distinguishing between sound and unsound banks, added to the network of contractual relationship linking them together, can spread the run across the entire banking system. The process has certain self-fulfilling aspects (Diamond and Dybvig 1983): concerned about the lack of funds, people withdraw from the bank, causing a lack of funds.

In the case of markets and the evaporation of market liquidity, the same happens. Liquidity constraints and doubts about the creditworthiness of counterparties lead to the freezing of the secondary market and determine a general retrenchment. Again, in as self-fulfilling mechanism, anticipations of large pending orders, by precipitating sales, can cause the evaporation of market liquidity (Bernando and Welch 2004).

The second common feature is that liquidity crises are not 'meteorite strikes' (Borio 2009), but derive from the combination of a build-up in risk-taking and the associated overextension of balance sheets over a prolonged period. Thus, the build-up of financial imbalances have unmistakable signs in the growth of (overt and hidden) leverage, generally low-risk premia and volatilities, and buoyant asset prices.

'Artificial liquidity' characterizes the build-up of the crisis. Specifically, liquidity and risk-taking are self-reinforcing: the weakening of funding liquidity constraints during a phase of expansion encourages greater risk-taking by facilitating position-taking and an increase in exposures. This improves market liquidity and increases asset prices. The consequence is that volatility and risk premia decrease, determining a further easing of funding liquidity constraints. If this mutually reinforcing process continues for too long, it leads to overextended balance sheets and self-destruction. So, market and funding liquidity seem to be at their highest precisely when they are most vulnerable, a phenomenon called the 'paradox of financial instability' (Borio 2007; Knight 2007, 2008). The subsequent reversal hits suddenly. This highlights the 'binary' nature of liquidity conditions and their pricing, in both time- and cross-sectional dimension. After being unusually low, liquidity premia increase, and after no differentiation between firms, market participants suddenly become more discriminatory in their pricing.

In addition, one characteristic of a liquidity crisis is related to the type of financial system. Specifically, Borio (2003) shows that, contrary to the widely-held view, the reliance on funding liquidity is higher in a market-based than in a bank-based (or intermediary-based) financial system.[11] A market-based financial system is 'funding liquidity hungry', given that the development of financial markets tends to increase, and not reduce, the demand for funding liquidity. Many observers expected the opposite, i.e. that the development of markets should reduce the reliance on funding liquidity, or in general the dependence on external funding. If the portfolios of economic agents include more tradable securities, their sales can replace external funding. Consequently, a market-based financial system was considered less vulnerable to liquidity crises. Specifically, this was based on two faulty convictions. The first related to the trading process and particularly the fact that it does not rely on funding liquidity. However, it strongly relies on it, since funding is necessary to take positions. Credit lines are a fundamental element in the provision of market-making services and a critical backstop for the issue of securities. In addition, trading provides a premium on mechanisms to address counterparty risk that can strain funding liquidity, such as collateral, margins and haircuts.

The second conviction related to market liquidity and its ability to remain robust even in a severe scenario, hence without amplifying the need for funding liquidity.

Both these convictions were disproved by the financial crisis of 2007–2009, which led to an unprecedented drying up of funding liquidity, as shown by the enormous strain placed on the interbank market and huge liquidity injections by central banks.

As a result of the above, there is clearly more reliance on funding liquidity in a market-based than a bank-based financial system. When a stress event appears and market liquidity evaporates, the demand for funding liquidity can skyrocket precisely when supply collapses. Secondly, financial intermediaries and markets are not alternative forms of finance. Their complementary nature is important and has grown over time (Borio 2003). Specifically, intermediaries, such as banks, have become increasingly dependent on markets as a source of income and for risk management, through hedging operations. Markets have become increasingly reliant on intermediaries for the supply of market-making services and funding liquidity to support their proper functioning. In addition, the capital base can ultimately support the operation of both markets and intermediaries (BIS 2005, 2009). Thus, intermediaries cannot replace markets, or vice versa. Neither is the 'spare tyre' of the other (Greenspan 1999). This became evident in the last financial crisis, where both markets and financial intermediaries faced stress scenarios at the same time. So, how can these crises be prevented or managed?

Prevention involves Payment and Settlement Systems (PSSs) and their role as a key yet limited element of financial infrastructure. Specifically, on the one hand, they are fundamental because if they are badly designed, they can deepen liquidity crises when they occur, in one of two ways (Borio and Van den Bergh 1993). Firstly, they can amplify concerns about counterparty risk when the arrangements do not allow the simultaneous exchange of instruments traded or centralized management of counterparty risk, via a central counterparty to the transactions. Secondly, they can amplify uncertainty about cash flows, receipts and payments whenever, for example, payment transfers can be revoked or be unwound under some conditions.

Yet, PSSs are limited for two reasons. In the first place, some of the mechanisms dealing with counterparty risk, by design, put pressure on liquidity, which needs to be properly managed. This is the case for Delivery versus Payment (DVP) and Payment versus Payment (PVP) arrangements, for Real Time Gross Settlements (RTGS) and tri-party repos. In addition and more importantly, PSSs are unable to address the build-up in risk-taking and underlying asset quality problems that invariably lie behind the most severe liquidity crises. Indeed, fool proofing may be ineffective if, paradoxically, confidence in the strength of the infrastructure encourages market participants to take greater risks.

The last financial crisis confirms this. In particular, it showed that PSSs work well during periods of strains, with the exception of the uncertainties associated with the exposures in the clearing and settlement of CDS contracts (Geithner 2008). Despite measures taken to strengthen this aspect of the infrastructure (Ledrut and Upper 2007), the opaque and decentralized nature of the OTC CDS market contributed to the strains in the financial system. Consequently, both the authorities and market participants have taken measures to establish a central counterparty for these contracts (Counterparty Risk Management Policy Group—CRMPG 2008; Financial Stability Forum—FSF 2008; Cecchetti et al. 2009).

So, the strengthening of PSSs is necessary, but not sufficient. To prevent liquidity crises, more measures are required, such as the improvement of buffers in the system. Two types of buffers are necessary. Both were included in the Basel III Accord of December 2010. One was the introduction of higher capital adequacy standards able to absorb the losses incurred by several banks during the subprime crisis. If Basel II had been implemented earlier, off-balance sheet vehicles would have been less common or would ultimately have been supported by more highly capitalized banks, owing to the greater capital requirements against these types of exposure. This would have reduced the likelihood, or at least the intensity, of the liquidity crunch. Nevertheless, higher capital buffers are not sufficient to prevent crises, but need to be completed by a second type of buffer, related to liquidity. For this reason, Basel III introduced, for the first time, two liquidity standards for banks: the Liquidity Coverage Ratio (LCR), to strengthen the short-term resilience of a bank's liquidity profile, and the Net Stable Funding Ratio (NSFR), which aims to prevent excessive maturity transformation or ensure long-term stable funding of active and off-balance sheet positions.[12]

Deposit insurance schemes, introduced to protect retail depositors in the event of bank failures, are another important instrument for the prevention of liquidity crises. These schemes have multiple roles, but academics tend to see them essentially as a means of preventing runs on banks (Diamond and Dybvig 1983). Indeed, the possibility of runs on otherwise solvent banks is concerning. If on the one hand, deposit insurance schemes are generally expected to enhance depositor confidence and minimize the moral hazard of bank conduct, on the other hand, too generous or lax schemes can promote risk-taking by banks and make financial systems vulnerable to crises (Demirgüç-Kunt and Detriagiache 2002; Barth et al. 2013; International Association of Deposit Insurers—IADI 2013, 2014). So, there is a widespread sense that they are not actually well-designed for the prevention of bank runs (Borio 2009). The topic is well researched, but remains controversial and open to further investigation.

The most obvious means for preventing a liquidity crisis is the action of the central bank in its role as liquidity provider. The existence of the central bank framework to provide liquidity is a 'double-edged sword'. Indeed, an effective central bank framework to supply liquidity to the banking system is necessary in order to address liquidity crises. However, the central bank provision of liquidity can determine the following trade-off: on the one hand, ex-post, it acts as a buffer and, for this reason, is activated when strains emerge; on the other hand, it can encourage banks to adopt more risky behaviour, since they know that they can rely on central bank support through the injection of liquidity to cope with potential future difficulties. Such an assumption can increase moral hazard. Indeed, during the financial crisis of 2007–2009, many troubled banks were saved by unprecedented liquidity injections by central banks, so achieving the right balance has become all the more important.

Finally, monetary (interest rate) policy can help to prevent liquidity crises by directly or indirectly influencing risk-taking behaviour by banks during the good times. Here, two aspects need to be considered. First, the relationship between unusually low policy rates and greater risk-taking: especially in the light of the subprime crisis, this is an important albeit neglected aspect of the monetary transmission mechanism and can be thought of as the 'risk-taking channel' of monetary policy (Rajan 2005; Borio and Zhu 2008; Farhi and Tirole 2009). The influence of interest rates on perceptions and attitudes towards risk can act in different ways: directly, through the interaction between the level of policy rates and strict rate of return norms or targets as well as via the reaction of the central bank, including its degree of transparency and anticipation of central bank support (reductions in policy rates) in the event of financial strains threatening the real economy; and indirectly, through the impact that asset prices, cash flows and profits can have on the measurement of risk and risk tolerance, and hence on risk premia (Borio 2009). Second, particular attention should be paid to understanding whether monetary policy is able to contrast the build-up of risk-taking and associated financial imbalances, even when near-term inflation appears to be under control. Yes, according to Borio and White (2004), and the Bank for International Settlements (BIS 2009). They argue that a strict focus on stabilizing near-term inflation, over one to two years, can unwittingly accommodate the build-up of financial imbalances, raising the spectre of broader financial strains, output weakness and unwelcome disinflation, if not outright deflation, further down the road, as the imbalances unwind. In extreme situations, it increases the danger of crippling monetary policy, where nominal interest rates are close to zero. Some evidence has emerged about the Japanese experience in the late 1980s–1990s and for more recent crisis.

Therefore, in the future, it may be necessary to keep monetary (interest rate) policy under control in order to prevent future bank liquidity crises. It seems that the central bank community is going in this direction (Carney 2009; Shirakawa 2009; Trichet 2009).

Notes

1. For a broad analysis of the subprime crisis, see Borio (2008), Calomiris (2008), Gorton (2008), Hellwig (2008), Kashyap et al. (2008), Brunnermeier (2009), and National Commission on the causes of the financial and economic crisis in the United States (2011).
2. Alan Greenspan was Chairman of the FED from 1987 to 2006.
3. Until 2015, China was the largest holder of US government debt securities. Since 2016, Japan has been top, followed by China. See: https://www.treasurydirect.gov/NP/debt/current.
4. American banks started to give subprime mortgage loans in the mid-1990s pressured to do so by the Clinton government's request and following some targeted regulatory initiatives. With reference to the latter, radical changes in the Community Reinvestment Act were made (in the 1990s) in order to create a system in which banks were assessed on the basis of the number of loans offered to low-risk customers. The aim was to provide a home to the poorest sector of the population (in particular, Hispanics, African Americans and immigrants in general) in order to promote greater integration. See Simkovic (2013).
5. Subprime borrowers are customers with a low credit score due to a low capacity to repay their debt as a consequence of difficulties in the past, such as payment delays, foreclosures, bankruptcies, etc. See: https://www.fdic.gov/about/comein/background.html.
6. The senior tranche is rated AAA, AA, or A; the mezzanine tranche is rated BBB, BB, or B; and the equity or subordinated tranche has a rating from CCC to D. The latter is called 'subordinated' because if the SPV defaults or the collateral (i.e. assets) underperforms, payments on senior tranches take precedence over payments on mezzanine and subordinated tranches.
7. In 1988, the BCBS introduced a Basel Accord on capital, known as Basel I, which required banks to keep capital (so-called regulatory capital) according to the specific risks taken on by the bank. The content of Basel I was then updated by subsequent documents known as Basel II (in 2004) and Basel III (in 2010). See Chapters 5 and 6 for further details on these Accords.
8. Credit Default Swap, the most common form of credit derivative, is a particular type of swap designed to transfer the credit exposure of fixed income products between two or more parties. In a CDS, the buyer of the swap (protection buyer) makes payments to the seller (protection seller) until the maturity date of a contract. In return, in the event that the debt issuer defaults or experiences another credit event, the seller agrees to pay the buyer the premium as well as all interest payments that would have been paid between that time and the maturity date. See ECB (2009b).

9. Mark-to-market or fair value accounting, refers to the accounting standard of assigning a value to a position held in a financial instrument based on the current fair market price for the instrument or similar instruments. See Wagner and Garner (2010).
10. See Chapter 6 for details on the new liquidity rules under Basel III.
11. In bank-based systems (such as Germany, France and Italy), banks play a leading role in mobilizing savings, allocating capital, overseeing the investment decisions of corporate managers, and providing risk management vehicles. In market-based systems (such as England and the United States) securities markets share centre stage with banks in channelling savings to firms, exerting corporate control, and easing risk management. As countries grow richer, financial markets play a more important role than banks.
12. See Note 10.

References

Afonso, G., Kovner, A., & Schoar, A. (2010, March). *Stressed, Not Frozen: The Federal Funds Market in the Financial Crisis* (Federal Reserve Bank of New York Staff Reports 437).

Anderson, R. G. (2008). *Paying Interest on Deposits at Federal Reserve Banks.* Economic Synopses, Federal Reserve Bank of St. Louis 30.

Ashcraft, A., Goldsmith-Pinkham, P., & Vickery, J. (2009, June). *MBS Ratings and the Mortgage Credit Boom.* Federal Reserve Bank of New York Report.

Baker, D. (2008). The Housing Bubble and the Financial Crisis. *Real-World Economics Review, 46,* 73–81.

Bank for International Settlements (BIS). (2005, June). *75th Annual Report.*

Bank for International Settlements (BIS). (2009, June). *79th Annual Report.*

Barth, J. R., Caprio, G., Jr., & Levine, R. (2013). Bank Regulation and Supervision in 180 Countries from 1999 to 2011. *Journal of Financial Economic Policy, 5,* 111–219.

Bernanke, B. (2007, August). *Housing, Housing Finance and Monetary Policy.* Federal Reserve Bank of Kansas City's Economic symposium, Jackson Hole, Wyoming.

Bernardo, A., & Welch, I. (2004). Liquidity and Financial Market Runs. *Quarterly Journal of Economics, 119,* 135–158.

Black, L., Hancock, D., & Passmore, W. (2009, August). *Core Deposit Funding of Subprime Mortgage and the Effect of Monetary Policy.* Washington, DC: Board of Governors of the Federal Reserve System.

Borio, C. (2003, December). Market Distress and Vanishing Liquidity: Anatomy and Policy Options. In A. Persaud (Ed.), *Liquidity Black Holes: Understanding, Quantifying and Managing Financial Liquidity Risk.* Also available (revised and updated) as (BIS Working Paper 158), 2004. Risk Publications.

Borio, C. (2007). Change and Constancy in the Financial System: Implications for Financial Distress and for Policy. In Reserve Bank of Australia (Ed.), *Financial System: Structure and Resilience*. Proceedings of a conference, Reserve Bank of Australia, Sydney.

Borio, C. (2008). The Financial Turmoil of 2007–? A Preliminary Assessment and Some Policy Considerations. *Revista de Estabilidad Financiera, 14*, 23–54.

Borio, C. (2009). *Ten Propositions About Liquidity Crises* (Bank for International Settlements (BIS) Working Papers 293).

Borio, C., & Nelson, W. (2008, March). Monetary Operations and the Financial Turmoil. *Bank for International Settlements (BIS) Quarterly Review*.

Borio, C., & Van den Bergh, P. (1993, February). *The Nature and Management of Payment System Risks: An International Perspective* (Bank for International Settlements (BIS) Economic Papers 36).

Borio, C., & White, W. (2004, August). Whither Monetary and Financial Stability? The Implications of Evolving Policy Regimes. In *Monetary Policy and Uncertainty: Adapting to a Changing Economy* (pp. 131–211). Proceedings of symposium sponsored by the Federal Reserve Bank of Kansas City, Jackson Hole.

Borio, C., & Zhu, H. (2008, June). *Capital Regulation, Risk-Taking and Monetary Policy: A Missing Link in the Transmission Mechanism?* (Bank for International Settlements (BIS) Working Papers 258).

Bottiglia, R., Gualandri, E., & Mazzocco, G. N. (2010). *Consolidation in the European Financial Industry*. Basingstoke (UK): Palgrave Macmillan.

Bruni, F., & Llewellyn, D. T. (2009). *The Failure of Northern Rock: A Multi-dimensional Case Study*. SUERF Studies—The European Money and Finance Forum.

Brunnermeier, M. (2009). Deciphering the Liquidity and Credit Crunch 2007–2008. *Journal of Economic Perspectives, 23*, 77–100.

Calomiris, C. (2008, August). *The Subprime Crisis: What's Old, What's New, and What's Next*. Paper presented at the Federal Reserve of Kansas City Colloquium, 'Maintaining Financial Stability in a Changing Financial System'. Jackson Hole, Wyoming, pp. 21–22.

Carney, M. (2009, August 22). *Some Considerations on Using Monetary Policy to Stabilize Economic Activity*. Remarks at the symposium on Financial stability and macroeconomic policy sponsored by the Federal Reserve Bank of Kansas City, Jackson Hole, Wyoming.

Cecchetti, S. G., Gyntelberg, J., & Hollanders, M. (2009, September). Central Counterparties for Over-the-Counter Derivatives. *Bank for International Settlements (BIS) Quarterly Review*.

Committee on the Global Financial System (CGFS). (1999, October). *A Review of Financial Market Events in Autumn 1998* (CGFS Report 12).

Counterparty Risk Management Policy Group (CRMPG). (2008, August). *Containing Systemic Risk: The Road to Reform* (The Report of the CRMPG III).

Demirgüç-Kunt, A., & Detragiache, E. (2002). Does Deposit Insurance Increase Banking System Stability? An Empirical Investigation. *Journal of Monetary Economics, 49,* 1373–1406.

Diamond, D., & Dybvig, P. (1983). Bank Runs, Deposit Insurance and Liquidity. *Journal of Political Economy, 91,* 401–419.

Dong, F., & Yi, W. (2017, August). *Flight to What?—Dissecting Liquidity Shortage in Financial Crisis* (Working Paper Series Federal Reserve Bank of St. Louis).

Dwyer, G. P., & Tkac, P. (2009). The Financial Crisis of 2008 in the Fixed-Income Markets. *Journal of International Money and Finance, 28,* 1293–1316.

European Central Bank (ECB). (2008, December). *The Incentive Structure and the "Originate and Distribute" Model.* Frankfurt am Main: European Central Bank.

European Central Bank (ECB). (2009a, December). *The Incentive Structure and the "Originate and Distribute" Model.* Frankfurt am Main: European Central Bank.

European Central Bank (ECB). (2009b, August). *Credit Default Swaps and Counterparty Risk.* Frankfurt am Main: European Central Bank.

Farhi, E., & Tirole, J. (2009). *Collective Moral Hazard, Maturity Mismatch, and Systemic Bailouts.* Mimeo.

Felton, A., & Reinhart, C. (2008, June). *The First Global Financial Crisis of the 21st Century* (Centre for Economic Policy Research (CEPR) paper).

Fender, I., Tarashev, N., & Zhu, H. (2008, March). Credit Fundamentals, Ratings and Value-at-Risk: CDOs Versus Corporate Exposures. *Bank for International Settlements (BIS) Quarterly Review.*

Financial Stability Forum (FSF). (2008, April). *Report of the Financial Stability Forum on Enhancing Market and Institutional Resilience.*

Geithner, T. (2008, June). *Reducing Systemic Risk in a Dynamic Financial System.* Remarks at the Economic Club of New York, New York.

Goodhart, C. (2007, October). *Luncheon Speech at the Institute of International Finance (IIF).* Washington, DC.

Goodhard, C., & Perotti, E. (2015, May). *Maturity Mismatch Stretching: Banking Has Taken a Wrong Turn* (CEPR Policy Insight 81).

Gorton, G. (2008, October). *The Subprime Panic* (National Bureau of Economic Research (NBER) Working Paper 14398).

Greenspan, A. (1999, September). Lessons from the Global Crisis. Remarks Before the World Bank Group and the International Monetary Fund. *Program of Seminars.* Washington, DC.

Hellwig, M. (2008, November). *Systemic Risk in the Financial Sector: An Analysis of the Subprime-Mortgage Financial Crisis*. Max Plank Institute for Research on Collective Goods, Mimeo.

Holt, J. (2009). A Summary of the Primary Causes of the Housing Bubble and the Resulting Credit Crisis: A Non-technical Paper. *The Journal of Business Inquiry, 8*, 120–129.

International Association of Deposit Insurers (IADI). (2013). *Enhanced Guidance for Effective Deposit Insurance Systems: Mitigating Moral Hazard*. Basel: International Association of Deposit Insurers.

International Association of Deposit Insurers (IADI). (2014). *IADI Core Principles for Effective Deposit Insurance Systems*. Basel: International Association of Deposit Insurers.

Kashyap, A., Rajan, R., & Stein, J. (2008, August). *Rethinking Capital Regulation*. Paper prepared for the Federal Reserve Bank of Kansas City Symposium at Jackson Hole.

Knight, M. D. (2007, February). *Now You See It, Now You Don't: Risk in the Small and in the Large*. Speech delivered at the Eighth Annual Risk Management Convention of the Global Association of Risk Professionals.

Knight, M. D. (2008, February). *Now You See It, Now You Don't: The Nature of Risk and the Current Financial Turmoil*. Speech delivered at the Ninth Annual Risk Management Convention of the Global Association of Risk Professionals.

Lastra, M., & Wood, G. (2010). The Crisis of 2007–09: Nature, Causes, and Reactions. *Journal of International Economic Law, 13*, 531–550.

Ledrut, E., & Upper, C. (2007, December). Changing Post-trading Arrangements for OTC Derivatives. *Bank for International Settlements (BIS) Quarterly Review*.

Levitin, A. J., & Wachter, S. M. (2012). Explaining the Housing Bubble. *The Georgetown Law Journal, 100*, 1177–1258.

Litan, R. E. (2010). *In Defense of Much, But Not All, Financial Innovation* (Weiss Center Working Papers 10).

Madalino, A., & Peydrò, L. (2009, September). *Bank Risk-Taking, Securitization, Supervision and Low Interest Rates: Evidence from Lending Standards*. Frankfurt am Main: European Central Bank.

National Commission on the Causes of the Financial and Economic Crisis in the United States. (2011, January). *The Financial Crisis Inquiry Report*. Official Government Edition.

Pozen, R. C. (2009, November). Is It Fair to Blame Fair Value Accounting for the Financial Crisis? *Harvard Business Review*.

Rajan, R. J. (2005, August). *Financial Markets, Financial Fragility, and Central Banking*. Paper presented at 'The Greenspan Era: Lessons for the Future'—Symposium sponsored by the Federal Reserve Bank of Kansas City, Jackson Hole, Wyoming.

Ruozi, R., & Ferrari, P. (2013). *Liquidity Risk Management in Banks*. Economic and Regulatory Issues. Heidelberg: Springer.

Segoviano, M., Jones, B., Linder, P., & Blankenheim, J. (2013, November). *Securitization: Lessons Learned and the Road Ahead* (International Monetary Fund (IMF) Working Paper 255).

Shirakawa, M. (2009, June). *Some Thoughts on Incentives at Micro- and Macro-Level for Crisis Prevention*. Remarks at the Eighth BIS Annual Conference, Financial and macroeconomic resilience—Revisited, Basel.

Simkovic, M. (2013). Competition and Crisis in Mortgage Securitization. *Indiana Law Journal, 88*, 213–272.

Trichet, J. C. (2009, August). *Credible Alertness Revisited*. Speech delivered at the symposium on Financial stability and macroeconomic policy, sponsored by the Federal Reserve Bank of Kansas City, Jackson Hole, Wyoming.

Wagner, A., & Garner, D. (2010). Fair Value Accounting—Fact or Fancy? *Journal of Business and Economics Research, 8*, 35–38.

White, L. H. (2009). Federal Reserve Policy and the Housing Bubble. *Cato Journal, 29*, 115–125.

Zingales, L. (2008, October). *Causes and Effects of the Lehman Brothers Bankruptcy*. Oral Testimony Before the Committee on Oversight and Government Reform, United States House of Representatives.

CHAPTER 4

The Role of Central Banks and the Interbank Market in Managing Bank Liquidity During the Global Financial Crisis

4.1 Central Banks, the Interbank Market and Bank Liquidity Management

The GFC highlighted the importance of the role of central banks and the interbank market in fostering bank liquidity management. Central banks provide the necessary liquidity to the financial system as a whole, so that bank treasuries have adequate amounts to handle cash payments without any particular strain on the interbank market. In addition, central banks usually have a monitoring function and, in some cases, an address function for the money and interbank market, which is the other channel through which banks can rebalance their respective liquidity positions.

Modern central banks base their operations on final monetary policy objectives, intermediate objectives and tools. This is because the final monetary policy objectives, including price stability (the primary aim[1]) are not entirely under the control of the monetary authorities, as there are other exogenous variables that have a non-negligible influence on the final targets (such as raw material prices or wage dynamics in the labour market). Consequently, central banks give themselves a range of intermediate objectives (also known as operational objectives) that are easier to control and are addressed by the tools in their possession. In general, the monetary authorities set intermediate targets in terms of the annual growth of the monetary aggregate (M2 or M3),[2] or pursue a certain level of medium/long-term interest rates, or objectives relating

L. Chiaramonte, *Bank Liquidity and the Global Financial Crisis*,
Palgrave Macmillan Studies in Banking and Financial Institutions,
https://doi.org/10.1007/978-3-319-94400-5_4

to the exchange rate between the domestic currency and a particularly significant foreign currency. However, even the intermediate targets are not under the full and direct control of central banks, since several variables are beyond the influence of authorities and may shift interest rates, exchange rates or monetary aggregates away from desired values (for example, the supply and demand of foreign currency for the purchase of goods, services and financial assets mainly affect exchange rates; inflationary expectations affect medium/long-term interest rates, etc.). Consequently, central banks pursue monetary policy goals by using a range of instruments that commonly affect the amount of currency in circulation or short-term interest rates. However, the link between monetary policy and liquidity management is not limited to the refinancing and deposit opportunities provided by central banks to banks. Indeed, the monetary policy authorities are heavily involved in the proper functioning of the money market and, more generally, of the financial system, so that monetary policy impulses produce the desired effects on medium/long-term interest rates, and hence on the real economy. Therefore, in this context, the authorities are involved, in various ways, with the stability of the whole financial system, the containment of systemic risks and the efficient functioning of the interbank market. The latter is one of the most important and delicate segments of the money market with operators, including principally banks, engaged in negotiating financial resources to manage daily liquidity shortages arising in carrying out banking activity.[3] Under a microeconomic profile, the proper functioning of the interbank market is indispensable for orderly bank liquidity and treasury management. Moreover, an efficient interbank market, with depths, trade balances and adequate levels of transparency, is one of the essential requirements for the effective implementation of the monetary policy action of central banks.[4] Lastly, the significance of the interbank deposit market can be seen in the systemic implications that could arise from its malfunction, as almost all banks are interconnected by bilateral credit and debt relations originating in this market.

Before the outbreak of the subprime crisis, it was considered a safe and efficient market, due to the availability of numerous counterparties with whom contracts could be concluded at fairly homogeneous economic conditions. Therefore, the main issues regarding this market have not significantly interested scholars over the years. In particular, there have been few studies of the relationships between the structures and organizations of interbank markets, their proper functioning and systemic implications.[5] In addition, bank treasurers, almost universally, preferred to operate on non-regulated markets (OTC), characterized by low transparency and ad hoc exchanges.[6]

Finally, supervisory authorities at the international level failed to look at the interbank market in the general belief that it was self-regulating.

In the period 2007–2009, and again in the second half of 2011, numerous irregularities occurred in the interbank market. In particular, when the effects of the crisis began to bite, there was a collapse of confidence among intermediaries, volatility in interest rates increased considerably, trading volumes fell sharply and, at the same time, there was a significant shift to short-term contracts (overnight prevalence), and collateralized contracts, a preference for domestic counterparts (so-called home bias), and recurrent use of the central counterparty on repurchase agreement (repo) contracts. These trends intensified after September 2008, when the collapse of trust among intermediaries caused temporary shut-down of trading with maturities over three months due to the sudden withdrawal of banks from the market, an unprecedented circumstance in financial crises in the recent past.

In response to the global financial turmoil, rapid deleveraging,[7] and the consequent dramatic slowdown in economic activity, the main central banks tried to subdue the role of the interbank market typically by adopting non-conventional measures which enabled bank treasuries to access liquidity without recourse to the traditional interbank financing channel, avoiding drastic consequences for the global financial system.[8]

Over time, the roots of financial crises has increasingly been seen to depend on the interbank market, the main transmission 'belt' of central bank monetary policy, based on open market operations aimed at influencing overnight interest rates and the real economy. The efficiency of the money market, and in particular of the interbank market, is an essential prerequisite for the proper functioning of the banking system. Its gradual paralysis showed how, overall, this segment can be regarded as anything but efficient and secure. The interbank market, under normal conditions is an efficient means for redistributing local liquidity shocks, at the most acute moment of the subprime crisis, became a formidable channel for the propagation of insolvency within the financial system through the dense network of existing interbank relationships.

On the basis of the above, the subprime crisis was an epoch-making event both because it forced central banks, for the first time, into full-scale coordination with the synchronized adoption of extraordinary measures, and because of the profound processes of change in the interbank market. Hence, this chapter opens (Sects. 4.2 and 4.3) with the operational framework of the three major central banks involved in the crisis (the ECB, FED and Bank of England), and the exceptional liquidity management instruments that were forced to put in place to cope with the crisis; the second part (Sects. 4.4 and 4.5) traces the main theoretical contributions of the interbank market role in the transmission of financial crises, with a focus on the functioning of this market in the GFC.

4.2 The Liquidity Management Instruments of Leading Central Banks

The main central banks of Western countries may have the same ultimate goals and some of the tools used to pursue them, but adopt various techniques to interact with bank treasuries, to target interest rates and achieve the desired level of monetary restriction. Therefore, this section now turns to the techniques with which the three most important central banks involved in the GFC (ECB, FED, and Bank of England) influence the overall liquidity in the financial system under their control.

The ECB and the national central banks of Euro zone countries are responsible for the single monetary policy of the euro. The main objective of monetary policy, established by the treaty setting up the European Community, is the maintenance of price stability.[9] Secondly, without compromising the primary objective, the Eurosystem is called upon to support the economic policies of the European Community as a whole.

With regard to the impact of the ECB's monetary policy instruments on bank liquidity management, it should first be noted that all Eurosystem policy operations are carried out with euro area banks as counterparts. Unlike other areas in the world, for example the United Kingdom, the Frankfurt authorities operate on the financial system solely through the banking channel, since banks have a central role within the financial system of the euro area. The recent financial crisis led the ECB to review this practice.

The Eurosystem's monetary policy is implemented by three instruments: open market operations, counterparty operations and the mandatory reserve (ECB 2011). With reference to the frequency, the purpose and the procedures adopted, open market operations currently include main refinancing operations, longer-term refinancing operations, fine tuning operations, and structural operations.[10] Open market operations have the important aim of targeting interest rates, determining liquidity conditions in the market and signaling monetary policy orientation. The Eurosystem carries out its monetary policy action without imposing conditions on interest rates other than market rates, taking care not to distort competition between the various banks in the area. Hence, open market operations are mainly carried out through main refinancing operations and, to a lesser extent, through longer-term refinancing operations into which the Eurosystem injects liquidity, obtaining in return eligible assets as guarantee from the banks, with the forward commitment to replenish the liquidity and return the guaranteed assets. Both transactions are conducted through auctions: main refinancing operations are carried out through variable rate auctions with a minimum bid rate; while longer-term refinancing operations usually take place at variable rate auctions without a minimum rate. The main refinancing operations and the longer-term refinancing operations are by far the most important, both for the large volumes of liquidity involved in these transactions and because they take place systematically according to a predetermined schedule. In particular, the main refinancing operations, which provide most of the necessary refinancing to banks, take place on a weekly basis and last for a week; longer-term operations, which provide a small amount of liquidity, take place every month and, until the GFC, lasted three months. The minimum interest rate for key refinancing operations (the so-called official discount rate, ODR) is of crucial importance in signaling monetary policy orientation, as it represents the minimum rate for banks to take part in weekly Eurosystem auctions and, more generally, influence money market rates.

Counterparty transactions, including marginal lending operations and deposits with the Central Bank, are the second policy instrument adopted by the ECB. They are overnight standing facilities, through which those banks that have unexpected surpluses or liquidity deficits can do deposits with the Central Bank or obtain loans secured by the Eurosystem for a single day. Banks use such liquidity management tools when it is difficult to find the liquid resources they need elsewhere, typically on the interbank market, or when they are not able to place any excess liquidity they have on the market in question. On the interbank market, interest rates for overnight deposits with the Central Bank and marginal lending operations are respectively the lower and upper limits of the corridor of interest rates in the money market. Therefore, by adjusting the width and position of the rate corridor, the ECB contributes signals monetary policy orientation and restricts the fluctuation of interest rates in the overnight market within the corridor. There are no quantitative limits for marginal lending operations and overnight deposits with Central Bank.

Finally, the mandatory reserve is the instrument used by the Eurosystem to stabilize interest rates in the money market and to create and dilute a structural liquidity requirement. Specifically, at the aggregate level, in order to meet reserve requirements the banking system is required to take part in open market operations where liquidity amounts and minimum rates are determined by the Eurosystem. Two mechanisms are available to minimize the implicit burden on banks due to the need to allocate part of their own funds to a special account at a national central bank in the Eurosystem, bringing the yield of the liquidity required to be allocated as reserve, closer in line with market conditions. Firstly, the sums deposited in reserve accounts are remunerated at the minimum rate established by the Eurosystem for the main refinancing operations, the reference rate for the entire money market. Secondly, Eurosystem reserves can be fully mobilized, as the banks are required to meet an average monthly requirement within a period of maintenance. It follows that banks have the power to withdraw resources from reserve accounts if there are more opportunities for employment on the interbank market and vice versa. In such cases, cash deposits must be made later in the monthly maintenance period and higher than the daily average. Full mobilization of the mandatory reserve creates a more intense and continuous link between official rates and interbank market rates, which tend to tally with official rates under extended liquidity conditions.

In order to address the risks that may arise from the possible failure of a banking counterparty in monetary policy operations, the ECB requires that all transactions involving liquidity in the system, i.e. intraday credit operations, be carried out with adequate safeguards. The financial crisis of 2007 led to unprecedented changes in the area of eligible assets and to a further expansion of assets used in monetary policy operations.[11]

Moving on to the FED, in relation to its role as monetary policy authority, the Federal Reserve Act establishes its aims as the pursuit of full employment, price stability and moderate long-term rates. These are not prioritized or expressed in figures. The FED carries out several banking channel operations with the explicit intent of influencing the supply and demand of base money (Board of the Governor of the Federal Reserve System 2005). Specifically, the FED possesses three monetary policy instruments impacting on interest rates in the interbank market, which in turn affect medium/long-term interest rates: open market operations, the discount rate and the mandatory reserve.

As for the Eurosystem, open market operations by the FED are the main tool available to increase or decrease the amount of cash in circulation. These transactions take place in the form of repurchase agreements in which the Central Bank purchases or sells liquidity against US government securities or securities issued by primary federal entities, either temporarily or definitively. Unlike in the euro area, the FED is involved with a very small number of primary dealers, which subsequently distribute liquidity to the market. In addition, open market operations by the FED are restrained, take place daily frequency and apply different rates to counterparties, depending on the collateralized assets (Cheun et al. 2009).

In deciding whether to buy or sell government bonds to raise or reduce the monetary base, the main variable that the FED takes into account is the federal funds rate, i.e. the interest rate that banks apply to other banks for the overnight loans of federal funds (i.e. bank reserves deposited with the FED). Therefore, in practice, the Federal Open Market Committee (FOMC), responsible for the operational conduct of monetary policy, identifies a target value for the rate on federal funds and, consequently, determines whether to buy government bonds, through repurchase agreements, to increase the monetary base, reducing the level of rates, or vice versa if the FED intends to reduce the bank liquidity. However, the rate of interest on federal funds is determined on the basis of market supply and demand, and therefore the FED can only try to push the rate in the desired direction, without necessarily pursuing a value established by the monetary authority. In the past, rather than setting a federal fund rate target, the FOMC pursued quantitative targets in terms of the volume of reserves to hold.

The second instrument available to the FED is the discount rate, i.e. the interest rate applied to discount window lending to banks by the regional banks of the Federal Reserve. The discount rate usually stands at 100 basis points above the target rate for federal funds in order to encourage banks to resort to the interbank market rather than refinancing at the central bank. The FED's discount window is similar to marginal refinancing operations in the Eurosystem. However, unlike marginal refinancing operations, the banks that make up the federal reserve offer three separate discount windows depending on counterparty solidity—primary, secondary and seasonal credit—with different interest rates. Specifically, primary credit line refinancing provides short-term loans, usually overnight, to counterparties considered solid. Banks that do not meet the requirements for primary credit may apply for funds under secondary credit at more expensive rates. Lastly, seasonal credit is a financing line for smaller intermediaries, which need more liquid resources in particular periods of the year.

Finally, the FED requires banks to deposit a percentage of their funding as a mandatory reserve. The coefficient of the reserve is established directly by the FED Board of Governors and, unlike in the euro area, is updated regularly. The minimum thresholds for the calculation of reserves and the related deductibles are also updated annually. For bonded banks these reserves, deposited at the FED, represent assets that are traded daily in the federal funds market. Therefore, the demand for funds on the federal funds market is determined by the obligation to comply with mandatory reserve constraints, but also by the fact that reserve accounts are used to settle payments. In addition, in particular circumstances, banks may ask for federal funds to obtain excess reserves.

Lastly, with reference to the British system, the Bank of England is tasked with monetary policy, the stability of the financial system and acting as lender of last resort.

The Bank of England pursues price stability as a monetary policy objective. In a subordinate position, the Bank is committed to supporting the government's economic goals, including growth and employment.[12] As in various Anglo-Saxon countries, the Bank of England adopts a monetary policy framework based on inflation targeting. With this approach, the government sets an annual inflation target, while the central banker has a wide margin of discretion in defining operational objectives and instruments for achieving that goal. Communication is a crucial element in United Kingdom (UK) inflation targeting strategy: if the actual inflation rate is more than 1 percentage point above the preset value, the Governor of the Bank of England is required to write an open letter to the Chancellor of the Exchequer, explaining the reasons for the deviation and the measures the Bank intends to take to bring inflation back to its target level.

The Bank of England's operating target is the level of short-term interest rates on unsecured deposits that the Bank influences through two-week open market operations, using mainly UK- government bonds as collateral (Bank of England 1999). In particular, the Bank of England conducts monetary policy by offering liquidity at the official rate for repurchase transactions determined by the Monetary Policy Committee of the Bank. The open market operations can be short-term, carried out on a weekly basis and on a fixed or long-term basis, with a monthly variable rate of three, six and twelve months. As in the US, the Bank of England conducts open market operations with a very small number of counterparties (Cheun et al. 2009). In addition, the range of assets available in the GFC was restricted to securities issued by the state or by primary public entities.

In addition, the British Authority also offers both standing and funding facilities with overnight maturity. Finally, since May 2006, the Bank of England has introduced a voluntary contractual reserve.

4.3 The Monetary Policy Actions Used by Leading Central Banks in Response to the GFC

The GFC caused central banks around the world to make extraordinary efforts to maintain acceptable liquidity conditions within their own financial systems. However, unlike other central banks, the Eurosystem, the FED and the Bank of England were forced to adopt extraordinary measures both in interest rate manoeuvering and by introducing new tools to allow the banking system to find adequate liquid resources, to avoid systemic crises and, more generally, to prevent the collapse of the financial system. The operation of all three institutions was significantly changed by the crisis. Therefore, this section now focuses on the monetary policy action of three of the main monetary authorities in the world, with the aim of highlighting critical areas and the corrective measures that can be adopted.

With reference to the Eurosystem, since 2007, its main interventions to counter the crisis of markets and to facilitate the distribution of liquidity among banks, can be divided into seven timeframes.[13]

The first phase was from August to September 2007. At the beginning of August 2007, when the financial crisis began, the world economy was expanding. Hence, central banks conducted a non-expansive monetary policy, partly because of the fears of the US real estate bubble bursting. On 9 August 2007, three BNP Paribas mutual funds declared they were unable to meet redemptions by selling securitized securities. As a result, concerns in the securities market secured by US real estate mortgages quickly spread to the euro area and other segments of the financial market. Doubts about the solidity of counterparties in the interbank market and a general increase in liquidity risk pushed the overnight interest rate in the euro area from 4.10% to about 4.70%. The ECB initially sought to counteract the tensions with ordinary tools. It intervened immediately to ensure orderly conditions in the money market of the euro. Specifically, it decided to inject additional liquidity through overnight fine-tuning operations, carried out two extra long-term refinancing operations (lasting six months) in addition to ordinary monthly payments, and placed a higher liquidity volume on the system through main refinancing operations. Therefore, in the first phase of the crisis, until mid-September 2007, the ECB responded to events by increasing volumes of liquidity through conventional instruments and sought to reassure the markets whilst reminding the market in its press releases that its statutory aim was to ensure price stability in the medium term.

In the second period, from mid-September 2007 to mid-September 2008, the money market continued to be unusually volatile, with significant consequences on bank liquidity management. Liquidity in the interbank market drained rapidly and the volume traded, especially in the unsecured markets, fell dramatically. A measure of increased liquidity and counterparty risks in interbank market transactions can be seen from the differentials between Euribor interest rates (non-collateral interbank loans) and Eurepo (guaranteed loans).[14] These differentials, usually close to 10 base points, reached 90 base points at the end of 2007, pushing the crisis to a much higher level than in the past.

Against this backdrop, the ECB continued to increase its volume of liquidity by refinancing operations, while reducing the surplus by approximating the mandate reserve maintenance period (an operational strategy called front-loading in central bank language). The amounts granted in longer-term refinancing operations also increased in the period. More generally, dictated by the turbulence of the financial environment the ECB used the tools available with greater flexibility, by increasing liquidity at the beginning of the compulsory reserve maintenance period. In addition, in order to provide financing opportunities for longer maturities, rare in the money market, in April and July 2008 the Eurosystem completed two longer-term semi-annual refinancing operations, renewing the extraordinary operations carried out at the beginning of the crisis. Finally, in this period, the size of the money market crisis and the increased systemic risk led central banks to greater monetary policy coordination. In December 2007, the ECB entered into agreements with the FED to allow the exchange of liquidity in their respective currencies, through swaps, to reduce tensions in short-term markets. Specifically, the Eurosystem preferred FED Term Auction Facilities (repurchase agreements by auction), offering dollars in return for eligible assets in its financing operations. These cooperation agreements were renewed and extended in 2008.

Overall, in the period under review, despite the tensions in the interbank market and the consequent funding difficulties of many banks, the ECB put in place operations aimed at overcoming the monetary stalemate, whilst stressing its statutory objective of price stability. After keeping interest rates on hold from the beginning of the crisis, in July 2018, the ECB raised the official rate by 0.25 points to contain inflationary pressures, a decision that was controversial and heavily criticized. At the same time, the excess reserves held by euro area banks in the Eurosystem were kept in line with pre-crisis levels, as shown by the fact that in the early stages of the crisis there was no general perception of difficulties in finding liquid resources, but a greater selectivity in the credit rating of counterparties in the interbank market, as well as a total increase in the liquidity risk premium.

The third phase of the crisis covers the period between mid-September and 8 October 2008. Around mid-September 2008, two events happened: the sale of Merrill Lynch to Bank of America and the failure of Lehman Brothers. So, two of the four global investment banks that had survived the market turmoil so far disappeared. Specifically, the failure of Lehman Brothers on 15 September 2008 generated significant fears of a systemic crisis. There was a significant increase in counterparty risk, a rise in the spread between unsecured and guaranteed loans and a collapse in the volume on the interbank market of unsecured deposits, while interbank collateral transactions increased significantly.

In order to restore confidence in the money market, the ECB carried out four fine-tuning operations between 15 and 24 September 2008, injecting 165 billion euros into the system. At the same time, the amounts allocated to leading refinancing operations were increased.

The fourth phase of the crisis, between 8 October 2008 and 7 May 2009, was certainly the most complex for the Eurosystem, both in terms of liquidity management to prevent a collapse in the money market and for the conduct of monetary policy. Following the bankruptcy of the Lehman Brothers investment bank, faced with turmoil and the real risk of a systemic crisis, the ECB initially showed a certain degree of restraint with official rates at 4.25% after the increase in July 2008. Specifically, on

2 October 2008, the ECB decided to keep rates unchanged, saying that, despite the slowdown in economic activity, annual inflation remained above the level consistent with the stability of prices. Only six days later, with close to paralysis in the monetary market, the ECB started to reduce interest rates, leading to a 1% fall in refinancing rates in May 2009, the lowest ever reached. In the 8 October 2008 press release, the ECB reviewed the previous analysis of inflation risks, arguing that in the euro area the upward risks to inflation had further decreased.[15] The decision to reduce the monetary policy reference rate was coordinated by the ECB and the FED, the Swiss National Bank, the Bank of Canada, the Bank of England and the Sveriges Riksbank, which all adopted similar measures.

At the meeting of 8 October 2008, the Governing Council of the ECB also decided on two temporary measures, fundamental for restoring the proper functioning of the interbank market. First, the ECB reduced the rate of the corridor on counterparty-based operations from 200 to 100 basis points, thereby reducing to 50 basis points the spread between the minimum rate of the main refinancing operations and the rates on the two standing facilities. This became necessary when the large amounts of liquidity injected by the ECB failed to reach the interbank market. Banks in the area feared that they would not be able to find additional liquid resources if needed and held large amounts of liquidity in excess of their needs. In the absence of liquid and risk-free alternatives, euro area treasury banks deposited excess reserves with the Eurosystem. The ECB measure, revoked on 21 January 2009, reduced the volatility of the Eonia rate[16] and the cost-opportunity of holding excess reserves, but also reiterated the burden of resorting to marginal refinancing operations, which had become relatively less expensive than in the past.

The other important measure decided by the ECB in October 2008 consisted in carrying out main refinancing operations through fixed-rate auctions, with full award of the amount at the main refinancing rate. In this way, given the severity of the situation, the Eurosystem temporarily waived the control of the amount of currency in circulation, thus putting in strong discussion its inflation control strategies. In the same month, October, the fixed-rate tender procedure without import limits was extended to longer-term refinancing operations. These choices were a major attempt by the ECB to combat the inefficiencies of the interbank market, enabling it to inject any amount of liquidity at pre-established rates. Simultaneously, a similar measure was adopted with regard to refinancing in US dollars and Swiss francs, offering refinancing opportunities at different maturities.

In addition, during this period, the ECB decided to extend the range of eligible assets for monetary policy operations to the maximum, accepting BBB as the minimum credit rating for securities taken as collateral. The rating for new issues of ABSs to be used as guarantees was left at A and raised to AAA in January 2009, pending the illiquidity of such instruments. From November 2008 on, the Eurosystem also granted euro-denominated negotiable debt instruments in US dollars, sterling or yen, provided that issuers were headquartered in the European economic area. The new eligible assets included time deposits made with the Eurosystem in the context of liquidity drainage operations. Lastly, from 15 October 2008 on, the ECB decided to further increase its long-term liquidity offer up to the first quarter of 2009 by remodeling this instrument and renewing the extraordinary operations already carried out.

Exceptional measures taken in the last quarter of 2008, on the one hand, prevented a systemic crises and bank runs, and on the other hand, bore witness to confusion in the money market, increasing the demand for liquidity from the Eurosystem by the banks. After the adoption of 'tap' liquidity injection through both main refinancing and longer-term refinancing operations, in the last quarter of 2008 the liquidity provided by these operations almost doubled. Longer-term operations grew more than proportionally while, at the same time, deposits with Eurosystem central banks also increased considerably. Finally, the Eonia rate gradually fell below the rate of the main refinancing operations.

Finally, the unconventional monetary policy measures adopted on and after 8 October 2008 led, among other things, to an expansion of the ECB balance sheet and to a re-aggregation of the principal amounts.[17]

The fifth phase of Eurosystem monetary policy action, which began on 7 May 2009 and ended in April 2010, was characterized by the identification of signals allowing for more liquidity. On that date, the Governing Council of the ECB decided to further reduce interest rates for main refinancing operations and marginal lending operations, maintaining the deposit rate at the central bank at 0.25%, with a view to provide a stimulus to the economy. Then the ECB introduced longer-term refinancing operations, with the total allocation of the required amounts, of annual maturity, alongside those of sixth months. The most controversial decision, given the ECB tradition was to buy covered bonds[18] of 60 billion euros in order to facilitate the credit flow to the economy, as did the FED and Bank of England, improving the risk profile of institutions holding covered bonds. Therefore, for the first time, the ECB decided not to operate exclusively through the banking channel, but to go directly to the markets. After weeks of internal debates at the Central Bank, the decision to buy covered bonds directly on primary and secondary markets did not attract the criticism of the Governing Council, as these bonds are particularly widespread in Germany, while they are almost unknown in other countries in the area, including Italy. Compared to other factors, it was considered that such evidence could have asymmetric effects on credit access opportunities in the euro area. The Covered Bonds Purchase Programme (CBPP), completed on 30 June 2010, was positively received by the markets because it contributed significantly to the recovery in the primary market of covered bonds.

The extraordinary transactions carried out and the strongly expansive monetary policy had evident effects over several months: in mid-May 2009, the spread between the Euribor rate and the Eonia swap rate,[19] both at three months, dropped to about 60 points, after reaching 180 basis points in October 2008. The level of interest rates on the interbank market fell significantly, while volumes on the interbank market increased (Papademos 2009). This spread was further reduced to 35 basis points between August and November 2009, while Eonia reached its minimum level of 0.299% in December 2009.[20] These signals led to the belief that, despite the crisis continuing to impact on asset quality, profitability and the asset balances of banks, the money market began to normalize. However, this did not mean that the euro area market would return in a few months or years to marginal spreads between collateralized and non-resident positions, or almost standardized risk premiums for counterparties with different deserve credit. Indeed, it was hoped that the money market would learn from the crisis and refine the techniques and procedures for a more analytical assessment of liquidity risk and counterparts in liquidity negotiations between banks. In this regard, there is no doubt that the ECB and other Eurosystem central banks and supervisors should play a role in encouraging the banking system to develop the most appropriate methods for assessing market liquidity risk, and, at the same time, the authorities should promote the creation of trading and settlement systems that are more responsive to the needs of the banks in the area.

In view of the improvement of the financial environment in the euro area in the second half of 2009, in December that year, the Eurosystem decided to step back some unconventional measures carried out during the crisis. In particular, it was decided to reduce the longer-term refinancing operations in the first quarter of 2010. However, the need to continue providing plentiful liquidity to the system led the ECB to maintain fixed-rate auction procedures with full awarding of amounts for the first quarter of 2010. Only in March 2010 did the Governing Council of the ECB decide to favour the standardization of liquidity conditions by establishing that, from the following month, regular longer-term refinancing operations, with a quarterly maturity, would be resumed at a floating rate, with a minimum bid rate of 1%.

The sixth phase was from April 2010 to the end of August 2012. It began when the ECB was forced to suspend the exit strategy of abandoning certain non-conventional measures, as a result of the tensions in Greek government bonds. The Eurosystem reintroduced the unlimited supply of liquidity in longer-term refinancing operations, reactivated dollar transactions and, above all, prepared a public and private securities purchasing programme to support the market segments particularly affected by the crisis (the so-called Securities Markets Programme, SMP). Specifically, the objective of the ECB programme was to ensure depth and liquidity in the debt securities market segments that were dysfunctional, and restore the proper functioning of the monetary policy transmission mechanism (ECB 2010). Therefore, through this instrument, the ECB's idea was to influence the liquidity of financial markets (by supporting the prices of certain assets) without altering monetary liquidity, as such asset purchases are sterilized through fine-tuning operations. Alongside the SMP, approved in May 2010 (and ending in August 2012), the ECB decided to adopt new extraordinary measures during the period under consideration to deal with the sovereign debt crisis in 2011. Specifically, in the second half of 2011, the ECB was forced to purchase directly in the secondary market the government securities of countries like Spain and Italy, whose risk premiums had risen beyond the levels considered unenforceable, and, in December 2011, approved two extraordinary three-year long-term refinancing operations (LTROs) for unlimited volumes. The LTROs comprised a liquidity auction in which the ECB granted a loan to the requesting banks, with a duration of three to six months that could be extended up to three years with an interest rate equal to the average rate for leading refinancing operations calculated during the period of the transaction. In exchange, the ECB received a guarantee from banks (usually government bonds on loan).

There were only two LTRO auctions: the first on 22 December 2011, when 523 banks requested 489.191 billion euros, and the second on 29 February 2012, when 800 banks requested 529.53 billion euros.

Finally, the seventh and final phase (still ongoing) began with the approval in September 2012 of a new bond purchase plan called Outright Monetary Transactions (OMTs). Unlike the SMP, which was a temporary measure with a maximum limit of available resources, OMTs involve the unlimited purchase of government bonds. Specifically, they consist in the direct purchase by the ECB of short-term government bonds issued by countries with severe and accidental macroeconomic difficulties (conditionality requirement), i.e. the country has launched a financial aid or precautionary programme with the European Financial Stability Mechanism (EFSM). Therefore, the ECB has declared itself ready to provide unlimited monetary support provided that the beneficiary country is implementing a macroeconomic adjustment plan under European and international supervision. The objective of OMTs is to safeguard the channel of transmission of monetary policy for the euro area, i.e. to prevent strong tensions in the government bond markets leading to excessive increases in interest rates, which would in turn prevent banks and businesses from financing themselves at economically viable conditions and would accelerate the recessionary spiral of the country concerned up to default.

The latest phase also includes Targeted long-term refinancing operations (TLTROs), i.e. long-term liquidity injection by the ECB to support the real economy, launched in September 2014 through low-cost auctions with a four-year maturity. These operations are 'targeted' as the ECB's intention is to give liquidity to banks provided that it is used mainly to finance credit to small- and medium-sized enterprises (SMEs) and not to speculate on the bond market or real estate market, as happened with LTROs. The last TLRO auction took place in March 2017, by which the ECB invested more than 200 billion euros in the eurozone banking sector with a zero interest rate, which in some cases fell to −0.40%, depending on the bank's lending activity. This was the most 'generous' stimulus of TLTROs.

As stated above, it is interesting to focus on the monetary policy actions undertaken during the GFC by the other two major central banks, the FED and the Bank of England. Hence, the analysis now looks at their most significant interventions during the most acute period of the crisis, from 2007 to 2011.

The FED's response to the financial crisis was complex and far-reaching. Specifically, the FED worked very hard with existing tools, whilst adopting some exceptional policy tools. At the beginning of the financial crisis, the FED reacted, in the first instance, by decreasing interest rates several times. It first reduced the discount rate in August 2007 and subsequently revised the target rate on federal funds several times. The interest rate was reduced by 325 basis points until the spring of 2008 (Bernanke 2009). In October 2008, following the rescues of Merril Lynch and American International Group (AIG), and the bankruptcy of Lehman Brothers, the FOMC reduced the target rate on federal funds a further 100 points, coordinating with other six central banks, including the ECB. December 2008 saw another rate manoeuver through which the target value for federal funds was raised to a range of 0–25 basis points, the minimum level possible. In addition, to support the banking system, from 9 October 2008 on, the FED paid the required reserve and excess reserves.

Despite unprecedented cuts in the interest rate, in the US bank lending to the real economy heavily fell at the beginning of the crisis, due to the banks' difficulties in obtaining funding from the interbank market, combined with the drying up of the securitization market. Therefore, during the period 2007–2011, the FED adopted both new and old policy instruments over and above the reduction in interest rates causes by the structural crisis of the US bank business model.

Unable to further reduce interest rates, which had reached their minimum value, following the last rate cut in December 2008, the FED repeatedly claimed, that it would maintain this low level for a lengthy period. This was intended to cause a lowering of rates on longer-term maturities. Secondly, the FED decided to support the economy by implementing a so-called credit easing policy, based on credit injection in the economy by expanding the Central Bank's budget. It introduced new policy tools to expand credit offerings, in three categories (Bernanke 2009). The first subset of extraordinary instruments included the supply of short-term liquidity to healthy bank counterparties. As the lender of last resort, the FED created new monetary policy instruments, reduced the difference between the discount rate and target rate on federal funds to 25 basis points, and extended loan maturities through a discount window from one to ninety days. The new instruments also included term auction facilities, through which, with auction procedures, banks could refinance for up to three months; term securities lending facilities, which allowed primary counterparties to obtain loans from FED government bonds in exchange for less liquid assets; and primary dealer credit facilities, i.e. a dedicated credit line for these intermediaries.[21] At the same time, the FED signed 14 agreements with as many central banks as possible, committing themselves to swap contracts in which the FED gave dollars in exchange for local currency. In this way, central banks obtained dollars from the FED to lend to banks outside the United States. The measure aimed to alleviate pressures on collecting globally liquid resources in dollars. All the new monetary policy tools mentioned above required the supply by banks and primary dealers of special guarantees.

Despite the fact that during the crisis the FED's supply of liquidity to the banking system was and continues to be extensive, it has proved to be partially ineffective in view of the reduction in the supply of credit resulting from the liquidation of CPs and ABSs, both of which are crucial to the US financial system. Consequently, in order to solve problems arising from the significant fall in trading in certain key markets, from 2007 to 2011, the FED, developed a second set of instruments that required the direct involvement of the central bank in supplying liquidity to debtors and investors in markets considered strategic. In this context, the FED created a Commercial Paper Funding Facility (CPFF) enabling it to buy directly, from issued companies, high-rated commercial papers with a maturity up to three months. These interventions also aimed to limit investor escape from financial market segments considered important for the functioning of the US economy. In addition, from the beginning of 2009, the FED and the US Treasury have had the option of making loans with a maturity of three years secured by asset-backed securities with a minimum triple A rating. The Treasury allocated 20 billion dollars to cover the losses that would be registered on this credit line, thus limiting the credit risk to the FED for these transactions. In this way, the FED provided liquidity to financial intermediaries receiving as a guarantee illiquid securities for any transaction in the interbank market.

The third set of tools adopted by the FED during the period 2007–2011, involved the direct acquisition by the US Central Bank of longer-term financial assets, including securities originated by the securitization of subprime mortgage loans, bonds issued by government agencies specializing in the securitization of mortgages and government bonds. The positive effect of that decision on the markets is undeniable. According to Kohn (2009), the announcement and the subsequent implementation of these tools could have reduced the cost of thirty-year mortgage loans by 1 percentage point. However, the FED's easing credit policies, based on the increase in credit supply by the central bank and on the acquisition of financial assets led to a significant expansion of the FED's balance sheet. Between September 2008 and March 2010, the FED definitively purchased bonds issued by government agencies specializing in mortgages for 175 billion dollars, mortgage-backed securities guaranteed by these agencies amounting to 1250 billion dollars, and medium/long-term Treasury bonds for 300 billion dollars. By the end of 2011, the FED budget had reached 2945 billion dollars.

Lastly, the financial crisis also significantly struck the British banking system, altering its morphology. The changes caused the legislator to issue a new banking law in 2009 (the Banking Act). This law introduced, inter alia, a new Special Resolution Regime (SSR) for banks in crisis.[22]

As for the Eurosystem and the FED, the Bank of England's monetary policy action was also based on the reduction of official rates, on a more flexible use of existing instruments, and on the adoption of extraordinary measures.

With reference to interest rate manoeuvers, in the context of the financial crisis, the Bank of England maintained the rate at 5% until September 2008. Subsequently, it reduced the interest rate on several occasions, bringing it to 0.5% in March 2009. In addition, since March 2009, the Bank of England has adopted an extraordinary quantitative easing policy, directly injecting money into the financial system, trying at the same time to meet the inflation target.

With regard to the use of existing instruments and procedures, since December 2007, the Bank has carried out quarterly open market operations for larger and more frequent amounts than in the past. The range of eligible assets for these operations has also been increased, including, among other things, several government bonds with a minimum rating of AA3/AA-, securities issued by government agencies in the G10 countries, and ABSs with a minimum rating of AA-. The range of eligible assets has been extended since October 2008, including high-quality ABSs issued against corporate bonds and loans, as well as securities issued by banks under the government's credit guarantee scheme.[23]

Finally, as regards the extraordinary measures taken during the most acute phase of the crisis, on 20 October 2008, the Bank of England announced the introduction of a discount window facility to provide liquidity to the banking system. This new instrument gave banks the possibility to borrow, for a maximum of thirty days, British government bonds in exchange for a wide range of collateral (corporate debt securities, ABSs and covered bonds) after the payment of a fee that varies depending on the amount and the collateral provided. The duration of discount window operations was extended to one year in February 2009.

In addition, in January 2009, the Chancellor of the Exchequer introduced a new instrument, called the Asset Purchase Programme (APP). Its aim consists in the purchase of high-quality assets (such as commercial paper, corporate bonds, and long-term government bonds) directly on the markets, in order to increase liquidity in the credit market. Under the APP, if purchases are decided by the Executive, they are financed by the issue of additional government bonds, while if the purchase is decided by the Bank of England for monetary policy reasons, it is funded directly by the Bank, which issues new currency. By providing the direct recourse of the Bank of England to financial markets, the APP is consistent with the morphology of the UK financial system, where corporate financing via markets is much larger than elsewhere.

In 2009, the Bank of England was authorized to buy assets directly on the market for a total amount of 200 billion pounds, about 14% of GDP, thus creating a further monetary base. Additional purchases for a total of 125 billion pounds were authorized in October 2011 and February 2012. This led to steep growth in the Bank's budget, which in 2012 reached the highest value in relation to GDP for the last two centuries.

4.4 The Role of the Interbank Market in Financial Crises: Theories and Empirical Evidence

As an integral part of financial markets and a link between bank liquidity management and monetary policy, the interbank market has acquired increasing importance over time, although it appears to be more vulnerable than other markets to systemic risk (Sheldon and Maurer 1998). The orderly and efficient functioning of the money market plays a crucial role in liquidity management, especially in stressed situations characterized by the low transparency of banking assets, when liquidity hoarding on the unsecured channel and the inability to absorb liquidity needs on the one secured channel are both possible.

The analysis of financial crises over the last few decades has been characterized by a particular microeconomic approach, integrated into a framework of interbank relations, aimed at establishing the most appropriate structure for the financial system and the optimum forms of economic policy intervention. Based on this paradigm, the literature has focused on bank-centric economies where financial crises are essentially linked to the crisis of some banks (so-called bank-centred financial crises). Short-term interrelationships between individual banks have become increasingly important for the mutual exchange of liquid financial resources. The context of fund raising (mainly with short-term maturity) and of credit supply activities (principally with medium/long-term maturity) makes a bank more vulnerable to hasty withdrawals by savers, fearful of potential bankruptcy. Due to these sudden increases in the demand for repayments, banks may be required to liquidate at least part of their own loans, bearing the risk of large losses due to rapid disposals. As has often been observed in the past, in the absence of protective mechanisms and public safety interventions (the so-called safety net),[24] banks may be exposed to systemic risk and the main reason for this has always held a central place in the economic debate, attracting the attention of scholars, monetary authorities, supervisors and policymakers.[25]

In light of the above, a review of the main theoretical thinking concerning the role of the interbank market in the transmission of financial crises is in order. Microeconomic analysis gives the banking system the task of absorbing the liquidity risk latent in the economic system, and attributes to the money market, particularly the interbank market, the function of distributing liquidity shocks to the participants in the system (so-called liquidity insurance). However, in addition to being an expedient through which banks manage liquidity shortages by borrowing from other institutions, interbank relationships are also a vehicle for the transmission of a potential liquidity crisis to the entire system, through financial contagion.

Starting from the peculiarities of banking as a business activity, several recent theoretical contributors have explained crisis propagation mechanisms from one to several banks or from one to several geographical areas through the interconnections between banks in the interbank market for liquidity (and through participation in the payment system). The models in the literature explore systemic aspects, extending the examination to a context in which several banks operate simultaneously.

De Bandt and Hartmann (2000) distinguish between two major, independent or joint channels of propagation of shocks and spread of contagion in interbank markets: the channel of direct exposure and the information channel. The former refers to domino effects arising from connections in the interbank market or through the payment system.

The latter refers to bank runs by depositors operating in a context of imperfect information about the nature of the shock (idiosyncratic or systemic) suffered by the bank.

Adopting the approach of these two authors, the following analysis initially investigates the traditional literature on bank runs in order to understand the intrinsic fragility of a bank. Subsequently, the analysis is extended to models that deal explicitly with contagion, assessing the relevance of interbank exposure (and credit rationing).

With reference to classic bank run models, the general belief in the significant role of banking systems in the transmission of shocks to the entire economy is based on evident vulnerabilities in the coordination of depositors.

The important contribution of Diamond and Dybving (1983) is now considered a classic analysis of bank intermediation. They show that behind the crisis of a single institution there is the fact that banks usually keep in reserve only a part of the deposits collected to satisfy short-term liquidity demand. They also divide depositors of a bank into two groups: those patients and those impatient.

When bank customers demand deposited savings, these come satisfied according to the sequential criterion, so-called first-come-first-served rule. As long as they are patient customers to request the withdrawal of deposits, the consequences are not negative, given that the bank is prepared because it knows that the other part of customers will leave the deposits inside. The bank run phenomenon manifests itself when the fraction of impatient customers withdraws deposits in advance due to a liquidity shock. Therefore, the bank's expectations about the number of patient and impatient customers change, finding themselves in difficulty due to absence of liquidity necessary to satisfy the entire repayment request. Being known of liquidity necessary to satisfy the entire repayment request. Being known then that the bank will not be able to satisfy the entire request, it generates one a real rush to the bank to withdraw deposits, before the bank becomes insolvent. The bank's insolvency leads to its bankruptcy. If such situation should be repeated in several banks, the bank panic phenomenon would occur.

The above model identifies weaknesses that other contributors subsequently tried to overcome. Some authors focused on a different contagion channel in the banking sector: information. In this view, the runs of depositors are caused by the spread of new information on the sustainability of the investments made by the bank.

Gorton (1985) states that bank runs are rational and efficient when the access to information is complete (information-based). Otherwise, the presence of noise can make bank runs rational but inefficient. The underlying hypothesis of the model is that the interest rate on deposits is fixed and not renegotiable, and, therefore, a bank run occurs with the spread of perception that currency returns exceed those of deposits. Gorton argues that the problem of inefficiency can be solved by adding a suspension withdrawal clause to the deposit contract so that banks can report the status of their investments, in addition to the information already available.

Unlike Diamond and Dybvig (who put forward solutions to an incomplete information game), Postlewaite and Vives (1987) associate bank runs with a situation of full information (known as the 'prisoner dilemma') where depositors take their savings from the bank not for consumer needs but for personal interest. The model identifies bank runs as the only balance and exhibits some desirable features, such as the absence of exogenous events, that could affect the behaviour of agents.

In the model of Chari and Jagannathan (1988) contagion due to direct exposure takes place through a further information channel, comprising the observation by some customers of the length of queues at their bank branches (so-called long lines). There are two separate cases: in the first, some informed savers withdraw their savings on the basis of negative information about the future yields of the bank's assets. In the second, the withdrawal request occurs when customers individually experience a liquidity shock. In both circumstances, the subject that does not have adequate information on the effective distribution of informed and non-informed withdrawable savers, faces the problem of 'signal extraction' (not knowing the percentage of depositors with negative news on the profitability of the bank assets compared to those who need cash), according to which they should be encouraged to liquidate (or keep immobilized) their own investments. If the casual realization of these groups of individuals (informed and not) is unusually high, the situation could give rise to a bank run (even if there is no adverse information on future returns). The suspension of convertibility is considered an effective mechanism for reducing the social costs of liquidation (derived from massive savings withdrawals) as it is disadvantageous to those who require the repayment of their own funds to face an individual liquidity crisis.

Moving on to the modern literature on interbank contagion, it emerges that the propagation channels of shocks are not exclusively related to the production of the liquidity inherent in banking activity, or to depositor expectations or even some fundamentals. Contagion in the banking system may also arise from direct financial exposure between banks and towards wholesale counterparties (Freixas et al. 2000). The latter are generally better informed (compared to ordinary customers) and do not have insurance schemes on their deposits.

In order to analyze such cases, the Diamond and Dybvig approach has been extended to the analysis of the relationships between banks through the interbank lending network.

In light of the specific features of the crisis in the interbank market, numerous revisions of the Diamond and Dybvig model have recently been put forward as an example of accurate economic theory relating to financial crises. These studies analyze financial crisis from a systemic perspective, expanding the phenomena identified by Diamond and Dybvig at the level of single intermediaries to an integrated system of financial intermediaries. Despite their undoubted merits and the innovative aspects of these models, based exclusively on bank runs, the contributions (described briefly below) have several limitations since they assume (unrealistically) that financial crises are the outcome of rational behaviour, based on individual actions aimed at maximizing utility in a very short time period or over longer timescales.

Starting with the contribution of Diamond and Dybvig, Smith (1991) builds a model in which banking regulation is similar to that of the National Banking System and the information is complete. The reorganization of the banking system is more cost-effective as a solution reducing potential panic than alternative forms of protection, such as deposit insurance schemes (which generate perverse incentives in bank financing decisions). The results obtained by the author show that, given a specific regulatory context, the suspension of convertibility is bound to occur from time to time.

Based on the abundant literature on psycho-social aspects,[26] Chen (1999) combines traditional bank run models (mainly Diamond and Dybvig 1983; and Chary and Jagannathan 1988) extending them to systems characterized by a larger number of banks. In the initial period consumers decide whether to deposit their money in the bank which, in turn, invests its own funds in medium/long-term projects with uncertain returns. The author demonstrates that the failures of a small number of banks can have a negative effect on other institutions through the simultaneous presence of two transmission mechanisms:

the first-come-first-served rule, and the externalities of information on the trend of the bank's performance.[27] Therefore, Chen's findings are consistent with the empirical evidence that shows the key role played in bank runs by the disclosure of pessimistic information on the banks. With reference to the information channel, it is expected that some depositors receive detailed information on the trend of the bank's assets, on the basis of which they decide whether to leave their money invested with the bank or withdraw it. In the latter case, some banks may find themselves in difficulty. Due to the positive correlation between bank returns, depositors who do not have information on their own and other banks are forced to react to this signal. The presence of the second simultaneous channel (the first-come-first-served rule), as opposed to information, means that informed savers, who know the potential response of others, decide withdrawals in advance of others to avoid competitive and partially unsatisfied requests. This system leads to a negative payoff externality, i.e. the withdrawal of a depositor reduces the expected payoff for depositors who have not already withdrawn, and leads to a dual equilibrium, of which the bank run is the Pareto-dominant.

Informed agents act independently of the elements they have and do not even expect the spread of more accurate and updated information.

Aghion et al. (1999) support the thesis that banks invest in projects that are to some extent illiquid and, at the same time, face withdrawal requests from depositors during periods of uncertainty. If the withdrawals exceed the flows generated by the loans, the surplus can be found (apart from the interruption of the investments) on the interbank market. Therefore, if the liquid funds made available by the other intermediaries are sufficient, the risk of bankruptcy of individual operators is minimized. Conversely, the failure of a financial institution could be interpreted as a structural liquidity deficiency signal of the system and consequently spread panic among savers. In such a case, the crisis would infect the whole system.

De Bandt (1995) investigates the link between structure and the risk of a general collapse of the banking system. In his analysis, banks can invest in a risk-free or risky asset and promise to pay a fixed remuneration on deposits. The realization of returns on risky investments, with aggregate and idiosyncratic shocks, is privately observed by banks. The model is a multiple-bank type: within it two countries in the world are considered and the perception of the yields is found in $t=1$ and $t=2$. The unreliability of some banks to pay the promised remuneration in $t=1$

is the origin of fundamental bank failures. However, financial crises may be contagious because depositors use the information available to revise their beliefs about the state of the economy and may decide that a run on the banks is the best option. The generalized withdrawal of deposits from a bank may be interpreted by the other institutions in the system as a sign of the inability to repay the liabilities it holds to the (healthy) system. If such a perception is widespread, the crisis of some institutions may spread to the whole system.

Allen and Gale (1998) suggest a model of interaction based on 'four regions', within each of which banks, collecting deposits, meet their liquidity needs (more or less) through interbank transactions and invest in short/long-term non-risky projects. Therefore, the authors concentrate only on this transmission channel, excluding other propagation mechanisms. It is assumed that agents have complete information and do not concern themselves with the role of currency markets in spreading shocks. Liquidity shocks are random and local where the overall liquidity remains constant. Banks know the different states of nature and their probabilities, even though they do not know in which of them they are. The withdrawal of deposits by savers in a given region, in response to specific consumer needs, causes intermediaries to liquidate short-term investments and to require the liquidation of funds deposited with other institutions located in other regions. The option of the liquidation of long-term loans, is the most expensive and is resorted to only when the others (repayments obtained from expired short-term investments, and the settlement of interbank deposits with banks in other regions) are impossible. In this context, the interbank deposit market acts as an insurance mechanism between banks in different regions, allowing for the efficient distribution of liquidity risk, and limits the potential for bankruptcies, but only for as long as there is sufficient liquidity in the banking system.

It has been shown that interregional bank failures occur if the availability of short-term liquidity in the bank that suffers the shock is insufficient and the banks in other regions are hit by the demand for withdrawal by the intermediary involved. The authors support the hypothesis that the impact of the shock and its propagation depend on the structure of interbank loans: the more complete the market, the more stable the system. But if the loan structure is circular, failures may occur sequentially in all regions.

Freixas et al. (2000) argue that the possibilities for contagion stem from the network of relationships determined by financial contracts generated by transactions through the payment system, the interbank and derivatives markets. In their model the demand for liquidity is defined endogenously: panic is caused because depositors choose ex-ante the bank to deposit their funds, without knowing where their consumption needs will become manifest. These individuals may suddenly withdraw their deposited sums, giving up the predetermined return on the investments carried out by the bank as a result of the deposits received. Like Allen and Gale (1998), Freixas et al. also distinguish between different regions, imagining that only one bank operates in each. The fragility of the financial system is related to physical exposures caused by interbank lending, as a consequence of geographically uncertain consumer choices by depositors. Banks decide whether to invest long-term or store collected deposits. Subsequently, if some depositors decide to consume in a different location, they withdraw at least one part of the funds or make an interbank transfer order. To minimize the liquidation of long-term assets and to protect the returns from investments, banks execute these orders through special credit lines, then re-absorb in correspondence of the maturity of long-term investments. According to the results of the research, an efficient and credible interbank market is indispensable for the transfer of deposits from one bank to another located in a different geographical area, and therefore to maintain a level of trust that limits the contagion phenomena within the system, because it allows losses to be shared among a large number of intermediaries, reducing their impact and allowing the solvent (but illiquid) bank to survive, despite its inefficiency.

Flannery (1996) shows that uncertainty about the reliability of the available information on fundraising counterparties can lead banks (providers of funds) to apply very high rates by creating, simultaneously, an adverse selection mechanism against healthy banks, which may not be able to repay their interbank debt. During periods of recession this phenomenon could lead to the total disappearance of the interbank market.

Finally, Bhattacharya and Gale (1987) illustrate the essential role of the interbank market in redistributing liquidity within the national credit system, as well as on the international market among the leading markets. They suggest that rapid access to the market encourages participating banks to invest sub-optimally in liquid assets. This impulse creates a free-riding problem, as all participants are convinced that they will be able to supply themselves on the interbank market if a sudden liquidity need arises, potentially leading to liquidity drainage due to the lack of coordination between the different operators.

4.5 The Functioning of the Interbank Market During the Financial Crisis

For almost half a century, interbank markets were considered an example of efficiency and self-regulation. Liquidity was abundant, counterparty risks were deemed irrelevant: monetary authorities were able to govern the level of interest rates along nearly the entire maturity curve.[28] A strong contribution to the deposit supply and demand mechanism was given by the implicit guarantees offered by central banks and by the related market perception that no institution in major systemic countries would be allowed to fail due to international cooperation between the different monetary authorities.

The subprime mortgage crisis abruptly ended the favourable phase of limited variability and low-risk premiums, triggering the reorganization of monetary and financial markets. In the new configuration, tensions were rife in the interbank deposit market with an increase in spreads for bank bonds, indicating a higher funding cost for banks. Since August 2007, an unexpected increase in liquidity demand by banks, to meet their commitments to SIVs and for precautionary purposes, added to the perception of growing counterparty risk, caused tension on interbank markets. Uncertainty regarding the creditworthiness of each interbank counterparty is associated with both the opacity of some markets, particularly where credit derivatives (such as CDSs) shown in the Financial Statements of some banks are traded, and the consequently difficult evaluation of toxic securities (ABSs and CDOs) and the potential losses linked to these bonds.

The low liquidity of structured credit instruments and the issue of credit risk identification and measurement increased the difficulties of assessing counterparty risk and created initial tensions on the interbank market, immediately manifested in the form of a drop in the volumes traded, the increase in interest rates beyond short maturities, and flight to overnight, i.e. the concentration of volumes on overnight maturities. In the initial phase of the crisis, monetary policy rates and interbank market began to significantly diverge, irrespective of the will of the central banks.

Therefore, the gradual paralysis of interbank exchanges was not due to specific technical shortcomings in the trading markets but to a sharp drop in confidence among banks themselves, unwilling to lend each other funds for other than short periods due to the fear of becoming involved in the crisis of the debtor bank and/or to disclose to the market, or simply raise the suspicion of weakness in their liquidity position, via the trades they put on the table.

During the crisis, at least as far as the Italian market is concerned, episodes of distrust did not concern depositors, but the banks themselves. The diminished confidence in interbank market operators was not reflected solely in the reduced duration and volume of deposits and the greater selectivity of counterparties (as shown by the fall in exchanges between national and foreign intermediaries on an unsured basis), but led to a revision of the operation, which now involves both a greater use of collateralized loans and forms of bargaining through bilateral auction mechanisms or between a limited number of counterparts (request for quote, RFQ), as introduced by some electronic trading platforms. The reluctance of banks to exchange funds also translated into a sudden increase in deposit rates for the main currencies and interest differentials between deposits with and without collateral.

During the GFC, one of the most critical moments was reached in mid-March 2008, as a consequence of the liquidity crisis at Bear Stearns.[29] In the first quarter of 2008, CDS premiums[30] of the major international banks considerably increased.

The financial institutions believed to be most exposed to the crisis were based on the OTD model, due to the heavy write-downs of financial instruments for the transfer of credit risk, used extensively. Except for some intermediaries, rescued by public funds, for others the effect was indirect and reflected mainly the increase in funding costs.

After September 2008, the financial crisis accelerated: the strong tensions generated by this second wave rapidly swept aside Fannie Mae, Freddie Mac, Lehman Brothers, AIG, Merril Lynch, Washington Mutual, Wachovia, and Citigroup. During this phase, the interbank market, for a long-term period, was unable to distribute liquidity to banks, which faced serious difficulties in financing a variety of activities on the markets. Short-term interest rates (an indispensable reference point) gradually broke free of official rates, fixed by central banks. Despite the fact that the FED and ECB implemented expansionary monetary policy manoeuvers, there were no automatic adjustments in market conditions. The mismatches in monetary rates disoriented operators and authorities and forced the central banks to review operational rules and behaviour. In a situation of generalized distrust, operators with short-term surplus resources preferred to buy short-term government bonds and stipulate repurchase agreements, or use overnight deposit with the central bank. This exasperated attitude led to strong distortions. The short-term rates of government bonds and Eurepo rates, both thought of as secured, fell sharply, while the unsecured Euribor interbank rate showed a bullish trend in obvious conflict with the direction of the official rates established by the central banks.

As consequence of public bailouts and bankruptcies, the CDS premiums of the main international banks increased, bank stock prices collapsed, and the gap between the three month interbank deposit rate (three months Euribor) and the overnight indexed swap (OIS) rate,[31] the so-called Euribor-OIS spread, significantly expanded, reaching values close to 200 basis points in the first half of October 2008. In response to these tensions, banks, structural fundraisers in the capital market, revised their strategic liquidity management by redefining their degree of leverage. The disorderly process of deleveraging led to a reduction in loans to enterprises, householders and intermediaries (especially hedge funds) and further reduced the volumes traded on interbank markets.

In order to mitigate the tension in interbank markets, the main central banks carried out repeated operations, including with extraordinary instruments, aimed at injecting liquidity into the system and at ensuring its orderly functioning.

Notes

1. The ability to maintain stable prices on a sustained basis is a crucial prerequisite for increasing economic welfare and the potential growth of an economy.
2. The monetary aggregate called M2 is obtained from the sum of M1 (the sum of currency in circulation and overnight deposits), and deposits with an agreed maturity of up to two years, and deposits redeemable at notice of up to three months. M3 is the sum of M2, repurchase agreements, money market fund shares/units, and debt securities with a maturity of up to two years.
3. To manage their liquidity, banks can rely on two channels: the first, the private type, coincides with the interbank market; the second, the institutional type, is used to obtain or deposit liquidity at the Central Bank.
4. The transmission of monetary policy to the economic system starts with the money market. The characteristics of this market affect the ability of Central Banks to control very short-term interest rates, the operational target of monetary policy.

5. The money market structure significantly influences the liquidity risk of individual intermediaries and may give rise to systemic phenomena.
6. The exchanges are mainly over the counter, through bilateral and informal transactions that take place via telematic platforms or traditional communication tools (telephone, fax).
7. The changed market conditions and subsequent difficulties in obtaining resources pushed financial intermediaries into rapid deleveraging. However, the anticipation of a massive disposal of assets, on which these debt reduction plans are based, can generate negative spirals leading the intermediary into insolvency and to a drastic credit restriction to final debtors, with a devastating impact on the real economy.
8. Central banks play a role as a lender of last resort to the banking system when interbank and financial markets are inadequate liquidity providers to troubled banks.
9. With reference to monetary policy, the other ECB aims are: income growth, increased employment and the balance of foreign accounts.
10. There are four types of open market operations. The first are main refinancing operations. They play a pivotal role in fulfilling the aims of Eurosystem open market operations and normally provide the bulk of refinancing to the financial sector. The second type are longer-term refinancing operations aimed at providing counterparties with additional longer-term refinancing and can also serve other monetary policy objectives. The third type are fine-tuning operations, which can be carried out on an ad hoc basis to manage the liquidity situation in the market and to steer interest rates. In particular, they aim to smooth the effects on interest rates of unexpected liquidity fluctuations. Finally, structural operations are executed whenever the ECB wishes to adjust the structural position of the Eurosystem vis-à-vis the financial sector (on a regular or non-regular basis). For more details on these four operations, see ECB (2011).
11. For a comparative analysis of eligible assets from FED and the Bank of England before and after the crisis, to guarantee the Eurosystem, see Cheun et al. (2009).
12. For an overview of the monetary policy of the Bank of England and for the most recent measures adopted, see: http://www.bankofengland.co.uk/monetarypolicy/overview.htm, and the comparative analysis of the Bank for International Settlement (2009).
13. See ECB (2009) for a detailed review of Eurosystem monetary policy during the crisis.
14. Euribor is the rate offered to prime banks on euro interbank term deposits, while Eurepo is the average interest rate for secured money market transactions in the euro area.

15. See the ECB press release of 8 October 2008, available at: http://www.ecb.int/press/pr/date/2008/html/pr081008.html.
16. The Eonia rate is the average interest rate at which a selection of European banks lend one another funds denominated in euros where the loans have a maturity of one day. Eonia can thereby be seen as the overnight Euribor rate.
17. In 2008, the consolidated Eurosystem central bank balance sheet increased by about 60%. Over the same period, the budgets of the FED and Bank of England more than doubled. In April 2009, the Eurosystem budget amounted to 1.51 trillion euros, equivalent to 16% of euro area Gross Domestic Product (GDP). At the same date, the FED budget was 14% of US GDP (Papademos 2009).
18. Covered bonds are debt securities issued by a bank or mortgage institution collateralized against a pool of assets that, in the event of failure of the issuer, can cover claims at any point in time. Unlike ABSs and MBSs created by securitization, covered bonds continue as obligations of the issuer. In essence, the investor has recourse against the issuer and the collateral, sometimes known as 'dual recourse' (Lemke et al. 2013).
19. A swap at the Eonia rate is an agreement between two parties who commit to swap, for a predefined time period, a series of daily interest-rate payments at a floating rate (Eonia) in return for a series of daily interest payment calculated at a fixed rate specified in the agreement, the so-called Eonia swap rate.
20. See http://euribor-ebf.eu/euribor-eonia-org/eonia-rates.html.
21. A description of the salient features of the various facilities introduced by the FED is available at the following link: http://www.federalreserve.gov/monetarypolicy. For a critical review of the effectiveness of the measures taken, see Wu (2008).
22. For a detailed description of the special resolution regime, see Brierley (2009).
23. For the operation of the credit guarantee scheme, see the debt management office press release (http://www.dmo.gov.uk/documentview.aspx?-docname=cgs/press/mknotice08.pdf).
24. Certain forms of protection are represented by the deposit guarantee fund, the loan of last resort, the valuation of securities that in a specific period, due to the credit crunch or to a general crisis of trust, are worth much less than the value with which they are shown in the balance sheet (so-called impaired assets), and so on.
25. According to a widely consolidated view (Diamond and Dybvig 1983), systemic risk is endemic to the financial system, which is more exposed and vulnerable to contagion phenomena than other sectors of the economy, mainly due to the crises that may arise at the banking level. The role of financial markets, including the interbank market (which together with

intermediaries, payment and settlement infrastructures and trading mechanisms comprise the financial system), is deemd the most arduous task of systemic risk analysis.

26. In particular, the author recalls the concept of information cascade, which requires that individuals observe and imitate the behaviour of others, regardless of the private information signal they possess.
27. The results obtained by the author are consistent with the empirical evidence that testifies the key role played by the disclosure of pessimistic information on banks in the generation of the bank run.
28. The perception of the implicit guarantees supporting the interbank financing channel, which has increased over time, led to a weakening of the credit risk assessment mechanism. Weaker intermediaries could incur debt at the same conditions obtained from bigger and more solid banks. However, interest rates on unsecured bank loans were in line with those offered by central banks for secured loans.
29. The potential systemic implications prompted the FED to accentuate interest rate cuts and to provide, through JP Morgan Chase, a loan of twenty-eight days to Bear Stearns, which was technically not authorized to access the refinancing activity of the Central Bank, endorsing the JP Morgan Chase proposal to buy Bear Stearns within ninety days. Since then, there has been a partial recovery in equity markets and for the most risky corporate bonds.
30. The CDS premium is the price paid by an investor to cover the issuer's bankruptcy risk.
31. OIS rates are the interest rates applied to swap contracts where one counterparty receives a variable payment indexed to the interest rate for overnight unsecured interbank deposits and the other counterparty receives the fixed OIS rate.

References

Aghion, P., Bolton, P., & Fries, S. (1999). Optimal Design of Bank Bailouts: The Case of Transition Economies. *Journal of Institutional and Theoretical Economies, 155,* 51–70.

Allen, F., & Gale, D. (1998). Optimal Financial Crises. *Journal of Finance, 53,* 1245–1284.

Bank for International Settlement (BIS). (2009, May). *Monetary Policy Frameworks and Central Bank Market Operations.*

Bank of England. (1999, April). *The Trasmission Mechanism of Monetary Policy.*

Battacharya, S., & Gale, D. (1987) Preference Shocks, Liquidity, and Central Bank Policy. In W. A. Barnett & K. J. Singleton (Ed.), *New Approaches to Monetary Economics.* Cambridge: Cambridge University Press.

Bernanke, B. S. (2009, January 13). *The Crisis and the Policy Response*. Speech at London School of Economics, London. Available on: http://www.federalreserve.gov/newsevents/speech/2009speech.htm.

Board of the Governor of the Federal Reserve System. (2005, June). *The Federal Reserve System: Purposes and Functions*.

Brierley, P. (2009, June 5). *The UK Special Resolution Regime for Failing Banks in an International Context* (Financial Stability Paper). Bank of England.

Chari, V. V., & Jagannathan, R. (1988). Banking Panics, Information, and Rational Expectation Equilibrium. *Journal of Finance, 43*, 749–60.

Chen, Z. (1999). Banking Panics: The Role of the First-Come, First-Served Rule and Information Externalities. *Journal of Political Economy, 107*, 946–968.

Cheun, S., von Koppen-Mertes, I., & Weller, B. (2009, December). *The Collateral Frameworks of the Eurosystem, the Federal Reserve System and the Bank of England and the Financial Turmoil* (ECB Occasional Paper Series 107).

De Bandt, O. (1995). *Competition Among Financial Intermediaries and the Risk of Contagious Failures* (Working Papers, Banque de France n. 30).

De Bandt, O., & Hartmann, P. (2000, November). *Systemic Risk: A Survey* (ECB Working Paper Series 35).

Diamond, D. W., & Dybvig, P. H. (1983). Bank Runs, Deposit Insurance, and Liquidty. *Journal of Political Economy, 91*, 401–419.

European Central Bank (ECB). (2009, April). *Annual Report*.

European Central Bank (ECB). (2010, June). *Monthly Bulletin*.

European Central Bank (ECB). (2011, January). *The Monetary Policy of the ECB*.

Flannery, M. (1996). Financial Crises, Payment System Problems, and Discount Window Lending. *Journal of Money, Credit, and Banking, 28*, 804–824.

Freixas, X., Parigi, B., & Rochet, J. (2000). Systemic Risk Interbank Relations and Liquidity Provision by the Central Bank. *Journal of Money, Credit and Banking, 32*, 611–638.

Gorton, G. (1985). Bank Suspension of Convertibility. *Journal of Monetary Economics, 15*, 177–193.

Kohn, D. L. (2009, April 18). *Monetary Policy in the Financial Crisis*. Speech at the Conference in Honor of Dewey Daane, Nashville. Available on: http://www.federalreserve.gov/newsevents/speech/2009speech.htm.

Lemke, T. P., Lins, G. T., & Picard, M. E. (2013). Mortgage-Backed Securities. *Clark Boadman Callaghan*.

Papademos, L. (2009, May 27). The Role of the ECB in the Financial Crisis Management. Speech at the Conference on the Cost of the Crisis: Planning an Exit Strategy, London. Available on: www.ecb.int.

Postlewaite, A., & Vives, X. (1987). Bank Runs as an Equilibrium Phenomenon. *Journal of Political Economy, 95*, 485–491.

Shelder, G., & Maurer, M. (1998). Interbank Lending and Systemic Risk: An Empirical Analysis for Switzerland. *Swiss Journal of Economics and Statistics, 134,* 685–704.

Smith, B. D. (1991). Bank Panics, Suspensions, and Geography: Some Notes on the 'Contagion of Fear' in Banking. *Economic Inquiry, 29,* 230–248.

Wu, T. (2008, May). *On the Effectiveness of the Federal Reserve's New Liquidity Facilities* (Federal Reserve Bank of Dallas Working Paper 0808).

CHAPTER 5

Bank Liquidity Regulation Before the Global Financial Crisis

5.1 Liquidity Risk Management: Regulation Before the Financial Crisis

Before the outbreak of the financial crisis of 2007, regulators at the international level had not set up homogeneous rules of conduct for banks in terms of liquidity risk management, which was left to the broad discretion of individual national supervisory authorities. Specifically, in Basel I Accord (1988), the BCBS did not mention the liquidity risk banks could encounter while carrying out their business. Only in 1992 did the BCBS address the problem of ensuring minimum standards for managing this risk in international banks, but it was limited to a report setting out the best practices to measure and manage it (BCBS 1992). This document was subsequently upgraded in 2000, bringing the principles of liquidity risk management into line with developments in the operations of major international banks (BCBS 2000). Even this document, albeit outlining 14 principles of sound liquidity risk management, dealt purely with disclosure and was not an amendment to the Basel I Accord. In 2006, a joint study group formed by the BCBS, the International Association of Insurance Supervisors (IAIS) and the International Organization of Securities Commissions (IOSCO) published a report, once again highlighting the objective of sharing the best practices in place, without dictating guidelines to be implemented by the national systems of major industrialized countries (The Joint Forum 2006).

L. Chiaramonte, *Bank Liquidity and the Global Financial Crisis*,
Palgrave Macmillan Studies in Banking and Financial Institutions,
https://doi.org/10.1007/978-3-319-94400-5_5

Until the financial crisis of 2007, at international level, there was a broad consensus that liquidity risk should not be covered by specific capital requirements, given that it only indirectly affected the sphere of economic and financial equilibrium. Regulators thought that, unlike credit, market and operational risks, liquidity risk did not need to be covered by the equity capital of shareholders, but could be handled by maintaining an adequate volume of liquid items and items capable of being liquidated quickly, and by introducing monitoring processes and operating systems able to cope with a sudden liquidity deficit.

In line with this vision, in 2004, the BCBS published the Basel II Accord. Again, it did not introduce minimum requirements for liquidity risk under the first pillar.[1] However, in the second pillar of the Basel II Accord, for the first time, it obliged banks to adopt adequate systems for measuring, monitoring and controlling liquidity risk, taking into account the operational profile of the intermediary and the liquidity of the markets in which they operate. Therefore, it emphasized the need for credit intermediaries to possess policies and processes able, on a continuous and prospective basis, to measure and manage the net financial position, as well as the obligation to draw up emergency plans to deal with any crisis. Thus, the second pillar introduced a qualitative supervisory model and left the possibility for individual national regulators to consider further measures to monitor and prevent banking illiquidity. In addition, in the third pillar, relating to disclosure, Basel II left broad discretion to national supervisors in relation to the need to oblige banks to disclose their exposure to, and management of, liquidity risk.

Hence, before the GFC, the BCBS regulated liquidity risk management in a heterogeneous manner. In this light, it is now important to look at both the aims pursued by liquidity risk management process and its contents. It is aimed to optimize the relationship between costs and benefits linked to the creation or to the investment of liquidity, to minimize the cost of funding, to diversify the sources of deposits and lending, to keep the bank in solvency conditions in presence of a crisis. Overall, the liquidity risk management is a process finalized to minimize both the variability of the economic result, and the impact of liquidity risk on the regulatory and economic capital.

Then, focusing on the main components of liquidity risk management, a careful analysis of the literature and the practices of the financial industry reveals six building blocks in this process (BCBS 2000). The first component is the governance model, i.e. a structured and organic set of:

- aims, strategies and policies for liquidity risk management;
- an organizational structure for the management and monitoring of operational and structural liquidity;
- roles and responsibilities of the structures/functions involved in measuring and managing liquidity.

The first block is defined starting from the operational complexity of the intermediary, the peculiarities of the composition of assets/liabilities on the balance sheet, a definition of liquidity risk and a shared liquidity risk tolerance.

Operating limits system is another component of liquidity risk management. As for other types of risks, it is determined by specific regulatory constraints and is subject to a periodical and occasional review if the market conditions or tolerance to bank liquidity risk change. It is an autonomous block of liquidity risk management, bridging regulation and internal/external communications to the intermediary, between the subjects that manage the bank, operating units, and the different roles/organizational functions involved in liquidity management.

The third component comprises measurement methods in normal and adverse conditions (stress testing exercises). They include models to measure liquidity risk (differently based on the type of liquidity risk considered), the time period, frequency and the measurement conditions (normal or stressed). Stress testing exercises should not be merely accurate analyses of 'what if' (usually performed on a monthly or quarterly basis), but complex processes in which the results are discussed by the Risk Committee, in conjunction with related risk mitigation actions to be adopted and promptly communicated to the Board of Directors of the bank.

Another component comprises operational policy and response levers, including policy itself, the systems and instruments used to manage liquidity risk (such as financial planning, the eligible collateral system, the CFP, intraday liquidity management, transfer pricing for funds, the cushion of unencumbered high-quality assets[2]).

The fifth component comprises control activities. They include procedures, implemented at different hierarchical and functional levels of the organizational structure, aimed at monitoring operational and structural liquidity (the former predominantly by front-office systems; the latter especially by Asset and Liability Management—ALM); they assure the Board and Senior Management that the strategies and the policies in response to liquidity risk are carried out correctly (in the proper manner and by the expected times), complying with internal regulations and the relevant regulatory requirements.

The last block of liquidity risk management is internal communication and disclosure to the market. It comprises the following activities put in place in order: to monitor and control the situation of the treasury, liquidity reserves, day-to-day operations, and to facilitate targeted preventive interventions; to ensure continuous, up-to-date, frequent information flows between the units/functions involved in the liquidity risk management process in the forms and at the times that allow them to properly fulfil their responsibilities (internal reporting); in accordance with International Accounting Standards (IAS)/International Financial Reporting Standards (IFRS) accounting principles, to ensure adequate qualitative and quantitative disclosure (see Supplementary Notes in the Financial Statements) regarding the key dimensions of the liquidity risk management process.

Each of these building blocks is analyzed in detail in the following sections in order to capture their specific contents, giving shape and meaning to the entire bank liquidity risk management process. Finally, the chapter ends with the analysis the supervisors' role in the liquidity risk management process.

5.2 The Building Blocks of the Liquidity Risk Management Process

5.2.1 *The Liquidity Governance Model*

The liquidity governance model, one of the components of bank liquidity risk management, defines objectives, policies to be implemented, organizational structures and the roles and responsibilities of the various business actors.

The definition of the role of the Board of Directors is crucial, because it has to be fully aware of the nature and consequences of liquidity risk, of its characteristics and issues related to its identification, valuation, control and management. Sound supervisory practices and guidelines provide a good support in defining the roles and responsibilities of the actors involved in liquidity risk management.

Ideally, each bank has a strategy communicated to the entire structure for day-to-day liquidity management. The Board of Directors approves the strategy and the most important liquidity management policies. In addition, it ensures that top executives take general measures to monitor and control liquidity risk. When significant changes occur, they are promptly informed of the new liquidity situation.

The Board of Directors is responsible for ensuring that liquidity risk is properly identified, defined, measured and controlled. In addition, their duties include the definition of the level of bank liquidity risk tolerance and the consequent formulation of the liquidity management strategy. The latter should be set in line with business objectives, strategic direction and bank risk propensity, and should provide liquidity management in normal and stressful times; the communication and the sharing of the liquidity management strategy within the bank; approval of the limit system, operational mandates and the funding plan; the identification of the roles and responsibilities of the liquidity risk management unit and the allocation to the unit of the human resources and technologies needed to operate.

The Board of Directors approves the strategy and ensures that the Senior Management[3] converts it into clear management lines, operating standards, and systems that identify, measure, manage and control liquidity risk. The strategy should include specific liquidity risk management policies relating to the composition of assets and liabilities, the diversification and stability of funding sources, the various approaches of liquidity management in different currencies, cross-border operations, asset negotiability. Moreover, the Board of Directors is tasked with examining routine reports concerning liquidity positions and should be informed of any liquidity problems (such as increased funding costs or a concentration of funding sources, the dewatering of alternative sources of liquidity, a significant reduction in the cushion of unengaged and highly liquid assets) as soon as they arise. In addition, the Board of Directors should ensure that Senior Management takes appropriate corrective actions to solve these issues.

Senior Management is responsible for the development and implementation of the liquidity risk management strategy in line with the bank's risk tolerance level. In addition, supported by the Risk Management/Risk Committee, it recommends to the Board of Directors the liquidity management strategies and policies, the methods for analyzing and supervising the exposure of the bank to liquidity risk, the system of limits and operational mandates, and the funding plan. Within its operational mandates, Senior Management also carries out the operations required for the management of liquidity, issues operating instructions to bring management in line with the provisions of the Board of Directors, and informs the Board of possible encroachments of operating limits and, in conjunction with the finance Area/ALM Committee (Asset and Liability Committee, ALCO), recommends a return plan.

Banking practice usually attributes liquidity risk management to the ALCO, comprising all members of the business areas concerned with liquidity risk and with the task of establishing specific policies for managing this risk, ensuring that measurement systems are able to properly identify and quantify the exposure to liquidity risk and that reporting systems provide accurate and relevant information about the level and origin of the exposure. In large financial intermediaries, the Board of Directors decides the strategies and the related policies following the guidelines provided by the ALCO, while the verification of compliance of the limits set at the strategic and operational level is the job of a dedicated auditing body (internal audit). In addition, if a broad view of funding intervention prevails, engagement in the liquidity risk management process may include the division responsible for fund raising on the capital market. In addition, the distinction that some banks make between liquidity and treasury may be reflected in the organizational structure, delegating the responsibility to two separate units: one for long-term management and the other focused on the short term.

The liquidity governance model also involves the assignment of roles and responsibilities to a specific unit (the so-called Liquidity Risk Control Unit), which generally includes the following activities: the monitoring of indicators and compliance with operational limits, with consequent communication to Senior Management; verifying the adequacy/capacity of information systems to ensure effective liquidity management; monitoring the operation of the Finance Area in terms of liquidity; verifying the maintenance of adequate internal controls to protect the integrity of liquidity risk management and control; preparation of a (daily) report for Senior Management and the Board of Directors (at least monthly) on the performance of liquidity management; and drafting disclosure for liquidity management. The internal audit verifies the operating model for liquidity management and its effective implementation.

In general terms, in the case of groups with cross-border operations, the governance model is defined using either a centralized or decentralized approach (International Institute of Finance—IIF 2007), although in practice different models exist within a segment whose extremes are operational centralization and decentralization. The choice of the approach to follow depends on a number of factors, including the level at which policies, management procedures, measurement metrics and operating limit systems are designed and applied, and the measurement and manner in which liquidity can flow into the banking group.

There are several arguments in favour of each option (centralized vs. decentralized), all of them open to different interpretation (by extension and depth) within corporate organizations. Centralization can relate, for example, to the governance model as a whole, and/or policies and processes, and/or roles and responsibilities in liquidity risk management. The choice between centralized and decentralized is highly strategic, and strongly affects (CEBS 2007) potential restrictions on the transferability of assets and 'domestic' liquidity between intermediaries in the group which carry out cross-border activities, the localization of liquid assets, the applicability of regulatory frameworks that require quantitative requirements at a consolidated level, the impact that a sudden change in exchange rates and/or in the liquidity of a certain market may have on the economy of the entire group,[4] the definition of liquid assets and assets that can be liquidated quickly (supervisors in different countries establish differing sets of minimum criteria for assets to be included in this category), the management of the pool of liquid reserves in different currencies for refinancing with the various central banks that require financial guarantees in different currencies.

Each of the two options has advantages relating to the greater or lesser weight within the corporate organization. Banks that operate at a national level generally opt for a centralized approach compared to cross-border banking groups that offer greater autonomy to controlled entities in terms of developing liquidity policies. In the centralized approach, measurement rules, operational limits, medium- and long-term guidelines and the contingency funding plan are established at the central level by the parent company and subsequently passed top-down to the individual institutions in the group. On the other hand, based on the full responsibility of companies in the banking group, decentralized models are more widespread among international financial intermediaries characterized by cross-border operations. If, on the one hand, the organization of these structures reduces the complexity of liquidity risk management at a consolidated level, limiting the risks of contagion during a crisis, on the other hand, it often involves suboptimal funding costs, due both to the inability to offset positive and negative flows and the reduced depth of liquidity risk analysis carried out by each single unit of the group.

Nevertheless, the geographic area of markets (European, American, emerging) and (convertible, unconvertible) currencies can influence the organization managing liquidity risk (CEBS 2007). Unsurprisingly, supervisors emphasize the need for banks to adopt a measurement, monitoring and control system for liquidity in the major currencies. Banks must analyze its liquidity strategy for each currency (BCBS 2000).

The governance model used by banking groups is generally centralized: management of (strategic) structural liquidity is centralized at the parent/holding company level; the management of operational liquidity is centrally coordinated, but with a degree of local autonomy (regional centres/legal entities) whose intensity cannot be deduced from disclosure; and local units are responsible for compliance with regulatory constraints.

5.2.2 *The Operating Limits System*

The operating limits system, a further element of liquidity risk management, is a key instrument for monitoring and managing operational and structural liquidity given that its potential to contain the impact of liquidity risk provides early warning indicators of adverse and vulnerable situations, ensuring that banks are adequately prepared for stress situations. It includes target ratios provided by supervisory arrangements, and must be defined to allow banks to maintain an adequate net liquidity position over the short, medium and long term, and enough cash to operate under both normal and stressed conditions.

An effective operating limits system should be based on the operational complexity and the measurement methods applied by the intermediary and should be designed in the light of the following three directives:

- methods for defining (operational and structural) limits[5] and the perimeter for applicability.[6] The established limits must be relevant for the bank's business in terms of the type of activity carried out, the nature of the products provided, currencies and markets;
- internal communication methods where the various limits have been exceeded;

- monitoring frequency. Generally, operating limits are monitored daily, whereas structural liquidity risk is monitored on a monthly/quarterly basis; stress tests are subject to weekly/monthly reporting; contingent events are characterized by reports with nonstandard frequency. Monitoring is just one of the activities of the liquidity control system.

The operating limits system also establishes (internal and external) early warning devices, i.e. signals in advance, or at least promptly, of liquidity tensions. In the event of warning signals for one or more indicator, a process of additional monitoring, investigating the causes of alarm, and transition to crisis procedures can be triggered. Some examples of endogenous early warnings are: an increased concentration in assets or liabilities, a fall in asset quality, a decrease in profits or rapid growth in the volatility of financial assets. Instead, exogenous early warnings include market rumours about the bank's strength and reputation, its downgrading, a sharp drop in its stock prices (for listed intermediaries), an increase in the spreads paid by the bank and in the instruments issued, fewer funding opportunities or an increase in the demand for counterparty guarantees, an increase in the overall cost of funding, a reduction in lending lines by several banks, a decrease in the number of counterparties willing to deal with the bank, requests for early repayment, the deterioration of key indicators (such as loans on deposits, short-term liabilities on total assets, available liquidity, dependence on wholesale funding).

Operating limits are subject to review when market conditions or the risk tolerance of the bank change. They may relate to the absolute maturity gap, the volume of funding overnight in relation to total assets, liquid assets net of short-term liabilities, liquid assets and assets that can be liquidated quickly, net of the expected erosion in cases of stress, etc. In operational practice, many intermediaries set quantitative limits in terms of the overnight target for each local treasury and maximum cash outflow limits (for globally and locally operational liquidity), or the short-term gap, unsecured funding (for tactical liquidity); maximum imbalances of medium- and long-term structural liquidity and of regulatory ratios.

Generally, planning also includes concentration limits by type of fund-raising counterparty, the maximum exposure on the interbank market, some short-, medium- and long-term systemic indicators. Added to the latter are single-name concentration limits for trading and banking portfolios, provided by regulators for each funding channel and significant instrument/currency.

5.2.3 *Liquidity Risk Measurement*

Liquidity risk measurement is a particularly important component of liquidity risk management. As noted above, the type of liquidity risk most studied in the financial sector and where supervisors focus most of their attention is funding liquidity risk. So, until recently, intermediaries were interested only in the management of funding liquidity risk. However, changes in the competitive environment have obliged intermediaries to learn to manage the other type of liquidity risk, i.e. market liquidity risk.

Banks usually assess funding liquidity risk using measurement methods based on a stock-based, cash flow analysis or hybrid approach. No measurement metric has been widely agreed by academics, although in practice there seems to be a clear preference for cash flow approaches.

The stock-based approach aims to compute indicators based on the ratio between assets and liabilities, or to indentify net positions useful for the provision of liquidity measures, such as the loan to deposit ratio (LTD), the structural liquidity ratio (SLR), and the cash capital position (CCP).

The LTD, a financial structure indicator, is computed as the ratio between two typical components of the bank's balance sheet, i.e. customer loans and deposits. This ratio gives a summary and partial indication of the degree of bank liquidity risk. The information is 'partial' because the financial structure of a bank includes, among its assets and liabilities, items other than customer loans and deposits, giving rise to liquidity risks. In addition, the LTD gives 'summary information' because liquidity trends and the associated risk are not based only on the financial structure at a certain date. However, the LTD has the advantage of simplicity: it is easy to determine and read, can be derived from balance sheet data and allows comparisons to be made over time and with other banks. Values of this ratio above 1 mean that deposits provide full financial coverage to loans, less than 1 indicate that a portion of loans is financed with funds from other sources. However, what emerges is an initial rough guide without the complexity of liquidity risk measurement.

In order to adequately identify and quantify exposure and structural liquidity requirements, banks calculate a cumulated gap ratio or so-called SLR, by dividing assets by liabilities, both with a contractual maturity more than or equal to *n* years. SLR is often inferior to 1 due to maturity mismatching. Indeed, banks carry it out with different degree of intensity under conditions of relative illiquidity for their assets compared to those of the liabilities issued (the latter are subject to a high risk of repayment demands by subscribers or depositors). Very low values of this ratio are a signal of imbalances in the maturity structure of assets and liabilities.

In the calculation of SRL, gap profile analysis plays an important role, and this in turn essentially depends on some assumptions (often subject to formal validation by risk management) to determine the economic (rather than contractual) maturity of balance sheet items. The calculation of gap profiles with the above assumptions should provide an effective analysis of net requirements in order to highlight the appropriate financing interventions in terms of market and products.

Finally, the CCP was initially introduced by Moody's as an integral part of its rating assignments, to analyze the liquidity of a bank balance sheet (Moody's 2001). This indicator is computed as the (positive or negative) difference between liquid (or monetizable) assets and volatile liabilities. On the one hand, liquid assets include cash and free reserves held at the central bank, interbank loans, securities in the portfolio that are freely usable as collateral for secured loans the bank may require. In order to determine the corresponding amount of liquid assets, the value of securities is reduced by prudential haircuts which are normally applied in the provision activity of guaranteed loans. On the other hand, volatile liabilities include short-term deposits on the interbank market and the portion of on sight deposits considered unstable. The CCP gives a measure of the bank capacity to resist and, via its reserves, handle an unexpected increase in risk due, for example, to the inability of obtaining unsecured loans on the interbank market. To capture the relative value of CCP, the amount is divided by total assets. Thus, the CCP ratios of different banks can be compared over time.

In order to overcome the limits of the 'dichotomous' vision associated with the reclassification carried out to calculate CCP, the cash flow approach was introduced based on the use of the maturity ladder, constructed according to various hypotheses and methods. The reason banks use this approach is primarily to ensure that they continue to be able to meet their contractual obligations and, at the same time, measure and contain the implicit risks involved in maturity transformation through the introduction of a system of limits at the liquidity positions imbalances present on the temporal ranges of which the maturity ladder is composed.

This approach involves placing cash flows (incoming and outgoing) from the various balance sheet items, into certain future time ranges comprising the ladder, on the basis of their contractual or pending maturity and using a conservative approach. The timetable thus defined is an inertial representation for the purposes of liquidity risk measurement in a stable market scenario.

The assessment of the degree of equilibrium between incoming and outgoing cash flows is carried out by opposing them in each section of the maturity ladder, thus obtaining Marginal Liquidity Gaps (MLGs), and calculating Cumulative Liquidity Gaps (CLGs) indicating the net balance of needs or financial surplus over the time period considered. Negative MLG values, associated with very short-term maturities, mean that the bank is unable to cover the expected cash outflows with inflows. In this case, appropriate corrective actions are needed to ensure that the bank does not go into liquidity crisis. However, the picture emerging from this methodology is scarcely reliable as the cash flows associated with unencumbered assets are classified according to their contractual maturity. Thus, it overlooks the ability to use these cash flows as collateral to obtain new funding, including very short term.

The so-called adjusted maturity ladder is used to verify the daily maintenance of liquidity surpluses under stress conditions over a set time (the so-called survival period). The hybrid approach used for its construction, combining stock-based and mismatch-based models in an attempt to reduce the underlying limitations, assumes that potential outflows generated by sight balance sheet items and linked to future contingent scenarios, are prudently placed in the overnight area of the residual life pattern according to empirical evidence and/or behavioural models, rather than being classified according to their contractual maturity date.

As a tool to support liquidity management and measurement, the adjusted maturity ladder means that any negative financial needs are fully covered in the short-term period using a special liquidity buffer (LB). The latter principally comprises cash and assets that ensure in all likelihood liquidity creation in a very short-term period without excessive margins in stress circumstances or in the presence of a flight to quality.

The LB, the amount of which is defined on the basis of risk tolerance, should be sufficient to ensure the bank's survival for a set time (the so-called survival period target) without change to its business model. It means that the LB is represented by assets that are readily available for a limited time period without the need to change operations or use additional sources of funding over that period.

The LB is of the maximum value in periods of stress, when traditional funding channels are no longer accessible or cannot provide enough liquidity, where the bank also urgently needs to increase its liquidity in the short term.

The liquidity buffer is the short-term component of the counterbalancing capacity (CC), which is the ability of the bank, by its own actions, to counter, trends with a negative impact on the treasury and liquidity equilibrium: through both immediate intervention, covering liquidity gaps in the short-term and management policies and strategic guidelines which lead to additional liquidity sources or to changes and integrations of the activities aimed at improving impacts on financial flows and on the company's financial structure. The measures around which the CC is built include the CFP, i.e. the emergency plan for acquiring new funds in cases of particularly intense difficulties due, for example, to significant and unexpected stress conditions.

With reference to market liquidity risk measurement of this risk is a crucial aspect of overall liquidity risk management. Normally what is measured is the indicator of its lack or shortage, i.e. transaction costs. These can be defined as the costs resulting from changes in securities ownership, in other words, the sum of all the charges incurred by investors for trading in financial instruments. The higher the transaction costs required to trade an asset, the lower its liquidity. Specifically, transaction costs have two components: one explicit, i.e. the monetary payments for commissions and other charges imposed by the counterparty; and the other implicit, i.e. a suboptimum price. In turn, implicit costs comprise: the listed bid-ask spread which is the remuneration of the market-making service, measurable in percentage terms by reference to the mid-quote[7]; the market impact that derives from the fact that transactions of significant amount, in relation to the current market depth, tend to affect the price in an unfavourable direction in relation to the interests of those who gave rise to the exchange (i.e. the difference between the execution price of the transaction and what would have been the case if the transaction had not taken place). Opportunity costs, associated with the failure of a transaction, apply only to traders with more information, in so far as the value of this information declines over time. Such costs may arise from failure or partial execution or from a delay compared to the time when negotiation was decided. Opportunity costs occur if the market price moves in the opposite direction to the desired transaction, for example, the price decreases when the decision is taken to sell, and vice versa.

5.2.4 *Policies and Operational Levers*

After measurement, liquidity risk must be managed effectively with appropriate tools and techniques. These include: infra-day liquidity management, fund transfer pricing (FTP), the CFP, the collateral system, and retaining a cushion of unencumbered, and high-quality liquid assets. Below the analysis focuses on the main characteristics of these tools.

With reference to intraday liquidity management, in the last few years, the growing globalization of economies and changes in payment and settlement systems have contributed to increasing the demand for intraday liquidity. The precise management of intraday liquidity positions, promptly meeting settlement and payment obligations, contributes to the proper functioning of payment and settlement systems, both in normal and stress conditions.

Liquidity policies, generally focusing on the structural liquidity, manage key business lines, actions, controls, and activities on the basis of long-term goals, for which intraday liquidity management plays a crucial role. Indeed, for the intermediary, effective intraday liquidity management involves:

- continuous monitoring and control of intraday liquidity positions. It can help the intermediary to understand when to acquire further liquidity or limit outflows to meet the most critical payments; it can favour an efficient allocation of intraday liquidity, between the needs of the bank and those of its customers, and enable a rapid reaction to unexpected payment flows;
- the ability to measure expected daily cash inflows and outflows. Therefore, banks must know all the regulations of payment and settlement systems in which they are involved and identify key supply counterparts, time periods, days and circumstances in which such flows can reach their peaks;

- the ability to acquire sufficient intraday funds necessary to meet predetermined objectives (the central banks generally provide intraday credit lines to facilitate both banks and the proper functioning of payment and settlement systems);
- a clear assignment of roles and responsibilities;
- backup procedures able to minimize any operational problems (computer connections, unauthorized log-in, operating system issues, etc.) that could compromise the normal activities of the institution.

Another operational instrument of liquidity risk management is the FTP, which involves the application of a price or a fictitious internal cost (so-called transfer price) to be credited to liquidity sources found through various funding channels (on and off the balance sheet), and, conversely, to be charged to the investments linked to the multiple products, functions and activities of a banking group or an intermediary. The FTP, as a competitive and managerial lever, is crucial in measuring the profitability achieved by divisions, financial products and counterparties and, consequently, in indirectly influencing bank operations and risk appetite.

The FTP, as the interface between the commercial and financial aspects of the intermediary, also makes an appreciable contribution to liquidity risk management, implicit in individual products and in the operation of the business lines or of the intermediary as a whole. For this reason, the FTP framework must be consistent with governance, liquidity risk tolerance and the decision-making process of the intermediary. Especially for the most complex operational intermediaries, it provides an important support to financial planning and ALM.

The CFP is another tool that allows the intermediary to cope with sudden liquidity drainage, without incurring excessive extraordinary expenses, through the preliminary identification of a series of actions to be taken in case of adverse events, and the system of eligible collateral that can be used at the central bank to obtain liquidity. In this perspective, liquidity risk management goes beyond the diversification of the funding profile (in terms of instruments, counterparties, currencies), the control of maturity mismatching, maintaining access to payment systems, the careful monitoring of off-balance sheet commitments and contingent liabilities. The latter are ordinary liquidity management tools, while the CFP is a typical tool for liquidity management in extraordinary situations.

However, they should all be used in an integrated manner for the overall and coordinated management of the liquidity problem, which, by its very nature, requires the concerted attention of the various organizational units of the bank.

The principles of supervisors include the obligation on banks to have emergency plans (CFPs) for liquidity crisis management and procedures to cope with cash flow deficits in emergency situations, the management of collateral and their separation into unencumbered and encumbered assets.

With adequate projections, the emergency plan highlights cash flows and bank financing sources at specific future maturities and under stress. Therefore, its purpose is to protect banking capital from events that could impact deeply on the liquidity profile of the intermediary, by foreseeing and regulating the exceptional strategies that need to be activated in order to find sources of financing to face the emergency created by the events.

The bank should define its CFP on the basis of its complexity, risk profile and the role it plays in the financial system in which it operates, taking into account several factors, including: the impact of stressed market conditions on its ability to sell or securitize assets; the link between financial assets and liquidity; and the reputational effects associated with the implementation of emergency procedures. These factors should reflect the past experience of the bank or other intermediaries, market practice and the ratio with which the bank has performed stress tests. The emergency plan may include the definition of events triggering the implementation of the plan, the description of potential financing sources on the assets or liabilities side (sale of liquid assets, securitization, increase in deposits, prolongation of liability maturities, raising capital, suspension of dividends to parent companies), the increase of procedures indicating in detail how funds could be increased; the contract management procedure with external parties, such as bank counterparties, financial analysts, media and supervisory authorities.

Hence, the CFP is not only an operational lever of response to liquidity risk, but given that it is able, to some extent, to influence its outcome and depth, it can also be considered a genuine mitigation tool. For example, a CFP which provides sources of funding that are sufficiently diversified by geographical area and currency may enable a bank to overcome its funding tensions and so act as a stabilizer in a disrupted local market context.

From an operational point of view, the CFP browses the various additional sources of funding that need to be available in the event of liquidity shocks (the temporary mobilization of mandatory reserves, repurchase agreements with the central bank, loans from other banks, etc.), setting the order and priority in which they are to be activated. This order depends on the flexibility and cost of the various available sources, and on the type of shock taking place. While in the case of a specific shock, it makes sense to count on a certain volume of loans from other financial institutions (at least equal to the value of the securities that can be used as collateral, minus the haircut), a better response to a general market crisis is prompt action with the central bank to obtain extraordinary advances. From an organizational point of view, the CFP identifies the structures and actors responsible for the implementation of extraordinary funding policies in cases of shock, communicating and explaining to the market the difficulties encountered by the bank and the actions taken to overcome these problems. Usually, the medium- and long-term funding plan is established by the ALM function, which however must coordinate its work with financial planning,[8] management control and the treasury.

Emergency plans should be reviewed and tested periodically in order to ensure their effectiveness and operational feasibility. After approval by the Board of Directors, Senior Management updates the emergency plan every year and whenever the changing market or circumstances require.

Therefore, the objectives of the emergency plan are: to identify crisis signals, to establish strategies and intervention policies and to protect bank capital (IIF 2007). In order to achieve these goals, load or stress tests are carried out to accurately establish:

- adverse, but plausible events related both to firm-specific shocks (sudden reduction in credit lines granted to the bank, unexpected changes in the composition of deposits, increasing claims by depositors, downgrades of the bank rating, etc.) and systemic shock (economic downturn in leading industrialized countries, collapse of confidence between banks, a market crash, credit crunch, unexpected problems in the payment system). In operational practice, often only the first is considered and this makes the current emergency plans unsuitable to anticipate the size and duration of market shocks;

- the approaches to be used to estimate cash flow in the hypothetical scenarios (historical, statistical, judgment based)[9];
- the 'perimeter' of the load tests (at group level and/or at single operating unit level, of operating liquidity flows and/or structural liquidity);
- the time period, which is normally one month;
- frequency, usually monthly or quarterly.

The definition of an appropriate level of stress remains the main challenge for the liquidity risk manager. The results give management the starting point for the construction of the CFP, and for the analysis of the possible impact on cash flows, liquidity, profitability and solvency. Banks can use several approaches to predict the behaviour of cash flows in adverse conditions (historical, statistical, judgment based). They can be used to simulate the effect of individual risk factors, or to build worst-case scenarios where multiple risk factors act together, producing situations with high liquidity risk. The hypothetical scenarios must be adverse but plausible,[10] severe or prolonged, idiosyncratic or systemic. Overall, they must be such that, if they occur, the bank would not be able to survive beyond the predetermined time period. However, the lack of objective criteria and shared practices for the conduct of stress tests creates inequalities in treatment and makes it difficult to evaluate the ratio informing potential regulatory intervention in the event of any risk situations. Therefore, important guidelines were established for the definition of hypothetical scenarios underlying the stress tests, with regular reviews to ensure that the scenarios continue to be relevant and appropriate (especially in cases of changed market conditions, the nature, size, and complexity of its business model or activities, and based on the experience gained during previous stress situations).

As a liquidity management tool, collateral management is important. Collateral is both a potential source of funding and a form of risk mitigation. Therefore, it is essential that, in the current market scenario, the banking intermediary has an effective collateral management system. For this purpose, a bank needs to:

- continuously assess collateral eligibility as a guarantee for central banks (for intraday credit, overnight credit, and for standing facilities operations) and a major provider of funds;

- prudently diversify the collateral portfolio, carefully considering the risk of single-name concentration, the sensitivity of the market value of individual types of collateral, haircuts under normal and stressed conditions, the time needed to render the collateral liquid or replace it;
- carefully size the collateral portfolio to meet expected and unexpected financing needs and potential increases in required margins on various maturities, in view of the funding profile. Intermediaries that use derivative contracts should take into account the possibility that additional guarantees may be required as a result of changes in market positions, in the rating of the bank or in its financial position, without overlooking trigger events;
- define policies able to identify and assess collateral requirements,[11] and all available collateral resources,[12] for different periods of time;
- understand and address the legal and operational constraints underlying the use of collateral, including within control functions[13];
- define a global policy, approved by Senior Management, that includes a conservative definition of collateral and specifies the level of unencumbered collateral available to meet unexpected funding needs;
- implement policies and organize collateral system management in line with the organization of operations.

The allocation of the various available types of collateral should be optimized according to the needs, products, business units, places and currencies of the intermediary's operations.

Finally, a bank should maintain a cushion of unencumbered and highly liquid assets as collateral against a series of liquidity crisis scenarios, including those that involve the loss or unavailability of sources of both guaranteed and unsecured funding. This buffer is an effective tool of resistance to liquidity stress, given that these assets can be sold or pledged in order to obtain funds. Its size should be in line with the level of risk tolerance established by the bank and various stress scenarios should be envisaged in terms of duration, severity and the cash value that can be obtained from the assets, if sold or given as a guarantee.

In terms of the composition of the cushion, it should have a core of highly liquid and reliable assets, such as cash, government bonds, or similar instruments, as protection against, particularly severe stress scenarios. For less severe scenarios unencumbered assets are sufficient.

The negotiability of these assets depends on the stress scenario. However, some features tend to increase liquidity, such as the transparency of the structure and risk characteristics, the ease and certainty of evaluation, eligibility at the central bank, the depth of the market, the reputation of the bank and its presence in relevant markets.

The assets included in the cushion must not be subject to legal, regulatory or operational constraints since they should be able to be used freely, at any time, as new liquidity needs arise.

High-quality liquidity resources may belong:

- to the top level (cash, reserves at the central bank, government bonds);
- the second level (high-quality corporate bonds and covered bonds). The amount of the second level cannot be higher than the first.

When managing their liquidity stocks, banks should avoid holding large concentrations of individual securities and remove any legal, regulatory and operational obstacles to the use of these resources. The position and size of liquidity reserves within the banking group should properly reflect the structure and activities of the group in order to minimize the effects of any legal, regulatory and operational obstacles to using the liquidity buffer (CEBS 2009a).

Mostly during periods of stress, where traditional funding channels may become unavailable (or fail to provide sufficient liquidity), this cushion is of fundamental importance to meet liquidity needs.

5.2.5 Control Activities

In general terms, as part of the liquidity risk management process, control activities should reflect the environment and regulatory context in which the intermediary operates, the size and complexity of its organization, the nature and scope of its activities, its history and its culture. The activity is designed, with a reasonable degree of certainty, to achieve the following business objectives: the effectiveness and efficiency of operational activities, the reliability of financial information, compliance with current laws and regulations.

Control is a process, in the sense that it is intended not as an isolated event or unique circumstance and not a series of mechanical acts or controls performed automatically, but as a set of actions related to all business activities, carried out by the people involved. For this, a strong control culture should be fostered within the business organization, with the sharing of strategic objectives (throughout the company or in relation to specific activities) by different hierarchical levels, and the training of personnel with different roles in control activities.

Every bank must have an adequate internal control system for liquidity risk. The basic components of internal controls are reviews and independent evaluations. Where necessary, improvements should be made. The result of any reviews must be notified to the authorities.

Regulation requires investment in liquidity control systems, providing a broad margin of discretion to risk management in defining management models and control systems.

A sound internal control system for liquidity risk should include:

- careful monitoring of the environment;
- an adequate process for identifying and assessing liquidity risk;
- the definition of control activities (policies and procedures);
- adequate information and reporting system;
- continuous monitoring of compliance with established policy and processes.

The liquidity control function aims to: define the model for liquidity measurement; monitor operational and structural liquidity; define and perform stress test analysis; ensure coherence between the policies set by top management and operational risk management, with suitable processes and a proper rationale behind the measures adopted; achieve the established objectives and establish policies in the event of a crisis.

A bank should have the ability to monitor intraday liquidity positions in relation to expected assets and available resources. Frequent monitoring of positions during the day can help the bank to acquire additional liquidity or limit outflows in order to meet the most critical payments. In addition, control may enable the efficient allocation of intraday liquidity, covering the needs of the bank and its customers, and a rapid response to unexpected payment flows.

In the future, for liquidity management, all banks should introduce an increasingly stringent monitoring system based on the timely liquidity control, which includes future cash flow projections. Indeed, banks need to think of the future prospects of certain assets and liabilities, such as off-balance sheet exposures and demand deposits that may give rise to exogenous cash flows. 'Going concern' analyses are useful, but scenario analysis and stress tests related to forecasts and the activation of emergency plans (CFPs) are crucial.

The effectiveness of the monitoring system depends largely on the internal reporting system of the intermediary. Ideally, the management information system is used for day-to-day liquidity risk management to ensure compliance with established policies, procedures and liquidity limits. In order to effectively manage and monitor its liquidity profile, a bank must be able to calculate and promptly communicate to Senior Management and the Board intraday liquidity positions on a daily basis and over a series of longer time periods. To facilitate the monitoring of liquidity risk, the same organizational roles are involved in setting up the reporting criteria, specifying the field of application, methods used, frequency, and the parties responsible.

5.2.6 *Internal Communication and Disclosure*

The communications block consists in all the activities carried out in order to ensure continuous, updated and frequent information flows between the units involved in liquidity risk governance (internal reporting), and guarantee adequate qualitative and quantitative disclosure to the market.

Without complete, timely, and accurate information, the full value of the different levels of responsibility, and everyone's contribution to both the implementation of corporate strategies and the assessment of the adequacy and consistency of management cannot be insured. This is particularly the case in situations of financial turbulence in which the transmission of information, horizontally between structures, and vertically towards strategic supervisory and control authorities, enables appropriate risk management initiatives to be implemented and decisions to be taken in relation to the evolution of the market.

Liquidity risk reporting involves the various corporate functions/authorities. Delays or inaccuracies in internal information flows can compromise the significance and integrity of the information or simply slow down its reception, affecting the quality of the response from top management. As noted above, in order to facilitate the monitoring of liquidity risk, organizational roles must be involved in arranging and defining the reporting criteria, specifying the scope of application, methods used, frequency, and subjects responsible. However, from an operational point of view, with reference to reporting on internal liquidity risk, there is no consolidated market practice on frequency, responsible parties, depth, methods and the time required to include local in overall provisions (parties involved, instruments used). In addition, to effectively manage and monitor its liquidity profile, a bank must be able to calculate and promptly communicate to Senior Management and the Board, intraday liquidity positions on a daily basis and for a series of longer time periods. Clearly, proper liquidity management requires the production of reports with various frequencies (intradaily, daily, weekly, monthly, quarterly, etc.) integrating the management viewpoint with the regulatory framework, as useful for horizontal and vertical communication.

An effective business information system is fundamental for the decision-making process, including liquidity risk management. In order to facilitate the monitoring of liquidity risk, the Senior Management has to set a series of reporting criteria specifying the purpose, method and frequency of communication for the various members of the organization, such as the Board of Directors, the same Senior Management and ALCO. For risk management managers, reporting on risk measures are made on several periodic basis (intradaily, daily, weekly, monthly, quarterly) at each organizational level during normal periods, with increased communications during periods of stress. Any violation of the limits defined in the exposure to liquidity risk must be promptly notified to management bodies.

Reports should regularly include: a fund flow analysis, analysis of the funding gap and the maturity structure, a list of episodes in which established liquidity limits and regulatory ratios (including those specified by Basel III Accord) were exceeded, funding concentration (by counterparty, currency, instrument, funding channel), the evolution of the quality and value of liquid assets and assets that can quickly be liquidated (quality, quantity, evolution, location), an analysis of the market value of eligible collateral and related haircuts, the structure and composition of assets and liabilities (also useful for the analysis of financial equilibrium and structural liquidity), the dimensions and costs of the latest short-term liquidity supplies, the impact on the liquidity profile of securitization transactions, information on backup liquidity in case of stress and contingency liquidity needs, information on derivatives and other financial instruments.

With reference to disclosure to the market, the supervisor requires banks to provide public information on a regular basis to allow market participants to express an informed judgment about the soundness of its liquidity risk management process and liquidity situation. Banks should provide adequate information to the general public on a regular basis, and, in particular, to major banking and credit counterparties, without developing bilateral channels solely with leading lenders to overcome the issues related to rumours while failing to communicate with the market.

Public disclosure is based on both qualitative (bank liquidity) and quantitative information (necessary to understand the former). Some examples of qualitative information are: the definition of liquidity risk adopted, the organizational structure of liquidity risk management, an explanation of the responsibilities of the main organizational roles involved in liquidity management, an explanation of the measurement methods used and of stress testing (and hypothetical scenarios), and the frequency and type of liquidity risk reporting (including additional reporting in stress periods). Banking groups should indicate whether the treasury function and the liquidity risk management procedure are centralized or decentralized, and describe infra-group funding strategies.

Transparency reduces uncertainty and strengthens market discipline. In particular (Bauman and Nier 2004), it:

- encourages intermediaries to optimize the quality of liquidity management and, consequently, improves the public perception of the bank by reducing the cost of funding;
- promotes market discipline. Based on the homogeneous information, it allows the market to assess and compare the risk and return prospects of individual institutions, and the intermediary to handle perceptions of this, especially during periods of financial turbulence;
- prevents market failures caused by asymmetric information;
- can help to mitigate the volatility of securities issued by the bank.

Although a higher level of disclosure, at a systemic level, is desirable, the inclusion of information about liquidity and current limits among the public data may be counterproductive, exposing the bank to instability and reputational problems and to irrational contagion, by leading market operators to see all banks as equally risky.

Indeed, as widely demonstrated by the financial crisis of 2007, the market is not always in a position to distinguish healthy and weaker intermediaries based on considerations of sound and prudent management or the adequacy of risk policies and the organizational structure for liquidity risk. The presence of information asymmetries along with the negative externalities associated with the spread of systemic tension suggests that achieving a broad level of transparency in the liquidity conditions of an intermediary is advisable. In a normal operating environment (or on a going concern basis), the incentive provided by the control of the market might work well, but in a situation of systemic crisis involving idiosyncratic difficulties, it may reinforce instability.

The financial crisis was exacerbated by the uncertainty created by the lack of clear information on the liquidity of banks. Adequate transparency for management procedures and liquidity, not only would have made the context more understandable, but also would have encouraged intermediaries to adopt risk-averse behaviour. So, in order to increase transparency degree, it is necessary to define the level of granularity and completeness of the information to be disclosed so as to allow the market a reasonable appreciation of the bank's liquidity risk. This requirement also seems relevant in order to ensure a level playing field between intermediaries in different states and to minimize regulatory arbitrage as imposed on cross-border groups, due to the discretionary areas built into the regulations of these countries. The right balance is needed so information is both accurate and understandable, neither too brief nor too detailed.

Overall, there is no doubt of the importance of the disclosure of qualitative information on liquidity risk management, internal governance, measurement metrics, policies, risk management processes, information systems, internal controls and the number and experience of bank staff. This information provides a valuable aid to market participants in assessing the ability of each intermediary to manage liquidity in normal and stressed conditions. There are some perplexity and reluctance by the financial industry to disseminate quantitative information on liquidity risk. Some of it has a strongly strategic content, which is generally rather difficult to understand and banks fear that it is poorly interpreted, leading to improper comparisons between banks and erroneous conclusions about a bank's solidity and hence damage its image and reputation. Nevertheless, in view of the systemic benefits and individual operational realities, supervisors should encourage intermediaries to make clear, complete, and transparent quantitative information available to the public, helping market participants to evaluate their liquidity in quantitative terms.

At present, the main sources of disclosure for financial risks and the capital adequacy of intermediaries are the Supplementary Notes to

IAS/IFRS compliant Financial Statements and the third pillar of Basel II, which does not include an ad hoc information area for liquidity risk. Therefore, the information provided to the public regarding liquidity is limited to what is set out in the Supplementary Notes to the Financial Statements, which include: qualitative information concerning general aspects, management processes, and methods for measuring liquidity risk; and quantitative information relating to the residual durations of financial assets and liabilities, and a breakdown of financial liabilities by sector and territory.

In periods of financial turbulence and the massive use of securitization, it is even more important to ensure adequate liquidity risk disclosure in Financial Statements, with qualitative information on exposure, implications for the intermediary's liquidity profile, market management and measurement systems for market and funding liquidity risk, as well as quantitative information able to show the financial flows of the intermediary over significant time periods (in both number and extension).

The breadth and detail of the information should be commensurate with the exposure in relation to the overall operations of the intermediary or the extent of the risks imposed on them.

Under the provisions of the third pillar of Basel II, there is a gap in liquidity risk information that supervisors, after the subprime crisis, committed to filling in a short time. The Financial Stability Forum, the Basel Committee and the CEBS have always highlighted the need to guarantee the market an appropriate level of disclosure regarding banking liquidity (BCBS 2000; Financial Stability Forum 2008; CEBS 2009b). An adequate degree of transparency should ultimately strengthen the overall financial system. However, the following issues remain open: the controversial question of what information should be made public, the balance between too much and too little information, and the temporal lag in data communication. For all these issues, the role of banking intermediaries in finalizing disclosure actions and gradually strengthening the educational function of all stakeholders appears fundamental, if the market is to accurately distinguish between 'strong' and 'weak' intermediaries.

5.3 The Role of the Supervisors

The liquidity risk management process is shaped by the operational reality of the individual intermediary, but reflects the relevant regulatory framework. The task of the supervisory authority is to direct and accompany intermediaries in the effort to strengthen their liquidity governance arrangements without taking over their functions. Therefore, concrete organizational and operational liquidity solutions must be identified by the individual intermediary in relation to its operations and overall liquidity profile, in compliance with the related regulations and, if possible, with the principles and sound practices identified by supervisors. Supervisory action simply checks the effectiveness and suitability of the choices made by single intermediaries.

The authorities make an independent assessment of liquidity management. They require banks to have an effective system and to promptly notify sufficient information to assess liquidity risk, checking that the bank has adequate emergency plans.

In its independent valuation of the liquidity risk management process of an intermediary, the Supervisor verifies the internal process for measuring and managing liquidity risk to ensure that it complies with all its principles and market practice, taking into account any local risk factors, the regulatory environment and the structure of the reference market.

The independent valuation of liquidity management should cover:

- the effectiveness of managing the net financial requirements in stressed situations;
- the effective involvement of the Board of Directors and Senior Management, responsible for both effective liquidity risk management and the prompt and continuous input of information;
- the efficiency of liquidity risk measurement and monitoring, analyzing the techniques used and assumptions behind the estimate of future funding needs;
- the reasonable nature of the various 'what if' scenarios and the adoption, by Senior Management, of specific and significant actions to mitigate any vulnerability resulting from stress testing;
- how the intraday and overnight liquidity risk, arising from payment and settlement activities, is incorporated into the liquidity risk management process.

To carry out its supervisory and control activities, the authorities need to receive from sufficient information flows that can be integrated with market information and data that is specifically requested during stress periods.

If an intermediary has deficiencies in the liquidity risk management process, supervisors require urgent corrective action to be taken. The choice of the instrument and the time period for corrective action generally reflects the level of risk considered tolerable by the bank, the pursuit of solvency and soundness of the related financial system. The corrective actions required by an intermediary with excess liquidity risk, or intrinsic weaknesses in the liquidity risk management process, may include:

- a strengthening of liquidity risk management through the improvement of internal policies, controls or reporting to Senior Management and the Board of Directors;
- improvements to contingency planning, through robust stress testing able to develop a more effective CFP;
- a reduction of liquidity risk through filling the funding gap, the increase in unencumbered assets and assets that can be liquidated promptly;
- a reduction of acquisition and expansion activities;
- the demand for higher levels of capital. Although capital does not solve liquidity problems or make up for inefficiencies in liquidity risk management, the level of capital may affect the intermediary's ability to obtain liquidity on the market, especially during periods of crisis.

The efficiency of the process of assessing and controlling the liquidity profiles of intermediaries at the financial system level benefits from the exchange of information and from cooperation between public authorities, such as supervisors and central banks. For example, supervisors may provide central banks with information on their assessment of the liquidity risk of the banks they monitor. Central banks can help supervisors deepen their knowledge of the current market situation and of the risks of the financial system. Information on market conditions is particularly useful to supervisors in assessing the adequacy of the hypotheses used by banks when implementing stress testing and contingency funding plans. Cooperation between specifically liquidity supervisors also improves the regulation of the liquidity profile of an individual intermediary and the financial system as a whole.

In recent years, worldwide regulations have placed greater emphasis on the strengthening of the internal control system for liquidity risk management rather than on excessive quantitative requirements, based on the assumption that the internal development of liquidity risk measurement and management systems is the best way to ensure the continuous evolution of financial markets. The crisis, which reversed the ongoing deregulation highlighted the need to strengthen the prescriptive nature of the supervisory approach. Unlike in the past, market tensions have progressively increased the need to manage liquidity risk at the global level by the definition of shared operational approaches at a supranational level through greater cooperation.[14] This led to re-regulation including new regulatory practices, some introduced individually by supervisors and others developed internationally.[15]

Notes

1. The Basel II Accord comprises three pillars: the first relates to capital requirements, the second to the control activity of the supervisory authorities, and the third to market discipline.
2. A cushion of assets, characterized by a high level of liquidity and hence promptly negotiable, useful for the survival of an institution, especially during periods of stress.
3. Senior Management includes a limited number of people, for example, the President, Chief Executive Officer, General Manager and Secretary General, with responsibilities and authority over the entire company and responding directly to government authorities, which in some cases are a component.
4. Such changes can be generated by domestic factors or by the consequences of contagion due to turbulence in other markets (as was the case in the subprime crisis).
5. Usually, operating limits are defined in terms of the cumulative treasury gap net of any counterbalancing capacity; structural limits are defined in terms of the gap ratio between medium-/long-term assets and liabilities or in terms of ratio.
6. It refers to which balance sheet items must be included in operational and structural limits, on which buckets insist, what risk warning signals are included, with what alarm thresholds, etc.
7. Mid-quote, or mid-price, is the average of the best bid-price at which it is possible to sell securities, and the best ask-price, at which it is possible to buy them.
8. Starting from commercial strategies, it shows how to minimize structural and operational liquidity risks (while maintaining the funding costs), and impacts on customer fundraising and lending strategies.

9. The historical approach is based on events in the past occurring to the intermediary itself or to other intermediaries, in reference markets. The statistical approach, based on the historical information determines the impact on cash flows, through appropriate hypotheses for the distribution of risk factors. Finally, the judgment-based approach uses subjective conjectures formulated by the bank's top management together with risk management and treasury to come to an impact assessment for cash flows in adverse scenarios.
10. Stress testing should be based on the exceptional, but plausible events. Adverse scenarios that can increase liquidity risk include: bank runs, the temporary block of the interbank market, bank rating downgrades, etc.
11. These requirements are related not only to contractual positions, but also to new business, new activities, and to the impact that different stress scenarios may have on liquidity positions.
12. The knowledge of available collateral is crucial for intermediaries. They should verify whether liquidity obtained through unsecured short-term (wholesale) financing has been invested in unencumbered (freely negotiable) assets. Otherwise, intermediaries could be exposed to liquidity problems when their access to the capital market is limited. The market turmoil in 2007–2009 showed the importance of operators knowing whether an institution had access to funding at the central bank (both in terms of collateral available within the bank and of the conditions for the use of the collateral itself).
13. The widespread and growing use of collateral on the interbank market as well as more efficient and regular payment and settlement systems, lead to legal and operational problems that can have a significant impact on liquidity management. These issues need to be seriously evaluated by the control functions of the intermediary.
14. Before the liquidity crisis, the Basel Committee handle the liquidity risk merely by defining a series of best practices.
15. For example, UK regulatory changes as put forward by the Turner Review in 2009.

References

Basel Committee on Banking Supervision (BCBS). (1992, September). *A Framework for Measuring and Managing Bank Liquidity*. Basel: Bank for International Settlements (BIS).

Basel Committee on Banking Supervision (BCBS). (2000, February). *Sound Practices for Managing Liquidity in Banking Organizations*. Basel: Bank for International Settlements (BIS).

Bauman, U., & Nier, E. (2004). Disclosure, Volatility, and Transparency: An Empirical Investigation into the Value of Bank Disclosure. *Economic Policy Review, 10,* 31–45.

Committee of European Banking Supervisors (CEBS). (2007, August). *First Part of CEBS's Technical Advice to the European Commission on Liquidity Risk Management: Survey of the Current Regulatory Frameworks Adopted by the EEA Regulators.*

Committee of European Banking Supervisors (CEBS). (2009a, December) *Consultation Paper on Liquidity Buffers and Survival Periods.*

Committee of European Banking Supervisors (CEBS). (2009b, December). *Guidelines on Liquidity Buffers and Survival Periods.*

Financial Stability Forum. (2008, April). *Actions to Enhance Market and Institutional Resilience.*

International Institute of Finance (IIF). (2007, March). *Principles of Liquidity Risk Management.*

Moody's Investors Service. (2001, July). *How Moody's Evaluates US Banks and Bank-Holding Company Liquidity.* Global Credit Research.

The Joint Forum. (2006, May). *The Management of Liquidity Risk in Financial Groups.* Basel: Bank for International Settlements (BIS).

CHAPTER 6

The New International Liquidity Regulatory Framework for Banks

6.1 Liquidity Risk: Regulatory Issues

Liquidity risk management has evolved rapidly over the last few years. The rethinking of practices and techniques for identifying, measuring and monitoring this risk is closely linked to the regulatory reform introduced by the Basel Committee under the political input of the G20 and the Financial Stability Board (FSB).[1]

One of the lessons learned from the GFC is that minimum capital requirements are a necessary, but an insufficient safeguard for the stability of an intermediary. Indeed, despite the high levels of capital held before the financial crisis, many banks experienced serious difficulties as they did not have sufficient liquidity buffers. In this regard, the new Basel III rules (defined in 2010 and subject to amendments/additions during the observation period planned before their implementation) are a reasonable compromise between incentives to ensure prudent liquidity risk management and containing potentially restrictive effects on the financial system and the economy as a whole.

For a complete analysis of the new liquidity regulation which banks will have to comply with, the following sections focus on the liquidity risk rules introduced by the Basel Committee related to the following three categories of tools: common principles for sound liquidity management and supervision (Sect. 6.2), minimum standards of liquidity (Sect. 6.3), and monitoring tools to assess liquidity risk (Sect. 6.4).

L. Chiaramonte, *Bank Liquidity and the Global Financial Crisis*,
Palgrave Macmillan Studies in Banking and Financial Institutions,
https://doi.org/10.1007/978-3-319-94400-5_6

6.2 Common Principles for Sound Liquidity Management and Supervision

The crisis of financial markets and the instability of many systemic institutions led international supervisory bodies to analyze the factors behind these difficulties. In February 2008, the Basel Committee carried out an initial survey of the regulatory liquidity risk regimes in leading countries following the outbreak of the crisis. This survey, described in the document 'Liquidity Risk: Management and Supervisory Challenges' (BCBS 2008a), highlighted many common elements in the various systems, particularly the general objectives of the regulations (for example, in terms of proportionality, liquidity policies, stress tests, contingency funding plans); but it also highlighted the very different ways the high-level principles of the Basel Committee of 2000 (BCBS 2000, described in Chapter 5) were operationally translated into rules and guidelines in the various states. The February 2008 survey reported that in most jurisdictions, the intensity of controls increases for larger and systematically relevant intermediaries.[2] Supervisory approaches to liquidity risk supervision were classified into three main categories according to the prescription level of measurement, management and control methodologies adopted by intermediaries: quantitative, qualitative and mixed approaches. While the former requires the value of some parameters to be quantified and maintained within specific deadlines and certain minimum limits,[3] the latter focus on the internal risk management and control systems and regulation is limited to providing guidelines for the implementation of an effective control process. Finally, mixed approaches combine both approaches in an attempt to reduce the underlying limitations.

Although most of the approaches are in the latter category, with more or less accentuated nuances on quantitative or qualitative aspects, in recent years, world regulations have placed more emphasis on strengthening the internal control system for managing liquidity risk rather than on excessively prescriptive quantitative requirements. This assumes that the internal development of liquidity risk measurement and management systems is the best way to monitor the continuous evolution of financial markets. The crisis has highlighted the need to strengthen the prescriptive nature of the supervisory approach. Beyond this, compared to the past, market tensions have gradually brought to light the need to manage liquidity risk at the global and no longer the local level, through the definition of shared operational approaches supranationally through a strengthening of cooperation.[4]

The difficulties encountered by some banks are attributable to failure to comply with the basic principles of liquidity risk management. This is the main reason, in September 2008, the Basel Committee published the 'Principles for Sound Liquidity Risk Management and Supervision', aka 'Sound Principles' (BCBS 2008b), a document revising the 2000 version, 'Sound Practices for Managing Liquidity in Banking Organizations' (BCBS 2000). Specifically, the main weaknesses were the following:

- considering liquidity a secondary risk;
- liquidity management from an essential treasury point of view;
- the perceived unlikelihood of liquidity sources drying up, associated with the functioning of certain markets, for example, those relating to securitization, credit derivatives and securities loans;
- little attention given to the internal cost of liquidity: the most risky and highly liquidity-intensive business units benefited from the measurement of risk/return profiles;
- the weakness or absence of links between Risk Management, treasury units and business units;
- insufficient stress test exercises;
- the utter underestimation of the effects of reputational risks on liquidity.

Therefore, the best practices defined in September 2008 aimed to strengthen liquidity risk (funding risk) management both by banks and supervisors. The process of updating the Sound Principles was based on the recognition of the methodologies followed in each country in relation to the regulatory plan and controls. The banking industry was consulted and the most recent literature on the subject was reviewed.

The document preliminarily defines the concept of liquidity risk as 'the ability to fund increases in assets and meet obligations as they come due, at reasonable costs', or referring only to the risk of providing funding (so-called funding risk). It pays particular attention to the principle of proportionality. Although the document focuses on complex medium and large banks, its principles can be extended to all banks. Each principle should ensure adequate proportionality with the size and complexity of each bank and the role it plays within the financial sector of the country in which it operates.

The principles stress the importance of defining a robust system for managing liquidity risk that is well-integrated inside the bank. The primary objective is to increase the resistance of banks to liquidity stress.

Among other things, the principles seek to strengthen the following areas: the governance and management of liquidity risk in a stressful situation, transparency and communication to the public and the role of supervisors. Each of these areas, covered by the Sound Principles of September 2008, is reviewed below.

With reference to the governance of liquidity risk, the concept of tolerance to liquidity risk was introduced, as defined by the most senior corporate bodies. It is the main benchmark for the implementation of strategies and for the management of liquidity risk, including the consideration of OBS exposure, particularly those arising from securitization activities. An explicit provision was made regarding the adoption of a transfer pricing system with the aim of aligning the incentives of risk-taking units with the liquidity risk they determine by carrying out their activities. The ultimate goal is to make the allocation of liquidity costs mandatory for the various business units.

Also underlined was the importance of a Liquidity Risk Management structure aimed at facilitating the exchange of information between treasury units, risk control units and the various business lines. Finally, the liquidity risk management system was submitted to an independent internal audit process.

The principle was established for the identification, measurement, monitoring and control of liquidity risk: on a consolidated basis; for all activities above and below the line; for all currencies with a breakdown for the most important.

Particular importance was attributed to intraday liquidity risk, mainly associated with operations in the payment system and with the settlement system. No metric or reference model was explicitly taken into consideration. However, whatever the measurement systems adopted, banks need to adopt dynamic risk measures, for example, by estimating expected cash flows from financial statement amounts, and identifying the components of counterbalancing capacities by evaluating the bank's ability to access different sources of funding. In this context, carrying out systemic stress tests is important. The use of stress tests is partly aimed at defining strategic planning, the close monitoring of cash flows, monitoring the concentration of liquidity sources and liquidable assets, and the imposition or strengthening of operating limits. The ultimate goal is to maintain a robust buffer of non-committed, highly liquid assets to survive over a lengthy period of liquidity stress. As an example, the September 2008 document lists some suggestions for carrying out stress tests.[5]

Stress test methods must be strictly related to the definition of a CFP. Essential is the identification of a clear decision-making process within the CFP based on the actions to be taken, with the related scheduling, by those responsible for their activation, procedures for coordination and internal and external communication. In this case too, the document identifies a series of trigger events for actions to be taken.

With regard to transparency and public disclosure, the objective is to ensure that the information provided allows all interested parties to come to a detailed and reliable judgment on the liquidity risk management of the bank. Disclosure to the public increases the level of transparency, reduces uncertainty and reinforces market discipline. The information that a bank should make public is related to its organizational structure and the overall methodological framework for managing liquidity risk. Particular attention should be paid to the role and responsibilities of members of the Board, senior management and the various business units that contribute to liquidity risk management. The information should also concern the funding structure of the bank and the system of limits.

Finally, the Sound Principles reinforce expectations about the role of supervisors, including the need to intervene in a timely manner to solve shortcomings and the importance of ensuring constant communication with other supervisors within and beyond national borders. In particular, the supervisory authority must regularly carry out a complete review of the management of the liquidity risks of a bank in order to make sure it is able to withstand stress scenario given the role of the intermediary in the financial system.

On the basis of the results of these checks, the supervisory authority has at its disposal a series of tools to address any shortcomings identified in the process of assessing the liquidity risk of supervised intermediaries. The use of these tools must reflect the severity of the inadequacies found. Finally, cooperation and greater information sharing between the various authorities is recommended in order to increase the effectiveness of liquidity risk controls in the financial system. This collaboration is particularly useful during conditions of stress.

6.3 The Minimum Liquidity Standards of Basel III

To complement the principles of sound and prudent management set out in September 2008, the Committee further strengthened liquidity regulation by introducing two minimum quantitative requirements for bank liquidity risk. The new liquidity rules, defined in the Basel III document of 2010 together with more robust qualitative and quantitative capital rules (BCBS 2010a, b), were designed to achieve two distinct but complementary objectives. The first is to promote the short-term resilience of bank liquidity risk profiles by ensuring that they have sufficient high-quality liquid resources to overcome an acute stress situation of one month. For this purpose, the Committee developed a short-term indicator, the Liquidity Coverage Ratio (LCR). The second objective is to promote longer-term resilience by providing banks with more incentives to finance their businesses, drawing on a more stable funding base. The structural indicator, the Net Stable Funding Ratio (NSFR), with a time horizon of one year was developed to ensure that assets and liabilities have a sustainable maturity structure.

The new liquidity standards are applicable to all internationally active banks on a consolidated basis, but they can also be used to monitor the liquidity position of individual units, such as subsidiaries, in line with one of the principles discussed in the previous section, i.e. banks should actively manage liquidity exposures and funding needs within and across legal entities, business lines and currencies, taking into account the legal, regulatory and operational restrictions on the transferability of liquidity.

The LCR and NSFR, both described below, are essential parts of the reforms introduced by Basel III and together will increase bank resilience in the face of liquidity shocks, promote a more stable financing profile and improve the overall management of liquidity risk.

6.3.1 The Liquidity Coverage Ratio

The LCR, first included by the BCBS in December 2010 Basel III documents (BCBS 2010b) and subsequently revised in January 2013 (BCBS 2013a), is one of the Basel Committee's key reforms to strengthen global capital and liquidity regulations with the aim of promoting a more resilient banking sector. The LCR promotes the short-resilience of a bank's liquidity risk profile ensuring that it has sufficient non-captive high-quality liquid assets (HQLA),[6] consisting of cash or assets that can be converted into cash in private markets with little or no loss of value, to meet its liquidity needs over a period of thirty days in a liquidity stress scenario. The non-captive stock of

HQLA should at least allow the bank to survive until the thirtieth day of the scenario, within which it is assumed that appropriate corrective actions can be taken by the corporate bodies and supervisors, or that the bank can be liquidated in an orderly manner. It also provides the central bank sufficient time to take appropriate action, if it sees fit. As enshrined in the Sound Principles, given the uncertain timing of inflows and outflows, it is also expected that banks take into account potential misalignments over the thirty-day period and ensure that HQLA is available in sufficient quantity to satisfy any cash flow gaps over the whole period.

Determination of the LCR includes two elements (see the formula below): the value of the stock of HQLA under stress conditions (the numerator); and total net cash outflows over the next 30 calendar days (the denominator), the latter calculated according to the parameters outlined below.

$$\frac{\text{Stock of HQLA}}{\begin{array}{c}\text{Total net cash outflows over the next 30 calendar days}\\ (=\text{total cash outflows} - \text{total cash inflows}: \ 75\% \text{ of total cash outflows})\end{array}} \geq 100\%$$

The standard requires that, without financial tensions, the ratio cannot fall to lower than 100% (i.e. the stock of HQLA is at least equal to total net cash outflows) on an ongoing basis since the stock of unencumbered HQLA is meant to ward off liquidity stress. During periods of financial stress, however, banks can use their stock of HQLA so the ratio may fall below 100%, since in these circumstances maintaining the LCR at 100% could have undue negative repercussions on the bank and other market participants. Supervisors subsequently assess the situation and choose the most suitable response to the circumstances.

In particular, the decisions of supervisors regarding the use of HQLA should be based on the main objective and definition of the LCR. In their assessment, supervisors exercise their judgment based not only on the prevailing macro-financial conditions, but also on future assessments of macroeconomic and financial conditions. In shaping their response, they should be aware of the fact that some actions could be procyclical if applied in circumstances of market-wide stress. Supervisors should try to take these considerations into account consistently, regardless of jurisdiction. Specifically, they should:

- promptly assess conditions, and if necessary take action to address potential liquidity risk;
- consider different responses to individual cases in which the LCR falls below 100%. Any potential supervisory response should be proportionate to the cause, entity, duration and frequency of the shortfall;
- in determining the appropriate response, take into account various firm- and market-specific factors, as well as other factors related to domestic and global frameworks and conditions. These factors include:
  - the reasons why the LCR has fallen below 100%, for example, the use of the stock of HQLA, the impossibility to rollover funding or large unexpected draws on contingent obligations. Other reasons could be linked to overall credit, funding and market conditions (including liquidity in credit, asset and funding markets), which affect individual banks or all institutions, regardless of their specific situation;
  - the extent to which the decline in LCR is due bank-specific or due to market-wide stock;
  - the overall health status and risk profile of a bank, including assets and positions with other supervisory requirements, internal risk management systems, controls and other management processes;
  - the size, duration and frequency of the decrease in HQLA;
  - the potential contagion to the financial system, as well as the possible reduction in the flow of credit or market liquidity due to the measures aimed at maintaining an LCR of 100%;
  - the availability of other sources of financing, such as central bank funding, or other measures by prudential authorities;
- have a range of tools to use to address an LCR below 100%. Banks are authorized to use their stock of HQLA in both idiosyncratic and systemic stress events, but the response of supervisors in the two cases may differ;
- ensure that responses are consistent with the overall approach to the prudential framework.

Although the LCR threshold is a minimum of 100%, the Committee decided to opt for its gradual application, similarly to the requirements of Basel III regarding capital adequacy. Specifically, the LCR was introduced as planned on 1 January 2015, but the minimum requirement was initially 60%, to be gradually raised each year reaching 100% on 1 January 2019 (see Table 6.1). This gradual approach aims to ensure that the introduction of the LCR does not cause significant disturbances to the orderly strengthening of banking systems or to the ongoing financing of economic activity.

In terms of the details of LCR components, with reference to the numerator (stock of HQLA) the Committee established that assets may be deemed liquid and of high quality, if they can be converted into cash easily and immediately with little or no loss of value. The liquidity of an asset depends on the underlying stress scenario, the volume to be monetised and the time period considered. Nonetheless, there are certain assets that even in times of stress are more likely to generate funds in the markets for sale or repos without incurring large discounts due to fire-sales. Specifically, the stock of HQLA must comprise assets with the following features:

- low risk. Less risky assets tend to be more liquid. High creditworthiness of the issuer and a low degree of subordination increase an asset's liquidity. Low duration,[7] a low level of legal and exchange risk are all factors that improve the liquidity of an asset;
- ease and certainty of valuation. The liquidity of an asset increases if market participants are more likely to agree on its value. Assets that are standardized, homogeneous and simply structured are generally more fungible, promoting liquidity. The formula for determining the price of a high-quality liquid asset must be easy to calculate and not depend on restrictive assumptions. Furthermore, the inputs into the pricing formula must be publicly available. This condition in practice excludes most structured and exotic products;
- low correlation with risky assets. The stock of HQLA should not be subject to the risk of (high) adverse correlation (wrong-way risk). For example, assets issued by financial institutions are more likely to be illiquid during periods of liquidity stress in the banking sector;
- listed on a well-established exchange. This characteristic increases the asset's transparency.

Table 6.1 The timetable of the introduction of the LCR

	1 January 2015	*1 January 2016*	*1 January 2017*	*1 January 2018*	*1 January 2019*
Minimum LCR (%)	60	70	80	90	100

Source Adapted from BCBS (2013a)

In addition to the above features relating to the assets, others are related to the market, including:

- activity and size. At all times assets should have active markets for sale or repo, which requires:
  - historical evidence of the size of the market and its depth, such as low bid-ask spreads, high trading volumes, and a high number of diversified market participants. The diversification of market participants reduces the concentration of the market and increases the reliability of its liquidity;
  - a robust infrastructure. The presence of multiple committed market makers increases liquidity guaranteeing the willingness to buy or sell HQLA;
- low volatility. Assets with a relatively stable price and reduced tendency to sharp price decreases over time are less likely to trigger forced sales to meet liquidity requirements. The volatility of traded prices and spreads are simple proxy measures of market volatility. There should be historical evidence of the relative stability of the market terms (obtained, for example, from prices or haircuts) and of the volumes traded during periods of tension;
- flight to quality. Historically, during systemic crises, the market has generally preferred these types of assets. In this regard, a simple measure that could be used is the correlation between proxies of market liquidity and tensions in the banking system.

As can be seen from these characteristics, liquid assets are considered of 'high quality' when, if sold or used in repos, their ability to generate liquidity remains intact even in periods of severe idiosyncratic and market tension. Lower quality assets do not usually meet that test. If a bank attempts to obtain liquidity under severe market stress via lower-quality assets, it has to accept substantial discounts due or significant haircuts to offset the high market risk. This could not only undermine the market confidence in the bank, but also generate mark-to-market losses for banks that hold similar instruments and exacerbate the pressures on their liquidity positions, causing further fire sales and reductions in prices and market liquidity. In these circumstances, private market liquidity for these instruments is likely to disappear quickly.

Ideally, HQLA (with the exception of level 2B assets as described below) should also be eligible as collateral at central banks[8] for intraday

Table 6.2 HQLA categories

Stock of HQLA—items	*Factors (%)*
Level 1 assets:	100
• Coins and bank notes	
• Qualifying marketable securities from sovereigns, central banks, PSEs, and multilateral development banks	
• Qualifying central bank reserves	
• Domestic sovereign or central bank debt for non-0% risk-weighted sovereigns	
Level 2 assets (maximum of 40% of HQLA)	
Level 2A assets:	
• Sovereign, central bank, multilateral development banks, and PSE assets qualifying for 20% risk weighting	85
• Qualifying corporate debt securities rated AA– or higher	
• Qualifying covered bonds rated AA– or higher	
Level 2B assets (maximum of 15% of HQLA):	
• Qualifying RMBS	75
• Qualifying corporate debt securities rated between A+ and BBB–	50
• Qualifying common equity shares	50
Total value of stock of HQLA	

Source Adapted from BCBS (2013a)

liquidity needs and overnight liquidity facilities. In the past, in severe conditions, central banks have provided additional support to the supply of banking system liquidity. The eligibility at the central bank should, therefore, increase confidence in the fact that banks hold assets that can be used at times of stress without damaging the broader financial system. This, in turn, increases confidence in the safety and soundness of liquidity risk management in the banking system.

It should be noted, however, that eligibility at the central bank is not in itself a sufficient condition for classifying an asset as HQLA.

The types of assets that can be included in the stock of HQLA are of two types, 'Level 1' and 'Level 2' (see Table 6.2). The assets in each category are those that the bank holds on the first day of the stress period, regardless of their residual maturity. Level 1 assets can be included to an unlimited extent, while Level 2 assets can only comprise up to 40% of the stock. Level 1 assets are as follows:

- coins and banknotes;
- reserves at the central bank (including those required),[9] to the extent that central bank policies allow their use in times of stress;

- negotiable securities representing claims on, or guaranteed by, sovereign entities, central banks, public sector entities (PSEs), the Bank for International Settlements, the International Monetary Fund, the European Central Bank and European Community, or multilateral development banks,[10] and meet all the following conditions:
  - a 0% risk-weight under the Basel II Standardized Approach for credit risk;
  - they are traded in large, deep and active repo or cash markets characterized by a low level of concentration;
  - a proven record as a reliable source of liquidity in the markets (repo or sales) even under stress conditions; and
  - difference from the obligation of a financial institution or an affiliate[11];
- for sovereigns with a risk-weight other than 0%, sovereign or central bank debt securities issued in domestic currencies by the sovereign issuer or the central bank of the country in which the liquidity risk is being taken, or in the bank's home country; and
- for sovereign entities with a risk-weight different from 0%, domestic sovereign or central bank debt securities issued in foreign currencies, for a maximum amount equal to the amount of net cash outflows of a stressed bank denominated in the currency in question and stemming from the bank's operations in the jurisdiction where the bank's liquidity risk is being taken.

Level 2 assets include so-called Level 2A assets and, at the discretion of national authorities, certain additional assets, called Level 2B assets. Any Level 2B asset permitted by the supervisors may constitute at most 15% of the total stock of HQLA. Moreover, they must be included in the calculation of the maximum limit of 40% imposed on Level 2 assets.

Level 2A assets include:

- marketable securities that represent claims on, or guaranteed by, sovereign entities, central banks, PSEs or multilateral development banks, which satisfy the following conditions:
  - a 20% risk-weight based on the Basel II Standardized approach for credit risk;
  - they are traded in large, deep and active repo or cash markets, characterized by a low level of concentration;

- a proven record as a reliable source of liquidity in the markets (repo or sale) even during stress conditions (undergoing a 10% maximum price drop or further haircut not exceeding 10 percentage points over a period of thirty days during a relevant significant liquidity stress period);
- a difference from the obligation of a financial institution or any of its affiliated entities;

- corporate debt securities (including CPs)[12] and covered bonds[13] that meet all the following conditions:
  - in the case of corporate debt securities: are not issued by a financial institution or by any of its affiliated entities;
  - in the case of covered bonds: are not issued by the bank itself or by any of its affiliated entities;
  - they have received a long-term credit rating of at least AA– from an acknowledged external credit assessment institution (ECAI) or, failing this, an equivalent short-term rating; or, failing this, an internal evaluation of the likelihood of default (PD) corresponding to a credit rating no lower than AA–;
  - they are traded in large, deep and active repo or cash markets, with a low level of concentration;
  - a proven record as a reliable source of liquidity in the markets (repo or sale) even under stress conditions, suffering a maximum price drop or a further haircut not exceeding 10% over a period of thirty days during a period of significant liquidity stress.

Level 2B assets include:

- residential mortgage-backed securities (RMBS) which satisfy all the following conditions, subject to a 25% haircut:
  - not issued by, or with underlying assets comprising mortgages granted by the bank itself or by any of its affiliated entities;
  - a long-term credit rating no lower than AA from an approved external credit rating agency or, failing that, a short-term credit rating of equivalent quality;
  - they are traded in large, deep and active repo or cash markets, with a low level of concentration;
  - a proven record as a reliable source of liquidity in the markets (repo or sale) even during stressed market conditions (undergoing a maximum price drop of 20% or a maximum further haircut

of 20 percentage points over a period of thirty days during a significant liquidity stress period);
  - based on a portfolio of underlying assets consisting exclusively of residential mortgages, with no structured products;
  - rely on 'full recourse' residential mortgage loans (in the case of foreclosure the borrower is obliged to pay off any negative difference between the proceeds from the sale of real estate and the amount of the debt) with a maximum loan-to-value ratio (LTV) of 80% on average at issuance;
  - securitization is subject to 'risk retention' rules that require issuers to maintain an interest in the assets they securitize;
- corporate debt securities (including CPs) that satisfy all the following conditions, with a 50% haircut:
  - not issued by a financial institution or by any of its affiliated entities;
  - with a long-term credit rating between A+ and BBB− from a recognized ECAI or, failing that, an equivalent short-term credit rating; or, failing that, an internal evaluation, a PD corresponding to a credit rating between A+ and BBB−;
  - they are traded in large, deep and active repo or cash markets, with low level of concentration;
  - a proven record as a reliable source of liquidity in the markets (repo or sale) even during stressed market conditions (undergoing a maximum price drop of 20% or a maximum increase in haircut of 20 percentage points over a period of thirty days during a significant liquidity stress period);
- common equity shares that satisfy all the following conditions, with a 50% haircut:
  - not issued by a financial institution or by any of its affiliated entities;
  - traded on a stock exchange and centrally cleared;
  - included in the major stock index in the home jurisdiction or where the liquidity risk is taken, depending on the supervisory authority of the jurisdiction for the index;
  - denominated in the domestic currency of the jurisdiction where the bank is located or in the currency in which the liquidity risk is taken;
  - traded in large, deep and active repo or cash markets, with a low level of concentration;

– a proven record as a reliable source of liquidity in the markets (repo or sale) even during stressed market conditions (undergoing a maximum price drop of 40% or further haircut of 40 percentage points over a period of thirty days during a period of significant liquidity stress).

As shown in Table 6.2, each component of the numerator must be multiplied by a specific weighting factor ranging from 100% for more liquid assets to 50% for less liquid assets.

The denominator of the LCR, i.e. 'total net cash outflows',[14] is defined as total expected cash outflows minus total expected cash inflows over the next thirty-calendar days in the specified stress scenario. The scenario for this requirement is based on the experience during the GFC after 2007 and includes both idiosyncratic shock at the level of individual institutions, and systemic shock. It indicates significant tension, but not catastrophic events. Specifically, the scenario for the LCR simulates the combination of an idiosyncratic and market-wide shock involving:

- the withdrawal of a portion of retail deposits;
- a partial loss of unsecured wholesale funding capacity;
- a partial loss of secured, short-term financing with certain collateral and counterparties;
- additional contractual outflows which would derive from a downgrade in the bank's public credit rating by up to three notches, including collateral posting requirements;
- an increase in market volatility that affects the quality of collateral or potential future exposure to derivatives, requiring larger collateral haircuts or additional guarantees, or leading to other liquidity needs;
- unexpected uses of irrevocable liquidity and unused credit lines the bank has made available to customers;
- the potential need for the bank to repurchase debt securities or to fulfil non-contractual obligations in order to mitigate reputational risk.

Hence, many of the shocks of the crisis that began in 2007 are incorporated into a single significant stress scenario where a bank should have sufficient liquidity to survive for up to thirty-calendar days.

Total expected cash outflows, the first component of the LCR denominator, are calculated by multiplying the outstanding balances of the various categories or types of liabilities and OBS commitments by the rates at which they are expected to be collected or used (see Table 6.3). Several items make up total expected cash outflows, including the retail

Table 6.3 Total cash outflows calculation in LCR

Cash outflows—items	*Factors (%)*
Retail deposits	
Demand deposits and term deposits (less than 30 days maturity):	
• Stable deposits (deposit insurance scheme meets additional criteria)	3
• Stable deposits	5
• Less stable retail deposits	10
Unsecured wholesale funding:	
Demand and term deposits (less than 30 days maturity) provided by small business customers:	
• Stable deposits	5
• Less stable deposits	10
Operational deposits generated by clearing, custody and cash management activities	25
• Portion covered by deposit insurance	5
Cooperative banks in an institutional network (qualifying deposits with the centralised institution)	25
Non-financial corporates, sovereigns, central banks, multilateral development banks, and PSEs	40
• If the entire amount fully covered by deposit insurance scheme	20
Other legal entity customers	100
Secured funding:	
• Secured funding transactions with a central bank counterparty or backed by Level 1 assets with any counterparty	0
• Secured funding transactions backed by Level 2A assets, with any counterparty	15
• Secured funding transactions backed by non-Level 1 or non-Level 2A assets, with domestic sovereigns, multilateral development banks, or domestic PSEs as a counterparty	25
• Backed by RMBS eligible for inclusion in Level 2B	25
• Backed by other Level 2B assets	50
• All other secured funding transactions	100
Additional requirements, among which, for example:	100
Net derivative cash outflows	
Total cash outflows	

Source Adapted from BCBS (2013a)

deposits run-off, which in turn includes on demand and term deposits (with a maturity of less than thirty days), placed with a bank by a natural person. Retail deposits are 'stable' or 'less stable' portions of funds, as described below, with listed minimum run-off rates for each category. The run-off rates for retail deposits are minimum floors, with higher run-off rates established by individual jurisdictions as appropriate to capture depositor behaviour in a period of stress in each jurisdiction.

Stable deposits, to which a run-off rate of 3% is applied (against the general rate of 5%), are the amount of deposits that are fully insured[15] by an effective deposit insurance scheme or by a public guarantee that provides equivalent protection.

Less stable deposits include deposits that are not fully covered by an effective deposit insurance scheme or by a sovereign deposit guarantee; high-value deposits; deposits from sophisticated investors or high net worth individuals; deposits that can be quickly withdrawn; and foreign currency deposits, as determined by each individual jurisdiction. The minimum expected run-off rate for less stable deposits is 10%.

Another item in total expected cash outflows is unsecured wholesale funding. For the purposes of the LCR, this is defined as the liabilities and general obligations to non-natural persons (legal entities, including sole proprietorships and partnerships) and are not collateralized by legal rights to specifically designed assets owned by the borrowing institution in the case of bankruptcy, insolvency, liquidation or resolution. The wholesale funding included in the LCR corresponds to all funding sources that can be revoked within the LCR horizon of thirty days or with earliest possible contractual maturity date within this horizon (such as maturing term deposits and unsecured debt securities), as well as funding with indefinite maturity. It includes all funding received with options exercisable at the investor's discretion within the thirty-calendar day horizon. For funding with options exercisable at the discretion of the bank, supervisors should take into account reputational factors that could limit the bank's ability not to exercise the option.[16] In particular, where the market expects the repayment of certain liabilities before their legal final maturity date, banks and supervisors should behave in this way for the purpose of the LCR and include these liabilities as outflows.

For the LCR, unsecured wholesale funding is classified according to the perceived sensitivity of lenders to the rate offered as well as the credit standing and solvency of the borrowing bank. This sensitivity depends on the type of lender and on their level of sophistication, as well as on their operational relationships with the bank. Below the run-off rates are listed for each category in the scenario under examination. Specifically, unsecured wholesale funding includes:

- sight deposits and time deposits (with maturities of less than thirty days) provided by small business customers, weighted at 5% if stable or 10% if considered less stable;
- operational deposits generated by clearing,[17] custody[18] or cash management[19] activities. These funds can receive a 25% run-off factor only if the customer is substantially dependent on the bank and if the deposit is required for such activities;
- deposits in institutional networks of cooperative banks, or a group of legally autonomous banks operating within a statutory structure of cooperation with common strategic focus and brand, where specific functions are performed by central institutions or specialist service providers. A 25% run-off rate can be given to the amount of deposits of member institutions or specialist central service providers;
- all deposits and unsecured funding from non-financial corporate customers (not classified as small business companies) and from (both domestic and foreign) sovereign entities, central banks, multilateral development banks and PSE customers that are not held specifically for operational purposes. The run-off factor for these funds is 40%. However, the unsecured wholesale funding provided by non-financial corporate customers, sovereigns, central banks, multilateral development banks and PESs in the absence of operational relationships may receive a 20% run-off factor if the entire amount of the deposit is fully covered by an effective deposit insurance scheme or by a public guarantee that provides equivalent protection;
- finally, all deposits and other funding from other institutions (including banks, securities firms, insurance companies, etc.), fiduciaries,[20] beneficiaries,[21] conduits and special purpose vehicles, affiliated entities of the bank[22] and other entities that are not specifically held for operational purposes (as defined above) and not in the previous three categories. The run-off factor for these funds is 100%.

Total expected cash outflows also include secured funding, defined as the liabilities and general obligations guaranteed by legal rights on specifically designated assets belonging to the borrowing institution, which can be exercised in the case of bankruptcy, insolvency, liquidation or resolution. The run-off factor to be applied to this category is a minimum of 0%, for any maturing secured funding transactions with the bank's domestic central bank, and a maximum of 100%, for all other maturing transactions, including those where a bank has satisfied customers' short positions with its own long inventory.

One last group, defined as 'additional requirements', has to be considered for the calculation of total expected cash outflows. The various items include, for example, cash outflows for derivative transactions, for which the run-off factor is 100%.

As already mentioned, in order to determine total net cash outflows, total expected cash inflows must be subtracted from total expected cash outflows. When calculating available cash inflows, the bank should only consider contractual inflows (including interest payments) from outstanding exposures that are fully performing and for which the bank has no reason to expect a default over the time horizon of thirty days. Contingent inflows are not included in total net cash inflows. Banks and supervisors need to monitor the concentration of expected inflows from all the wholesale counterparties within bank liquidity management in order to ensure that their liquidity position does not depend excessively on the arrival of expected inflows from one or a limited number of wholesale counterparties. In order to prevent banks depending solely on the expected inflows to meet the liquidity requirement and to ensure a minimum level of HQLA, the amount of inflows that can offset outflows is subject to a ceiling of 75% of total expected cash outflows as calculated in the standard. This means banks must maintain a minimum stock of HQLA with 25% of total cash outflows.

As shown in Table 6.4, cash inflows include:

- secured lending, including reverse repos and securities borrowing agreements. Specifically, a bank should assume that maturing reverse repurchase or securities borrowing agreements guaranteed by Level 1 assets are rollover and do not give rise to any cash inflow (0%). Maturing reverse repurchase or securities lending guaranteed by Level 2 HQLA lead to cash inflows equivalent to the relevant haircut for the specific assets. It is assumed that a bank does not rollover maturing reverse repurchase or Securities borrowing agreements secured by non-HQLA. It could, therefore, receive

Table 6.4 Total cash inflows calculation in LCR

Cash inflows—items	*Factors*
Maturing secured lending transactions backed by the following collateral:	
Level 1 assets	0%
Level 2A assets	15%
Level 2B assets	
• Eligible RMBS	25%
• Other assets	50%
Margin lending backed by all other collateral	50%
All other assets	100%
Credit or liquidity facilities provided to the reporting bank	0%
Operational deposits held at the other financial institutions (include deposits held at the centralised institution of network of co-operative banks)	0%
Other inflows by counterparty:	
• Amounts to be received from retail counterparties	50%
• Amounts to be received from non-financial wholesale counterparties, from transactions other than those listed in above inflow categories	50%
• Amounts to be received from financial institutions and central banks, from transactions other than those listed in above inflow categories	100%
Net derivative cash inflows	100%
Other contractual cash inflows	National discretion
Total cash inflows	

Source Adapted from BCBS (2013a)

back 100% of the cash related to those agreements. Secured loans granted to customers for the purpose of taking leveraged trading positions (margin loans) should also be considered as a form of secured lending; however, in this case banks may recognixe no more than 50% of contractual inflows resulting from maturing margin loans made against non-HQLA collateral. This treatment is consistent with the hypotheses outlined for guaranteed funding in the section dedicated to outflows;

- committed facilities. No credit or liquidity facility or other contingent funding facility the bank holds at other institutions for its own purposes are assumed to be capable of being drawn. These facilities receive a 0% inflow rate, i.e. in this scenario, the inflows from committed credit or liquidity facilities are not considered.

This is to reduce the risk of contagion (when liquidity shortages at one bank cause shortages at others) and reflects the risk of other banks failing to honour credit facilities or deciding to incur the legal and reputational risk of non-compliance in order to preserve their own liquidity or reduce their exposure;

- other inflows by type of counterparty. For all other types of transactions, whether secured or unsecured, the inflow rate is determined on the basis of the counterparty. In order to reflect the need for a bank to conduct ongoing loan origination/rollover with different types of counterparties, even in times of stress, a series of limits apply to contractual inflows by counterparty type. When considering loan payments, the bank should only take into account inflows from fully performing loans. This category includes:
  - inflows from retail and small business customers. This scenario assumes that banks receive all payments (including interest payments and instalments) from retail and small business customers that are fully performing and contractually due within the thirty-day horizon. At the same time, however, it is assumed that banks continue to provide loans to this type of client at a rate of 50% of contractual inflows. This results in a net inflow of 50% of the contract amounts;
  - other wholesale inflows. This scenario assumes that banks receive all payments (including interest payments and instalments) due within the thirty-day horizon of performing contracts with wholesale customers. Banks are also expected to continue the lending activity to wholesale clients at a rate of 0% of inflows for financial institutions and central banks, and 50% for all other entities, including non-financial corporates, sovereigns, multilateral development banks, and PSEs. Hence, the share of inflows is 100% for financial institutions and central banks, and 50% for non-financial wholesale counterparties;
  - other cash inflows, including:
  - from derivatives, to which a 100% inflow rate is applied;
  - other contractual cash inflows. The percentages of inflow for each type are determined by supervisors in each jurisdiction.

The LCR is an essential component of the liquidity risk monitoring approach, but needs to be integrated with detailed prudential assessments of other aspects of the liquidity risk management system adopted by the bank, in accordance with the Sound Principles, with the NSFR (analyzed in Sect. 6.3.2), and with the use of monitoring tools (described in Sect. 6.4). In addition, supervisors may require an individual bank to adopt more stringent requirements or parameters depending on its liquidity risk profile and the assessment made by the authorities themselves in compliance with the Sound Principles.

6.3.2 *The Net Stable Funding Ratio*

With Basel III (BCBS 2010a, b) the BCBS introduced not only the LCR, but also a structural indicator, the NSFR, which requires banks to maintain a stable funding profile in relation to the composition of their assets and off-balance sheet (OBS) assets. A sustainable financing structure aims to reduce the likelihood that disruptions to a bank's regular sources of funding erode its liquidity position and increase its risk of bankruptcy, potentially leading to broader systemic tensions. The NSFR avoids excessive recourse to short-term wholesale financing, promotes a better assessment of funding risk across all on- and OBS items, and promotes funding stability. Ultimately, the NSFR was introduced with the aim of discouraging banks from over-maturity transformation, i.e. excessive recourse to unstable funding sources to finance their main assets, often illiquid.

In 2010, after an initial period of observation, the Committee undertook a review of the experience with the NSFR, addressing any undesirable consequences on the functioning of the financial markets and the real economy, and fine-tuning the ratio with regard to key aspects, including: the impact on retail business activities; the short-term matched funding of assets and liabilities; the analysis of sub-one-year buckets for both assets and liabilities. On the basis of the review, in October 2014 the Committee published the final version of the NSFR (BCBS 2014b).[23] The NSFR is defined as the ratio between the amount of available stable funding (ASF) and the required amount of stable funding (RSF), a ratio that has to remain continuously at a no less than 100% (see the formula below). The ASF is the portion of capital and liabilities considered reliable over the time horizon considered by the NSFR, i.e. up to one year. The RSF of a specific institution depends on its liquidity and the residual maturities of the various assets held by the institution, as well as its OBS exposures.

$$\frac{\text{Available Stable Funding (ASF)}}{\text{Required Stable Funding (RSF)}} \geq 100\%$$

The ASF, the numerator of the NSFR, is measured according to the expected degree of stability of liabilities, which includes the following two characteristics:

- the contractual maturity of its liabilities. The NSFR is generally calibrated on the assumption that longer-term liabilities are more stable than short-term liabilities;
- the different propensity of the various lenders to withdraw their funding. The NSFR is calibrated on the assumption that short-term deposits (with a maturity of less than one year) placed by retail customers and the funding provided by small businesses customers are more stable than wholesale funding with the same maturity provided by other counterparties.

Specifically, the ASF is calculated, firstly, by assigning the carrying value of an institution's capital and liabilities to one of five categories, as shown in Table 6.5. The amount assigned to each category is then multiplied by an ASF factor. The stabler the liability considered, the higher the ASF factor applied. The total ASF is the sum of the weighted amounts.

The first category includes liabilities and capital instruments with an ASF factor of 100%, i.e.:

- the total amount of regulatory capital before the application of capital deductions, excluding the proportion of additional capital instruments (Tier 2) with residual maturity of less than one year;
- the total amount of any capital instrument (not included above) with an effective residual maturity of one year or more, but excluding any instruments with explicit or embedded options that, if exercised, would reduce the expected maturity to less than one year;
- the total amount of secured and unsecured borrowings and liabilities (including term deposits) with effective residual maturities of one year or more. Cash flows falling below the one-year horizon, but arising from liabilities with a final maturity of more than one year do not qualify for the 100% ASF factor.

Table 6.5 ASF calculation in NSFR

Components of ASF category	*ASF factors (%)*
Total regulatory capital (excluding Tier 2 instruments with residual maturity of less than one year)	100
Other capital instruments and liabilities with effective residual maturity of one year or more	
Stable non-maturity (demand) deposits and term deposits with residual maturity of less than one year provided by retail and small business customers	95
Less stable non-maturity deposits and term deposits with residual maturity of less than one year provided by retail and small business customers	90
Funding with residual maturity of less than one year provided by non-financial corporate customers	50
Operational deposits	
Funding with residual maturity of less than one year from sovereigns, PSEs, and multilateral and national development banks	
Other funding with residual maturity between six months and less than one year not included in the above categories, including funding provided by central banks and financial institutions	
All other liabilities and equity not included in the above categories, including liabilities without a stated maturity (with a specific treatment for deferred tax liabilities and minority interests)	0
NSFR derivative liabilities net of NSFR derivative assets if NSFR derivative liabilities are greater than NSFR derivative assets	
'Trade date' payables arising from purchases of financial instruments, foreign currencies and commodities	

Source Adapted from BCBS (2014b)

The second category of liabilities considered for the calculation of the numerator of the NSFR are liabilities with a 95% ASF factor comprising 'stable' (as defined in 6.3.1) non-maturity (demand) deposits and/or term deposits with residual maturities of less than one year provided by retail and small business customers.

The third category consists of liabilities defined as 'less stable' (as defined in 6.3.1) non-maturity (demand) deposits and/or term deposits with residual maturities of less than one year provided by retail and small business customers. These liabilities have a 90% ASF factor.

The fourth category, to which a 50% ASF factor is assigned, includes:

- funding (secured and unsecured) with a residual maturity of less than one year provided by non-financial corporate customers;

- operational deposits;
- funding with a residual maturity of less than one year from sovereigns, PSEs, and multilateral and national development banks;
- other funding (secured and unsecured) not included in the categories above with residual maturity between six months and one year, including funding from central banks and financial institutions.

Finally, the last category includes liabilities to which a 0% ASF factor is assigned, namely:

- all other liabilities and equity categories not included in the above categories, including other funding with a residual maturity of six months from central banks and financial institutions;
- other liabilities without a stated maturity. This category may include short positions and open maturity positions. Two exceptions are made for liabilities without a stated maturity:
  - deferred tax liabilities, which should be treated according to the nearest possible date on which such liabilities could be realized; and
  - minority interest, which should be treated according to the term of the instrument, usually in perpetuity.

Hence, these liabilities are assigned either a 100% ASF factor where the effective maturity is one year or greater, or 50%, where the effective maturity is six months or over and less than one year;

- NSFR derivative liabilities net of NSFR derivative assets, if NSFR derivative liabilities are larger than NSFR derivative assets;
- 'trade date' payables arising from purchases of financial instruments, foreign currencies and commodities (i) are expected to be settled within the standard settlement cycle or period that is customary for the relevant exchange or type of transaction, or (ii) have failed but are still expected to settle.

Moving on to the denominator of the NSFR, the RSF is measured on the basis of the broad characteristics of the liquidity risk profile of an institution's assets and OBS exposures. It is calculated firstly by classifying the carrying value of an institution's assets in the eight categories listed in Table 6.6. The amount assigned to each category is subsequently multiplied by the corresponding RSF factor. The more liquid

Table 6.6 RSF calculation in NSFR

Components of RSF category	*RSF Factors (%)*
Coins and banknotes All central bank reserves All claims on central banks with residual maturities of less than six months 'Trade date' receivables arising from sales of financial instruments, foreign currencies and commodities	0
Unencumbered Level 1 assets, excluding coins, banknotes and central bank reserves	5
Unencumbered loans to financial institutions with residual maturities of less than six months, where the loan is secured against Level 1 assets, and where the bank has the ability to freely rehypothecate the received collateral for the life of the loan	10
All other unencumbered loans to financial institutions with residual maturities of less than six months not included in the above categories Unencumbered Level 2A assets	15
Unencumbered Level 2B assets HQLA encumbered for a period of six months or more and less than one year Loans to financial institutions and central banks with residual maturities between six months and less than one year Deposits held at other financial institutions for operational purposes All other assets not included in the above categories with residual maturity of less than one year, including loans to non-financial corporate clients, loans to retail and small business customers, and loans to sovereigns and PSEs	50
Unencumbered residential mortgages with a residual maturity of one year or more and with a risk weight of less than or equal to 35% under the Standardised Approach Other unencumbered loans not included in the above categories, excluding loans to financial institutions, with a residual maturity of one year or more and with a risk weight of less than or equal to 35% under the standardised approach	65
Cash, securities or other assets posted as initial margin for derivative contracts and cash or other assets provided to contribute to the default fund of a CCP Other unencumbered performing loans with risk weights greater than 35% under the standardised approach and residual maturities of one year or more, excluding loans to financial institutions Unencumbered securities that are not in default and do not qualify as HQLA with a remaining maturity of one year or more and exchange-traded equities Physical traded commodities, including gold	85

(continued)

Table 6.6 (continued)

Components of RSF category	*RSF Factors (%)*
All assets that are encumbered for a period of one year or more NSFR derivative assets net of NSFR derivative liabilities if NSFR derivative assets are greater than NSFR derivative liabilities 20% of derivative liabilities All other assets not included in the above categories, including non-performing loans, loans to financial institutions with a residual maturity of one year or more, non-exchange-traded equities, fixed assets, items deducted from regulatory capital, retained interest, insurance assets, subsidiary interests and defaulted securities	100

Source Adapted from BCBS (2014b)

the asset, the higher the RSF factor applied. The total RSF is the sum of the weighted amounts added to the amount of OBS activity (or potential liquidity exposure) multiplied by the associated RSF factor.

The most liquid category, to which a RSF factor of 0% is assigned, includes:

- coins and banknotes immediately available to meet obligations;
- all central bank reserves (including required reserves and excess reserves);
- all claims on central banks with residual maturities of less than six months;
- 'trade date' receivables arising from the sale of financial instruments, foreign currencies and commodities that (i) are expected to be settled within the standard settlement cycle or period that is customary for the relevant exchange or type of transaction, or (ii) have failed but are still expected to settle.

The second group of assets, weighted at 5%, includes:

- marketable securities representing claims on sovereigns, central banks, PSEs, the Bank for International Settlements, the International Monetary Fund, the European Central Bank and the European Community, or the multilateral development banks that are assigned a 0% risk-weight under the Basel II standardized approach for credit risk;
- certain non-0% risk-weighted sovereign or central bank debt securities.

The third category of assets includes unencumbered loans to financial institutions with residual maturities of less than six months (as defined in 6.3.1), and where the bank has the ability to freely rehypothecate the collateral for the life of the loan. These assets are given a 10% RSF factor.

The fourth group includes assets weighted at 15%, as follows:

- marketable securities representing claims on sovereigns, central banks, PSEs or multilateral development banks that are assigned a 20% risk-weight under the Basel II standardized approach for credit risk;
- corporate debt securities (including CPs) and covered bonds with a credit rating equal or equivalent to at least AA−;
- all other unencumbered loans to financial institutions with residual maturities.

The fifth group, with a 50% RSF factor, includes:

- RMBS with a credit rating of at least AA;
- corporate debt securities (including CPs) with a credit rating of between A+ and BBB−; and
- exchange-traded common equity shares not issued by financial institutions or their affiliates;
- any HQLA as defined in the LCR that are encumbered for six months or more and less than one year;
- all loans to financial institutions and central banks with residual maturity of six months or more and less than one year;
- deposits held at other financial institutions for operational purposes;
- all other non-HQLA not included in the above categories with a residual maturity of less than one year, including loans to non-financial corporate clients, loans to retail customers and small businesses, and loans to sovereigns and PSEs.

The sixth group of activities, weighted at 65%, includes:

- unencumbered residential mortgages with a residual maturity of one year or more that would qualify for a 35% or lower risk-weight under the Basel II standardized approach for credit risk;
- other unencumbered loans not included in the above categories, with a residual maturity of one year or more that would qualify for a 35% or lower risk weight under the Basel II standardized approach for credit risk.

Assets assigned an 85% RSF factor comprises:

- cash, securities or other assets posted as the initial margin for derivative contracts and cash or other assets provided for the default fund of the central counterparty (CCP);
- other unencumbered performing loans that do not qualify for the 35% or lower risk weight under the Basel II standardized approach for credit risk and have residual maturities of one year or more, excluding loans to financial institutions;
- unencumbered securities with a maturity of one year or more and exchange-traded equities, which are not in default and do not qualify as HQLA according to the LCR;
- physical traded commodities, including gold.

The last and least liquid group of assets, for which a 100% RSF factor is expected, include:

- all assets that are encumbered for a period of one year or more;
- NSFR derivative assets net of NSFR derivative liabilities, if NSFR derivative assets are larger than NSFR derivative liabilities;
- non-performing loans, loans to financial institutions with a residual maturity of one year or more, non-exchange-traded equities, fixed assets, items deducted from regulatory capital, retained interest, insurance assets, subsidiary interests and defaulted securities;
- 20% of derivative liabilities (i.e. negative replacement cost amounts).

Finally, the calculation of the denominator of the NSFR, i.e. the RSF, needs to take OBS exposures into account. Many potential OBS liquidity exposures require little direct or immediate funding, but can lead to significant liquidity drains over a longer period. The NSFR assigns an RSF factor to various OBS assets in order to ensure that institutions hold stable funding for the portion of OBS exposures that may be expected to require funding within one year.

The NSFR identifies OBS exposure categories based on a commitment to a credit or liquidity facility or some other contingent funding obligation. Table 6.7 illustrates the specific types of RSF factor.

In line with the roadmap specified in the Basel III document of 2010, revised in October 2014 (BCBS 2014b), the NSFR became a minimum requirement from 1 January 2018.

Table 6.7 OBS categories in NSFR

OBS category	*RSF Factors*
Irrevocable and conditionally revocable credit and liquidity facilities to any client	5% of the currently undrawn portion
Other contingent funding obligations, including products and instruments such as: • Unconditionally revocable credit and liquidity facilities • Trade finance-related obligations (including guarantees and letters of credit) • Guarantees and letters of credit unrelated to trade finance obligations • Non-contractual obligations such as: – potential requests for debt repurchases of the bank's own debt or that of related conduits, securities investment vehicles and other such financing facilities – structured products where customers anticipate ready marketability, such as adjustable rate notes and variable rate demand notes (VRDNs) – managed funds that are marketed with the objective of maintaining a stable value	National supervisors can specify the RSF factors based on their national circumstances

Source Adapted from BCBS (2014b)

6.4 Monitoring Tools to Assess Liquidity Risk

The two liquidity indicators described in the previous sections do not represent the whole of a bank's liquidity profile. Therefore, the Committee also prepared a series of monitoring tools in order to strengthen and further promote global consistency in the supervision of liquidity risk. These instruments are complementary to LCR and NSFR and should be used for the regular monitoring of bank exposures to liquidity risk and for the notification of such exposures between supervisors in the domestic and host countries. In particular, these indicators aim to:

- identify a mismatch of maturities between inflowing and outflowing liquidity for certain time periods. This measure shows the extent to which a bank depends on maturity transformation in the context of existing contracts;

- evaluate funding concentration, with particular reference to counterparties, instruments and currencies. The indicator is intended to identify the sources of wholesale funding of such importance that their failure would lead to liquidity problems. Therefore, it encourages the diversification of funding as recommended in the Sound Principles of the Committee (BCBS 2008b);
- measure the amount of available unencumbered assets that can be used as collateral to raise additional liquidity in markets and/or from central banks. It should give banks (and authorities) greater awareness of the potential capacity to obtain additional guaranteed funding, taking into account that in a situation of tension, this capacity may decrease;
- calculate the LCR in all significant currencies. Recognizing that exchange rate risk is a component of liquidity risk, the LCR must be calculated for each significant currency, in order to monitor and manage the overall level and trend of a bank's currency exposure. This enables banks to monitor potential currency misalignment issues;
- identify in advance potential liquidity strains highlighted by the market. High-frequency market data with little or no time lag may be used as early warning indicators to monitor potential banks liquidity difficulties. In this regard, it is useful to monitor premiums on CDSs and stock prices, as well as further information on the ability of individual banks to finance themselves on the wholesale markets and at the price applied.

In applying these indicators, supervisors have to take action whenever a negative trend in measurements reveals the presence of potential liquidity problems, the liquidity position has deteriorated or the absolute value indicates a current or potential liquidity problem.

Finally, an area in which further work on monitoring tools has been carried out concerns intraday liquidity risk. The objective of the LCR is to promote the short-term resilience of the liquidity risk profile of banks, but does not include intraday liquidity in its calibration (BCBS 2013a). Therefore, in April 2013, in consultation with the Committee on Payment and Settlement Systems (CPSS),[24] the BCBS developed a set of quantitative tools to enable banking supervisors to monitor a bank's intraday liquidity risk and ability to meet payment and settlement obligations on a timely basis under both normal and stressed conditions (BCBS 2013b). The monitoring tools complement the qualitative guidance in the Sound Principles, dated September 2008.

Given the close relationship between the management of a bank's intraday liquidity risk and the smooth functioning of payment and settlement systems, the tools also benefit the central bank and other authorities responsible for the oversight of payment and settlement systems (overseers). The introduction of monitoring tools for intraday liquidity was intended to lead to closer cooperation between banking supervisors and overseers in the monitoring of the bank's payment behaviour. It is important to note that the tools were introduced for monitoring purposes only and internationally active banks must use them. National supervisors can determine the extent to which the tools apply to non-internationally active banks within their jurisdictions.

Notes

1. The FSB is an international body that monitors and makes recommendations about the global financial system. It was established after the 2009 G20 London summit in April 2009 as a successor to the Financial Stability Forum (FSF). The Board includes the G20 major economies, FSF members, and the European Commission. It is based in Basel, Switzerland.
2. Proportionality in supervisory action consists, in some cases, in requiring larger banks to hold a bigger liquidity buffer than smaller banks.
3. For example, quantitative indicators include so-called stock-based indicators, where cash flows respond more to a maturity mismatch logic, and so-called hybrids that take both aspects into account. For more details see Chapter 5.
4. Before the liquidity crisis, the Basel Committee addressed liquidity risk only by defining best practices (BCBS 2000).
5. For example, it is required to predict the escape of retail deposits or the unavailability of funding on guaranteed and non-guaranteed markets.
6. All assets in the stock must be 'unconstrained', i.e. free from legal, regulatory and contractual restrictions that limit the ability of the bank to liquidate, sell, transfer or allocate assets to a particular use. The assets should not be associated (explicitly or implicitly) with guarantees or provide credit support, or be designed to cover operating costs (such as leases and salaries).
7. Duration measures the price sensitivity of a fixed income security to changes in the interest rate.
8. In most jurisdictions, HQLA should be central bank eligible and liquid in markets during stressed periods. In jurisdictions where central bank eligibility is limited to an extremely narrow list of assets, a supervisor may

allow unencumbered, non-central bank eligible assets that meet the qualifying criteria for Level 1 or Level 2 assets to be included in the stock.

9. In this context, central bank reserves include overnight deposits with the central bank and term deposits with the central bank that: (i) are explicitly and contractually repayable on notice from the depositing bank; or (ii) constitute a loan against which the bank can borrow on a term or overnight but automatically renewable basis (only where the bank has an existing deposit with the relevant central bank). Other term deposits with central banks are not eligible for the stock of HQLA; however, if the expiry is within thirty days, the term deposit could be considered an inflow.
10. The Basel III liquidity framework follows the classification of market participants applied in the Basel II Framework, unless otherwise specified.
11. This requires the holder of the security not to have recourse to the financial institution or any of the financial institution's affiliated entities. Therefore securities, such as government-guaranteed issuance during the financial crisis, which remain liabilities of the financial institution, do not qualify for the stock of HQLA. The only exception is when the bank is also a PSE under the Basel II Framework where securities issued by the bank may qualify for Level 1 assets if all the conditions are satisfied.
12. In this respect, corporate debt securities (including CPs) include only plain-vanilla assets where valuation is readily available based on the standard methods and does not depend on private knowledge, i.e. are not complex structured products or subordinated debt.
13. Covered bonds are bonds issued and owned by a bank or mortgage institution and are subject by law to special public supervision designed to protect bond holders. Proceeds deriving from the issue of these bonds must be invested in compliance with the law on assets which, throughout the validity of the bonds, must be able to cover claims arising from the bonds and which, in the event of failure of the issuer, can be used on a priority basis for the reimbursement of the principal and payment of the accrued interest.
14. Where applicable, cash inflows and outflows should include the anticipated interest to be paid during the thirty-day time horizon.
15. 'Fully insured' means that, up to the deposit insurance limit, 100% of the deposit amount is covered by an effective deposit insurance scheme. Deposit balances up to the deposit insurance limit can be treated as "fully insured" even if a depositor has a balance in excess of the deposit insurance limit. However, any amount in excess of the deposit insurance limit is to be treated as 'less stable'.
16. This could reflect a case in which a bank may be considered to be under liquidity stress if it did not exercise an option on its own funding.

17. In this context, a clearing relationship refers to a service arrangement that enables customers to transfer funds (or securities) indirectly through direct participants in domestic settlement systems to final recipients. Such services are limited to the following activities: transmission, reconciliation and confirmation of payment orders; daylight overdrafts, overnight financing and maintenance of post-settlement balances; the determination of intraday and final settlement positions.
18. In this context, a custody relationship refers to the provision of safekeeping, reporting, processing of assets or the facilitation of the operational and administrative elements of related assets on behalf of customers in the process of transacting and retaining financial assets. Such services are limited to the settlement of securities transactions, the transfer of contractual payments, the processing of collateral, and the provision of custody-related cash management services. Also included are the receipt of dividends and other income, client subscriptions and redemptions. Furthermore, custodial services can include asset and corporate trust servicing, treasury, escrow, fund transfers, stock transfers and agency services, including payment and settlement services (excluding correspondent banking), and depository receipts.
19. In this context, a cash management relationship refers to the provision of cash management and related services to customers. Cash management services refer to products and services provided to a customer to manage its cash flows, assets and liabilities, and carry out the financial transactions required for the customer's ongoing operations. Such services are limited to payment remittances, the collection and aggregation of funds, payroll administration and control over the disbursement of funds.
20. In this context, fiduciary is defined as a legal entity that is authorized to manage assets on behalf of a third party. Fiduciaries include asset management entities such as pension funds and other collective investment vehicles.
21. In this context, a beneficiary is defined as a legal entity that receives, or may become eligible to receive, benefits under a will, insurance policy, retirement plan, annuity, trust or other contract.
22. Outflows on unsecured wholesale funding from affiliated entities of the bank are included in this category unless the funding is part of an operational relationship, a deposit in an institutional network of cooperative banks or the affiliated entity of a non-financial corporate.
23. Before release of the final NSFR document (October 2014), in January 2014 the BCBS published a consultative proposal (BCBS 2014a).
24. The CPSS serves as a forum for central banks to monitor and analyse developments in payment and settlement arrangements as well as in cross-border and multicurrency settlement schemes. Its members are senior officials responsible for payment and settlement systems in central banks. The CPSS Secretariat is hosted by the BIS.

References

Basel Committee on Banking Supervision (BCBS). (2000, February). *Sound Practices for Managing Liquidity in Banking Organizations*. Basel: Bank for International Settlements (BIS).

Basel Committee on Banking Supervision (BCBS). (2008a, February). *Liquidity Risk: Management and Supervisory Challenges*. Basel: Bank for International Settlements (BIS).

Basel Committee on Banking Supervision (BCBS). (2008b, September). *Principles for Sound Liquidity Risk Management*. Basel: Bank for International Settlements (BIS).

Basel Committee on Banking Supervision (BCBS). (2010a, December). *Basel III: A Global Regulatory Framework for More Resilient Banks and Banking Systems*. Basel: Bank for International Settlements (BIS).

Basel Committee on Banking Supervision (BCBS). (2010b, December). *Basel III: International Framework for Liquidity Risk Measurement, Standards and Monitoring*. Basel: Bank for International Settlements (BIS).

Basel Committee on Banking Supervision (BCBS). (2013a, January). *Basel III: The Liquidity Coverage Ratio and Liquidity Risk Monitoring Tools*. Basel: Bank for International Settlements (BIS).

Basel Committee on Banking Supervision (BCBS). (2013b, April). *Monitoring Tools for Intraday Liquidity Management*. Basel: Bank for International Settlements (BIS).

Basel Committee on Banking Supervision (BCBS). (2014a, January). *Basel III: The Net Stable Funding Ratio—Consultative Document*. Basel: Bank for International Settlements (BIS).

Basel Committee on Banking Supervision (BCBS). (2014b, October). *Basel III: The Net Stable Funding Ratio*. Basel: Bank for International Settlements (BIS).

CHAPTER 7

The Implications of Basel III Liquidity Regulatory Reform

7.1 Introduction

The aim of this chapter is first to analyse the operational implications of the Basel III liquidity requirements. Section 7.2 identifies conceptual channels through which the LCR and the NSFR are expected to exert their impacts, both at the individual bank (microeconomic) level and at the market (macroeconomic) level, underlining potential costs and benefits. Section 7.3 reviews the results obtained in the existing empirical studies of the impacts of liquidity requirements.

Second, the chapter aims to understand whether banks have already adapted to the new Basel III liquidity ratios and, if so, how. Section 7.4 focuses on the analysis of the results obtained from the Quantitative Impact Studies (QIS) carried out by the BCBS on a representative sample of banks.

7.2 Possible Strategies for Banks to Meet Basel III Liquidity Ratios: Costs and Benefits

To understand the micro- and macroeconomic effects of the Basel III liquidity standards shown by empirical studies (Sect. 7.3), the potential channels through which the LCR and the NSFR can affect bank behaviour need to be identified. It is also necessary to distinguish between

L. Chiaramonte, *Bank Liquidity and the Global Financial Crisis*,
Palgrave Macmillan Studies in Banking and Financial Institutions,
https://doi.org/10.1007/978-3-319-94400-5_7

LCR- and NSFR-associated channels, given that the two standards have different aims[1] and the ways each ratio is met are not always the same.

For the LCR, the channels through which this liquidity standard can impact on the bank behaviour are associated either with the asset side of the balance sheet (i.e. the numerator of the LCR) or the liabilities side (i.e. the denominator of the ratio). Bank-level assets-side channels of the LCR include the replacement of non-HQLA with HQLA, which may result in a shift away from holding loans towards government bonds. It potentially shortens the maturity of a bank's assets and these adjustments may be expected to lower the bank's credit risk. However, the replacement of non-HQLA with lower yielding HQLA and the shortening of asset maturities also lowers interest income.

On the liabilities side of the balance sheets, the LCR is expected to result in stable funding replacing non-stable funding, implying a lengthening of the maturity of liabilities. These liability adjustments may increase interest expenses, because more stable and longer maturity funding sources are associated with larger spreads and are therefore more costly. For OBS items, the LCR is expected to result in a reduction in contingent credit lines or liquidity facilities granted by the bank.

For the NSFR, banks can pursue a number of strategies to increase it with different implications (see King 2013; BCBS 2016). Alternatively, banks can increase the ASF (i.e. the ratio numerator), consisting of liabilities items, or decrease the RSF (i.e. the NSFR numerator), consisting of assets items.

Starting from the liabilities side, a bank can follow three strategies to increase the ASF and consequently the NSFR.

Firstly, a bank can decide to increase the share of its deposits, especially the stable rather than less stable deposits (strategy 1). As seen in Chapter 6, stable deposits are given a factor of 95%, because some are expected to run off in stressed conditions. Less stable deposits have a factor of 90% and include high-value deposits, deposits from high net worth individuals, deposits that can be withdrawn quickly (such as Internet deposits) and foreign currency deposits. While banks may wish to increase deposits, competition increases their cost. The ability to increase the NSFR by raising deposits is limited and depends on local conditions.

A second strategy through which banks can increase their ASF is by increasing the share of Tier 1 capital (strategy 2). Under Basel III, the predominant form of Tier 1 capital must be tangible common equity or instruments that are subordinated, have fully discretionary non-cumulative dividends and neither a maturity date nor an incentive to redeem (i.e. non-cumulative, perpetual preferred shares). Given this definition, any Tier 1 capital increases shareholder's equity and reduces the ROE. Theoretically, a bank's equity is the most expensive form of capital due to its higher risk and residual claim. Empirically, a bank's Tier 1 capital, as a share of total assets, is small, so a significant increase in equity would be required to raise ASF. Increasing equity is therefore likely to be the most expensive and least desirable strategy to improve the NSFR.

Third, banks may decide to extend the maturity of their liabilities, especially of wholesale funding, beyond one year (strategy 3). Liabilities with an effective maturity of more than one year receive a factor of 100% against 50% for wholesale funding below one year. Note that interbank borrowing is at 0%, as this source is not expected to be stable under stressed conditions. While debt maturity extension increases the numerator of the NSFR, it also raises interest expenses as the cost of longer-term wholesale funding is higher than shorter-term funding in most yield curve environments. All else being equal, higher interest expenses lead to a fall in net interest margins.

Overall, banks prefer to raise deposits (strategy 1) or to extend the maturity of debt (strategy 3) rather than issue equity (strategy 2) due to its higher cost.

As a complementary or alternative strategy to reducing ASF, banks can raise the NSFR above the minimum threshold of 100% by increasing RSF, which means reducing or modifying their assets. There are four possible strategies, as set out below.

First, banks can reduce RSF by shrinking their balance sheet through a reduction of their loan portfolio or selling assets funded at 100% (such as trading assets and fixed assets). The cost of reducing a loan portfolio may be high. Loans and mortgages are higher yielding assets where banks have a comparative advantage over other financial intermediaries (Strahan 2010). By replacing loans with more liquid securities, banks forego the loan spread and may incur a negative carry cost related to its capital cost. This strategy is likely to be more expensive and less attractive than other options.

For these options (such as the sale of other assets), any reduction in trading assets is associated with a fall in trading revenues, leading to lower non-interest income and profitability. Moreover, fixed assets may be required to support a bank's lending operations, so may not be feasible.

A second strategy to reduce RSF is a change in the composition of a bank's investments, either by selling lower-rated investments for cash or by replacing lower-rated with higher-rated investments. Cash and highly rated securities have a 0% factor, so no additional funding needs to be held against them. Both strategies, selling illiquid investments and holding more cash or more investments with less credit risk, are expensive, as these cash and AAA-rated securities would likely have a negative carry cost vis-à-vis the cost of capital. Replacement would reduce interest income, the cost being depending on the difference in returns. The ability to lower RSF by changing the composition of investments is limited by the quantity of investments compared to total assets. If the quantity of investments is small, banks may be required to change the composition of their assets more broadly.

A third strategy consists in the ability of a bank to change the composition of its loans. Here, there are two options. The first is to replace retail and corporate loans with mortgage loans. Under the NSFR, mortgage loans must be funded at 65% while retail and corporate loans require 85%. Everything else being equal, this weighting should lead banks to prefer mortgages loans over retail and corporate loans. The ability to switch between loan types depends on a number of factors that are beyond the scope of this study, such as the elasticity of loan demand, the availability of replacements and the competitive environment. The second option is to reduce the maturity of corporate loans to less than one year, which reduces their RSF factor to 50%. Thus, banks can be encouraged to increase the share of their corporate loans with a final maturity of under one year because they are less heavily weighted in the calculation of NSFR. While this change would benefit banks (reducing liquidity risk), it involves a cost for the bank's customers, who bear an increased rollover risk on their borrowing.

The last strategy is for banks to reduce the share of assets that must be funded at 100%. Specifically, it involves banks replacing assets with a high RSF factor with assets with a lower factor weight.

The above channels, through which liquidity requirements can affect a bank's behaviour, show the potential costs and benefits of Basel III liquidity regulation both at the micro- and macroeconomic level. At the microlevel they are easier to see where the cost and/or benefit is associated with the LCR and/or NSFR, whereas, at the market (macroeconomic) levels, effects are more difficult to attribute specifically to the LCR or the NSFR.

At the microeconomic level, the potential costs of liquidity regulation are summarized below.

Based on the above strategies to increase the LCR and NSFR, the introduction of the Basel III liquidity ratios may reduce aggregate bank credit in normal times through the following channels:

- the LCR may increase the opportunity cost of holding illiquid assets, which may translate into higher loan rates;
- both the LCR and NSFR may reduce the proportion of loans on bank balance sheets (by replacing loans with more liquid securities);
- the NSFR may reduce the average maturity of bank loans, which are less heavy for the calculation of the ratio and aim to reduce maturity transformation;
- both the LCR and NSFR may lead banks to increase lending charges to cover higher funding costs (due to the fact that both ratios are expected to result in stable funding replacing non-stable funding).

Moreover, both the LCR and NSFR may reduce net interest income. The latter may decrease due to the fact that banks should hold more HQLA (typically lower yielding assets), through the LCR, and due to the increase in stable funding (typically more costly), especially through the NSFR with the aim of reducing maturity transformation, one of the main causes of a bank's liquidity problems.

At the macroeconomic level, the potential costs could derive from the fact that changes in liquidity requirements should reduce interbank lending and maturity transformation, also impacting on aggregate borrowing. Lower borrowing reduces aggregate consumption and investment and, eventually, GDP.

Focusing on the potential benefit, at the microeconomic level, the introduction of the two liquidity ratios could reduce the likelihood of bank failure caused by liquidity shocks, especially due to the increase in the share of stable funding, reducing maturity transformation. In turn, improved resilience lowers both the likelihood of a financial crisis and reduces the size of the economic loss in the event that a crisis does occur. The benefit is the loss that is avoided through higher capital and liquidity requirements. Moreover, the increased stability of banks during a crisis period has two further potential positive microeconomic effects. On the one hand, the improved resilience of banks to shocks may lead to a less severe credit crunch during a liquidity crisis. On the other hand, liquidity requirements may increase net interest income, due to lower funding costs through a perceived reduction in risk and less likelihood of default.

All these benefits should increase the stability of the financial system (the macroeconomic benefit).

From the above, it is clear that the costs and benefits of the liquidity ratios identified at the theoretical level are also in conflict with each other. Therefore, the next section provides a detailed analysis of the current empirical evidence of the impact of the new requirements.

7.3 An Empirical Literature Review of the Impact of the Liquidity Requirements on Bank Behaviour

This section reviews the existing literature relating to the impact of Basel III liquidity ratios, both at the individual bank (microeconomic) and market (macroeconomic) levels. There are many studies on the effects of capital requirements, but relatively few on the effects of liquidity requirements. Partly, this is because capital requirements have been in place for some time and for more than one business cycle, while liquidity standards were implemented only after the recent financial crisis. Indeed, the LCR is partially implemented and the NSFR has yet to be introduced.

None of the empirical studies reviewed below attempts to assess both potential social costs and benefits simultaneously.

As highlighted in the previous section, the LCR and the NSFR can potentially impact on bank lending. At the theoretical level, Sect. 7.2 suggests that the effects vary according to the macroeconomic context. In normal times, they seem to lead to a reduction in bank credit. However, liquidity regulation may reduce the fall in bank credit in response to liquidity shocks, thereby resulting in a lower reduction in aggregate output associated with banking crises than otherwise would be the case.

From the current empirical evidence, most studies focus on the impact of the LCR (or similar indicator), but none appear to confirm a credit reduction by banks as a consequence of the introduction of the Basel III liquidity requirements. Specifically, some studies found no significant impacts of liquidity regulation on credit. They include Banerjee and Mio (2015) who investigated the causal effects on bank balance sheets of individual bank liquidity regulation, the so-called Individual Liquidity Guidance (ILG), imposed by the Financial Service Authority (FSA) in the UK in 2010. The ILG is similar to Basel III LCR, in that it required banks to hold HQLA to withstand both an acute bank-specific shock lasting for two weeks and a general funding shock for three months. Using a 'local projection method' (dividing the sample into pre-crisis and post-crisis periods), the authors found that the ILG led to the replacement of short-term intra-financial loans with HQLA, while lending remained nearly unchanged. As banks under the ILG increased the share of HQLA on average by 12 percentage points compared with banks exempted from the requirements, credit risk declined and made it easier for the banks to meet regulatory capital requirements. However, the authors emphasize that the latter result may have been driven by the UK's Quantitative Easing programme, possibly leading to a perfectly elastic HQLA supply curve.

As in the UK, even before the LCR and the NSFR established by Basel III, in the Netherlands, in 2003, the Dutch National Bank (DNB) introduced an ex post quantitative liquidity coverage ratio for Dutch banks (hereafter the DLCR) similar to the LCR. According to this rule, a bank's liquidity must exceed certain minimum requirements over periods of both one week and one month. The amount of liquidity required is determined according to assumptions related to deposit withdrawals, calls on contingent credit lines, and runoffs for wholesale and derivative funding. Bonner (2016) studied the effects of both capital and liquidity requirements in the Netherlands and found a similar replacement effect to the UK in terms of liquidity requirements. Due to the preferential regulatory treatment of government bonds in capital and liquidity requirements, banks replaced Dutch government bonds with other bonds (e.g. financial bonds, covered bonds and ABSs), which had a significant effect on capital requirements. In contrast to the findings for the UK, Bonner found that liquidity requirements impacted on private lending. With the revision of the DLCR in May 2011, liquidity requirements were tightened, as haircuts for all securities increased. Government bonds, however, became relatively more attractive, as the haircut for this asset class had increased by only 5% against 30% for almost all other bonds. In response, banks increased government bond holdings, and bank lending to the private sector declined by 3.1%.

Thus, the available empirical evidence from Banerjee and Mio (2015) and Bonner (2016) seems to suggest that national liquidity rules that resemble the LCR have had little, if any, impact on aggregate lending and, hence, on aggregate growth.

The findings of these two studies are consistent with the conclusions of three European Banking Authority (EBA) reports (2013, 2014, 2015) based on QIS data. These reports find that the LCR and the NSFR do not negatively affect lending to the real economy or GDP growth. In particular, banks have adjusted their LCR by reducing their intra-bank lending and increasing their HQLA holding, with no or very little impact on lending to non-financial corporates, retail and small- and medium-sized enterprise (SME) customers. These results appear to be due, at least in part, to the substantial 'softening' of both ratios during the course of the Basel negotiations and to the relatively low opportunity costs of compliance.

Finally, DeYoung and Jang (2016) use the loan-to-deposit ratio as a proxy for the NSFR and examine how US banks reacted to shocks to this ratio during the period 1992–2012. They estimate that US banks may respond to NFSR requirements by actively managing their funding and turning to larger amounts of stable funding, more so than actively managing their assets and turning to lower-yield (but higher-quality) assets. They also show that systemically important US banks manage liquidity less actively than community banks, hence the former have to adjust more to the NSFR.

On the other hand, some studies based on simulations have reached the opposite conclusions, suggesting a larger impact of liquidity requirements on lending. They focused only on the effect of the LCR and include a paper by De Nicolò et al. (2014) which analyses bank behaviour in a dynamic partial equilibrium model, and finds that adding liquidity requirements on top of capital requirements may severely hamper maturity transformation. In order to fulfil the additional requirements, banks are forced to use retained earnings to increase bond holdings (rather than use these funds to extend loans) or to reduce liabilities. Low capital requirements rather than no capital requirements at all can result in more lending, because it can be beneficial for banks to use the higher revenues from risky loans to build capital. However, for higher capital requirements, this alternative becomes too costly due to the assumption of decreasing returns to scale in lending, which then leads to a U-shaped impact of capital requirements on bank lending. In contrast, liquidity requirements lead to an increase in capital ratios by an inefficient increase in bond holdings. Although these actions increase bank safety, loans decline by 26%, due to a high elasticity of loan demand with respect to loan spreads. However, this result may be driven by the assumption that both deposits and prices are exogenous, i.e. by the usage of a dynamic partial equilibrium model.

Covas and Driscoll (2014) argue that partial equilibrium models are not well suited to identifying the magnitude of the impact of different regulatory requirements because they fail to take price effects into account. Using a non linear dynamic stochastic general equilibrium (DSGE) model, they show that taking price adjustments into account significantly diminishes the estimates of impacts made through partial equilibrium models. In particular, imposing an LCR requirement on top of a capital requirement of 6% decreases bank lending by 3%, whereas neglecting the price effects shows a 6% decline in lending. This effect is identical when the LCR is added to a capital requirement of 12%. In both cases, banks hold more securities and equity in response to the LCR and, as a result, their capital ratio increases by one percentage point. Doubling capital requirements from 6 to 12%, instead of imposing an LCR, reduces lending by less than 1%. However, these higher capital requirements have a strong impact on the holding of securities and equity ratios, which then leads to an increase in a bank's capital ratio of nearly 5%. The extent of the dampening effect depends on the characteristics of the bank and the design of the financial system. Indeed, the private sector might have a number of alternatives to bank loans (such as equity funding, supplier loans, issuance of corporate debt, and factoring/leasing).

Using a broader DSGE model that distinguishes between SME customers, large corporates, and investments in sovereign bonds, De Bandt and Chahad (2015) stress that liquidity requirements lead to an increase in household deposits. When the LCR moves from 60 to 85% of its target in four years, loans to SME customers decrease by 1%, while loans to large corporates, which also rely on bond funding, decrease by only 0.5%. The overall impact on GDP is in the same range as in previous studies.

Overall, all the studies based on simulations found a considerably larger impact of liquidity requirements on loans, with declines in credit ranging from 3 to 26%. However, these findings are often driven by specific assumptions, which are not in line with the findings of the empirical studies regarding banks adjustment strategies to liquidity regulation.

Finally, other authors find that liquidity requirements show that the costs arising from liquidity regulations in good times should be offset, at least partially, by a reduced fall in credit in crisis periods.

For example, Cornett et al. (2011), who estimate quarterly changes in new credit provision by US banks during the financial crisis compared to the pre-crisis period, found that banks with more contingent credit lines and banks with lower proportions of stable funding reduced their lending more during the crisis. These authors estimate that new credit fell by about US$500 billion in Q4 2008 and this reduction would have only been around US$87 billion if all the banks had the same level of liquidity risk exposure as the lowest quartile of the distribution of US banks. Hence, a binding liquidity requirement would have enhanced the ability of capital requirements to reduce the vulnerability of banks to this type of crisis.

Pessarossi and Vinas (2015) found similar results for France. Examining demand effects, they took advantage of the exogenous international interbank market freeze in 2007–2008 to assess the causal relation between French bank liquidity risk and lending. They provide evidence that banks with lower funding risk and a lower ratio of long-term loans to long-term funding and deposits provide more loans after the shock. This difference in lending only exists for the long-term loan supply.

Thus, the review of the empirical results from the studies summarized above suggests that neither lending nor output should be heavily affected by the imposition of the Basel III liquidity ratios.

In addition to lending, the LCR and NSFR may also impact net interest income. As stated in Sect. 7.2, at the theoretical level, the effects can be both negative, as a consequence of higher funding costs due to the increase in stable funding, and positive, because of lower funding costs as a result of the perception of an improved risk profile. The empirical literature on the impact of liquidity requirements on the net interest income is ambiguous. Up to now, there is no clear idea of whether net interest income increases or decreases in response to liquidity requirements. For example, King (2013) estimates that the implementation of the NSFR (or rather its proxy as developed by the author) could mean that the most cost-effective strategies to meet the regulatory minimum would be to increase the maturities of wholesale funding and increase the holdings of higher-rated assets, which together would reduce net interest income. From a sample of 15 countries based on Bankscope data and assuming banks increase liquid assets by 25%, King estimates that the interest margin would decrease by 70–80 basis points (i.e. 40% in 2013 data compared to the 2009 level).

In relation to the DLCR rule in the Netherlands (described above), Bonner and Eijffinger (2012) find that constrained banks (i.e. close to the liquidity requirement) pay and charge higher interest rates for unsecured interbank loans, especially for loans with maturities beyond thirty days. The results are consistent with the lengthening of funding maturity, but the evidence provided by the authors is inconclusive because several channels could explain this outcome.

Increased funding costs might also impose an indirect cost on bank lending. Using a fixed-effects panel regression for 26 Dutch banks between January 2008 and December 2011, Bonner (2012) investigated whether banks pass on increased funding costs to the corporate sector. He found that banks close to the liquidity requirement face higher funding costs in the interbank market, but these banks do not charge higher interest rates for corporate lending. The reason for this is the lack of pricing power that may result either from fierce competition among banks or the close relationships between banks and corporates in the Netherlands. Banerjee and Mio (2015) also found no evidence that banks increased the average interest rates on loans to the non-financial sector.

Chiaramonte (2015) came to the opposite conclusion. The author investigates the impact of the Basel III structural liquidity rule on bank profitability, taking into account, among other things, the cost of funding. The analysis focuses on a sample of commercial, cooperative and savings banks in the 28 countries of the European Union over the period 2004–2013. In contrast to the findings of recent related studies, the results of the empirical analysis show that the compliance of the NSFR threshold does not affect bank profitability, especially if the bank is small. Indeed, small banks, which generally comply with the structural liquidity rule, have higher profitability partly due to lower funding costs.

Finally, the last theoretical effect is the potential for Basel III liquidity ratios to improve the resilience to shocks of both individual banks and the financial system itself. A handful of recent studies focus on the ability of the new Basel III capital ratios or the new liquidity standards to reduce bank failures. Most attribute to the liquidity standards a positive effect in terms of stability. For example, Vazquez and Federico (2015) studied the connection between structural liquidity and leverage in bank balance sheets in the run-up to the global financial crisis, and the likelihood of subsequent failure. Based on a sample of US and European banks over the period 2001–2009, they show that banks with weaker structural liquidity and higher leverage ratios in the pre-crisis period were more likely to fail afterwards. Vazquez and Federico also find evidence of systematic differences between different types of bank. Smaller banks were more susceptible to failure because of liquidity problems, while large cross-border banking groups generally failed because of insufficient capital buffers.

A study by Chiaramonte and Casu (2017) came to similar conclusions. Focusing on a sample of banks headquartered in EU-28 member states over the period 2004–2013, they found that the EU banks that run into difficulties almost always had low structural liquidity. This result is consistent with the view that during the global financial crisis the key source of bank instability was excessive maturity transformation (see Gobat et al. 2014). Indeed, almost all banks that ran into difficulty had low NSFR, although their capital requirements were well above the statutory minimum (see BCBS 2014b).

Only, Hong et al. (2014), examining a sample of US commercial banks over the period 2001–2011, found that both the NSFR and LCR had limited effects on bank failures.

Putting these findings together, it could be argued that, on the basis of the information currently available, the welfare costs arising from liquidity regulation should be relatively small, and the numerous welfare benefits arising from reducing the likelihood and cost of bank failures considerable. The net social benefit of liquidity regulation may be expected to be significantly positive.

7.4 Bank Compliance with Basel III Liquidity Ratios: An Overview of Quantitative Impact Studies

Since 2010, every sixth month the BCBS publishes comprehensive QIS in order to monitor compliance with the Basel III capital and liquidity rules by a sample of banks. Information for the QIS is collected by national supervisors based on a representative sample of institutions in each of the 27 countries considered, in the following three geographical areas: Europe, the Americas and the rest of the world. Table 7.1 shows a sample of participating banks country by country, using the information from the Basel Committee's latest Basel III monitoring exercise, i.e. data as of 31 December 2016 (BCBS 2017).[2] Data were provided for a total of 187 banks, including 104 Group 1 banks and 83 Group 2 banks.

Table 7.1 Sample of participating banks by country*

Country	*Group 1 banks*		*Group 2 banks*	
	LCR	*NSFR*	*LCR*	*NSFR*
Europe				
Belgium	2	2	2	2
France	5	5	2	2
Germany	0	7	0	28
Italy	2	2	12	12
Luxembourg	0	0	1	1
The Netherlands	4	4	5	5
Russia	1	1	0	0
Spain	2	2	6	6
Sweden	4	4	1	1
Switzerland	2	2	1	1
Turkey	3	3	0	0
United Kingdom	4	4	4	4
Americas				
Argentina	0	0	2	2
Brazil	2	2	0	0
Canada	6	6	2	2
Mexico	1	1	6	5
United States	13	13	0	0
Rest of the world				
Australia	4	4	1	1
China	6	6	0	0
Hong Kong	0	0	0	0
India	5	5	4	3
Indonesia	0	0	2	2
Japan	16	16	3	2
Korea	6	6	2	2
Saudi Arabia	3	3	0	0
Singapore	3	3	0	0
South Africa	3	3	2	2
Total	97	104	58	83
of which: G-SIBs	30			

**Data* at 31 December 2016
Source Adapted from BCBS (2017)

Group 1 banks have Tier 1 capital of more than 3 billion euros, are active internationally and include all 30 banks designated as global systemically important banks (G-SIBs) by the FSB in November 2016 (FSB 2016), irrespective of their previous classification. All other banks are considered Group 2 banks (i.e. banks with Tier 1 capital of less than 3 billion euros or which do not operate internationally). Members' coverage of their banking sector is very high for Group 1 banks, reaching 100% coverage for some countries, while coverage is lower for Group 2 banks and varies by country. Banks were asked to provide data at the consolidated level. Hence, subsidiaries are not included in the analyses to avoid counting double.

This section presents the results of the monitoring exercises of the BCBS from 31 December 2012 to 31 December 2016 (i.e. the most recent data available at the time of going to press). Although QIS data are available from 2010 on, the analysis starts in December 2012 because from this date onwards BCBS reports provide not only global averages, but also a regional breakdown of many key metrics. Focusing only on the QIS results for the Basel III liquidity ratios, the following figures show the trend of the weighted average LCR and NSFR[3] for Group 1 banks, including the G-SIBs, and for Group 2 banks, over the period considered, both at the aggregate and regional levels. The last part of the section focuses on the variation in the components of the two liquidity standards in order to understand which of them caused the changes in the LCR and NSFR.

Figure 7.1 shows the weighted average LCR and NSFR for the sample of banks of Table 7.1 across reporting periods since end-December 2012. Group 1 bank LCR is increased from ratios reported in earlier periods. The weighted average LCR for these banks is 131.9% at end-December 2016. In the previous years, the ratio was about 121% in 2012–2013 and around 126% in 2014–2015. The same is true of the G-SIBs, but with slightly lower values. While Group 2 bank ratios trended lower for several periods, the weighted average LCR of 155.5% for these banks at end-December 2016 represents the highest ratio since the end-December 2012 reporting period. Additionally, the overall level of ratios for Group 2 banks remains higher than the level observed for Group 1 banks.

Figure 7.1 also shows NSFRs since end-December 2012. Group 1 banks, ratios increased from the ratios reported in earlier periods. The weighted average NSFR grew from 100% at end-December 2012 to

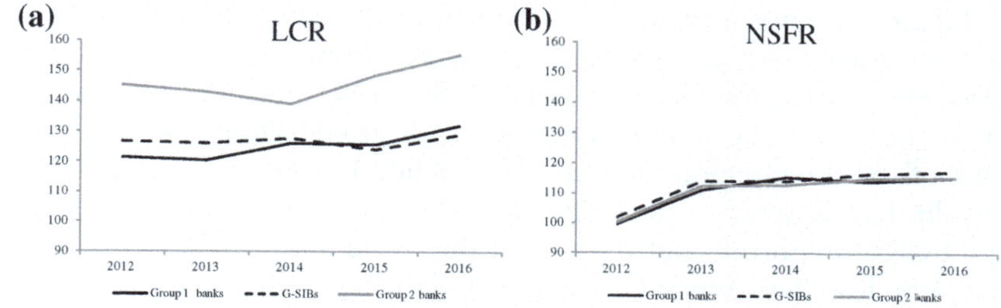

Fig. 7.1 LCR and NSFR* over time (in %)**
*The NSFR is calculated under different versions of the NSFR framework released in December 2010 (BCBS 2010), January 2014 (BCBS 2014a), and October 2014 (BCBS 2014b), respectively. Calculations performed according to the final standard approved by the Committee in October 2014 start with the end-December 2014 reporting period
**The time period considered is from end-December 2012 to end-December 2016
Source Adapted from BCBS 2017

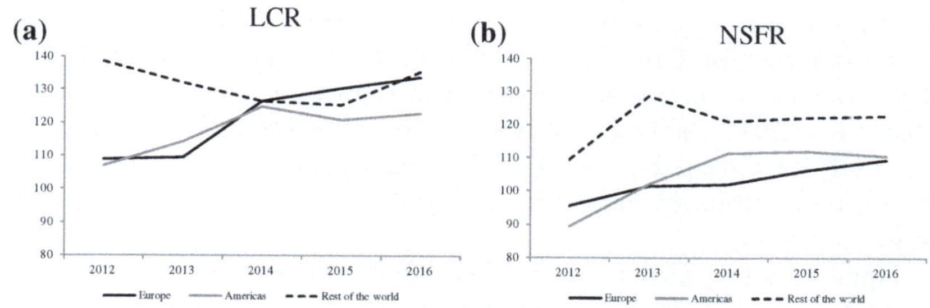

Fig. 7.2 LCR and NSFR* for Group 1 banks by region (in %)**
*The NSFR is calculated under different versions of the NSFR framework released in December 2010 (BCBS 2010), January 2014 (BCBS 2014a), and October 2014 (BCBS 2014b), respectively. Calculations performed according to the final standard approved by the Committee in October 2014 start with the end-December 2014 reporting period
**The time period considered is from end-December 2012 to end-December 2016
Source Adapted from BCBS 2017

115.5% at end-2016. Group 2 banks also display a growing trend for the NSFR in the same period, with very similar values. Unlike LCR, the weighted average NSFR values for Group 1 and Group 2 banks are very similar, with those of the G-SIBs slightly higher than both.

Figure 7.2 gives a regional breakdown of the weighted average LCR and weighted average NSFR over the reporting periods since end-December 2012, for Group 1 banks only (which include banks active internationally). The weighted average LCR at end-December 2016 for each of the three regions is over 120%. While Europe and the Americas initially had lower average LCRs than the rest of the world, the average LCRs for Europe and the rest of the world and, to a lesser degree, the Americas have tended to gradually converge. Regions with lower end-2012 average ratios increased significantly, particularly between end-2012 and December 2014. Interestingly the rest of the world had fluctuating LCR, at around 125% in December 2015, but also levels closer to 2012 at 136%.

The weighted average NSFR at end-December 2016 for Group 1 banks in each of the three regions is well in excess of 100%. Europe and the Americas, at around 110% at end-2016, have lower average NSFRs than the rest of the world, at 122.8%. NSFRs have improved in all three regions over the past four years, in particular in the Americas.

Figure 7.3 shows a breakdown of the period-to-period changes in the components of the LCR, i.e. the HQLA (the ratio numerator) and the total net cash outflows over the next thirty calendar days (the ratio denominator) over the reporting periods since end-December 2012. This suggests that the increases in weighted average LCR for Group 1 banks, G-SIBs, and Group 2 banks were mainly driven by continuous increases in HQLA, partially offset by increases in net outflows.

Figure 7.4 provides a regional breakdown of the results in Fig. 7.3 for Group 1 banks. It shows period-to-period changes in HQLA and net outflows, indicating that in each of the three regions, changes in HQLA have been a slightly more important driver of change in the weighted LCR, although both sources of change have been significant.

Figure 7.5 shows the percentage change in ASF and RSF, i.e. the components of the NSFR, over time. For all bank groups (Group 1 banks, G-SIBs, and Group 2 banks), there were significant positive changes in ASF, around 10 percentage points for the end-December 2013 reporting period, leading to across-the-board increases in the NSFR, sometimes over 10 percentage points.

Finally, Fig. 7.6 gives a regional breakdown of the evolution of the changes in ASF and RSF for Group 1 banks over time. For all regions, figures in 2013 reflect changes in the definition of the NSFR standard.

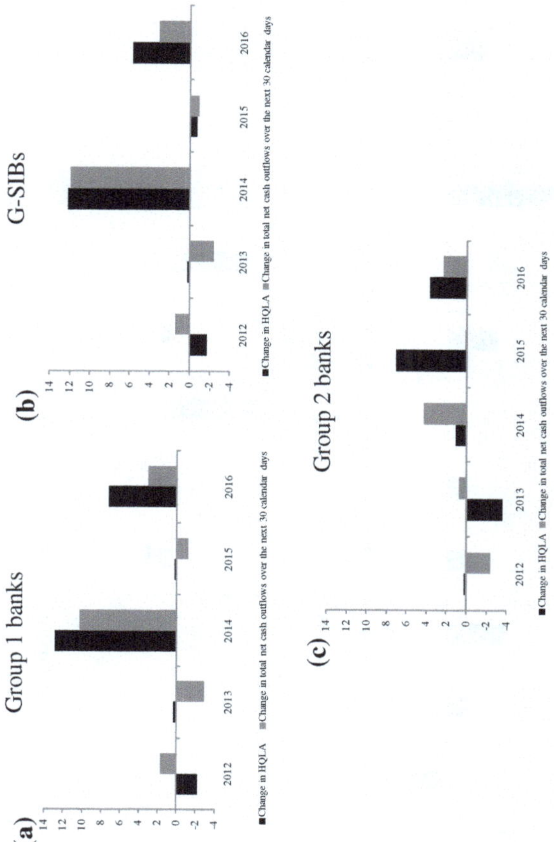

Fig. 7.3 Components of LCR by sub-sample banks (in %)*
*The time period considered is from end-December 2012 to end-December 2016
Source Adapted from BCBS 2017

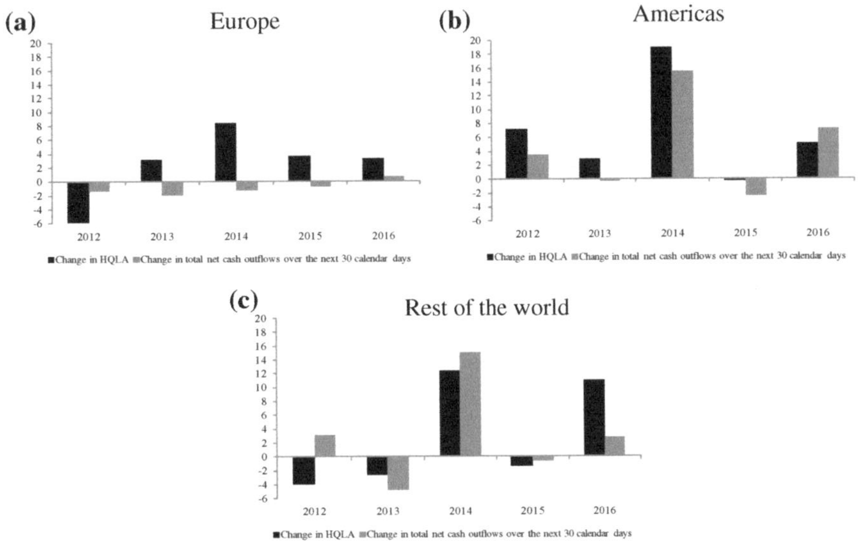

Fig. 7.4 Components of LCR for Group 1 banks by region (in %)*
*The time period considered is from end-December 2012 to end-December 2016
Source Adapted from BCBS 2017

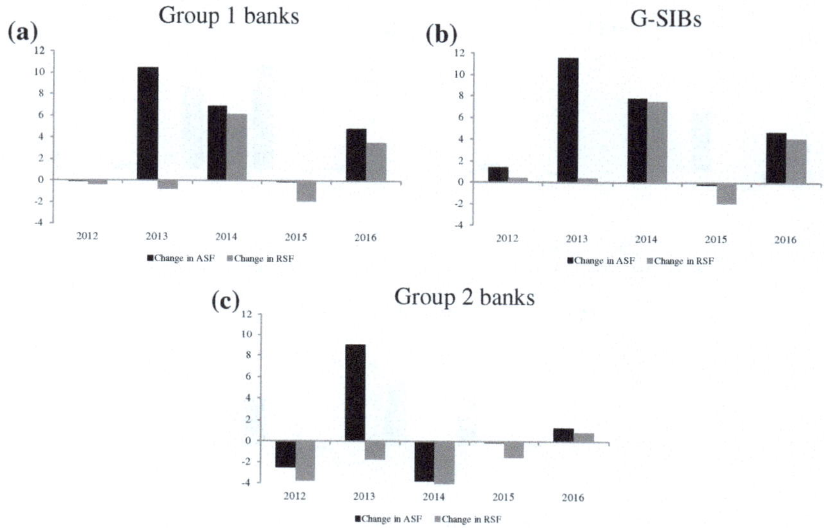

Fig. 7.5 Components of NSFR* by sub-sample banks (in %)**
*The NSFR is calculated under different versions of the NSFR framework released in December 2010 (BCBS 2010), January 2014 (BCBS 2014a), and October 2014 (BCBS 2014b), respectively. Calculations performed according to the final standard approved by the committee in October 2014 start with the end-December 2014 reporting period
**The time period considered is from end-December 2012 to end-December 2016
Source Adapted from BCBS 2017

The main impact of these changes was an increase in ASF for most banks. For the rest of the world, the denominator increased on average between 2014 and 2015, leading to a decrease in the NSFR, while in Europe the increase in NSFR was driven mainly by the decrease in the RSF. In the Americas, the change in ASF led to a downward trend from 2013 to 2015, but there was an increase in 2016. In general, for most periods, the positive change in ASF exceeds the increase in RSF indicating an increase in the NSFR ratio.

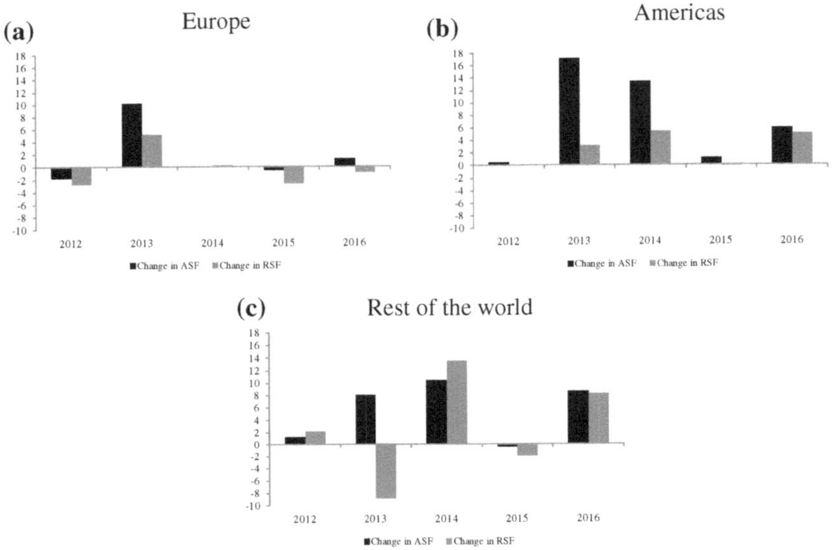

Fig. 7.6 Components of NSFR* for Group 1 banks by region (in %)**
*The NSFR is calculated under different versions of the NSFR framework released in December 2010 (BCBS 2010), January 2014 (BCBS 2014a), and October 2014 (BCBS 2014b), respectively. Calculations performed according to the final standard approved by the Committee in October 2014 start with the end-December 2014 reporting period
**The time period considered is from end-December 2012 to end-December 2016
Source Adapted from BCBS 2017

Notes

1. The LCR aims to ensure that banks have enough HQLA to withstand liquidity stress in the short term, while the NSFR aims to encourage banks to hold more stable and longer-term funding sources against their liquid assets, thereby reducing maturity transformation risk.
2. The data for Japan are for the end of September each year, as banks in that country report on a biannual basis, at the end of March and September, corresponding to the fiscal year-end period. The data for Canada are for a reporting date of 31 October each year, which corresponds to the end of the fiscal fourth quarter.

3. The NSFR is calculated under different versions of the NSFR framework released in December 2010 (BCBS 2010), January 2014 (BCBS 2014a), and October 2014 (BCBS 2014b), respectively. Calculations according to the final standard approved by the Committee in October 2014 start with the end-December 2014 reporting period.

References

Banerjee R. N., & Mio, H. (2015, July). *The Impact of Liquidity Regulation on Banks* (Bank of England Working Paper 536).

Basel Committee on Banking Supervision (BCBS). (2010, December). *Basel III: International Framework for Liquidity Risk Measurement, Standards and Monitoring*. Basel: Bank for International Settlements (BIS).

Basel Committee on Banking Supervision (BCBS). (2014a, January). *Basel III: The Net Stable Funding Ratio—Consultative Document*. Basel: Bank for International Settlements (BIS).

Basel Committee on Banking Supervision (BCBS). (2014b, October). *Basel III: The Net Stable Funding Ratio*. Basel: Bank for International Settlements (BIS).

Basel Committee on Banking Supervision (BCBS). (2016, March). *Literature Review on Integration of Regulatory Capital and Liquidity Instruments* (Working Paper 30).

Basel Committee on Banking Supervision (BCBS). (2017, September). *Basel III Monitoring Report*.

Bonner, C. (2012, December). *Liquidity Regulation, Funding Costs and Corporate Lending* (DNB Working Paper 361).

Bonner, C. (2016). Preferential Regulatory Treatment and Banks' Demand for Government Bonds. *Journal of Money, Credit and Banking, 48,* 1195–1221.

Bonner, C., & Eijffinger, S. (2012, December). *The Impact of the LCR on the Interbank Money Market* (DNB Working Paper 364).

Chiaramonte, L. (2015). Net Stable Funding Ratio e redditività bancaria: quali relazioni? *Bancaria, 10,* 31–49.

Chiaramonte, L., & Casu, B. (2017). Capital and Liquidity Ratios and Financial Distress: Evidence from the European Banking Industry. *The British Accounting Review, 49,* 138–161.

Cornett, M. M., McNutt, J. J., Strahan, P. E., & Tehranian, H. (2011). Liquidity Risk Management and Credit Supply in the Financial Crisis. *Journal of Financial Economics, 2,* 297–312.

Covas, F., & Driscoll, J. C. (2014, September). *Bank Liquidity and Capital Regulation in General Equilibrium*, 85. Washington, DC: Finance and Economics Discussion Series Divisions of Research & Statistics and Monetary Affairs Federal Reserve Board.

De Bandt, O., & Chahad, M. (2015). *A DSGE Model to Assess the Post Crisis Regulation of Universal Banks*. Mimeo, University of Paris Ouest and Banque de France-Autorité de Contrôle Prudentiel et de Résolution.

De Nicolò, G., Gamba, A., & Lucchetta, M. (2014). Microprudential Regulation in a Dynamic Model of Banking. *Review of Financial Studies, 7*, 2097–2138.

DeYoung, R., & Jang, K. Y. (2016). Do Banks Actively Manage Their Liquidity? *Journal of Banking & Finance, 66*, 143–161.

European Banking Authority (EBA). (2013, December). *Report on Impact Assessment for Liquidity Measures Under Article 509(1) of the CRR*.

European Banking Authority (EBA). (2014, December). *Second Report on Impact Assessment for Liquidity Measures Under Article 509(1) of the CRR*.

European Banking Authority (EBA). (2015, December). *Report on Net Stable Funding Requirements Under Article 510 of the CRR*.

Financial Stability Board (FSB). (2016, November). *2016 List of Global Systemically Important Banks (G-SIBs)*.

Gobat, J., Yanase, M., & Maloney, J. (2014, June). *The Net Stable Funding Ratio: Impact and Issues for Consideration* (International Monetary Fund (IMF) Working Paper 106).

Hong, H., Huang, J. Z., & Wu, D. (2014). The Information Content of Basel III Liquidity Risk Measures. *Journal of Financial Stability, 15*, 91–111.

King, M. R. (2013). The Basel III Net Stable Funding Ratio and Bank Net Interest Margins. *Journal of Banking & Finance, 37*(11), 4144–4156.

Pessarossi, P., & Vinas, F. (2015). *The Supply of Long-Term Credit After a Funding Shock: Evidence from 2007–2009* (Documents de travail du Centre d'Economie de la Sorbonne 73).

Strahan, P. (2010). Liquidity Production in 21st Century Banking. In A. N. Berger, P. Molyneux, & J. O. S. Wilson (Eds.), *The Oxford Handbook of Banking*. Oxford: Oxford University Press.

Vazquez, F., & Federico, P. (2015). Bank Funding Structures and Risk: Evidence from the Global Financial Crisis. *Journal of Banking & Finance, 61*, 1–14.

CHAPTER 8

Conclusion

Liquidity tensions during the GFC, which proved threatening to bank solvency and consequently stability, immediately attracted the attention of regulators and numerous bank scholars, all attributing the blame for these liquidity problems on the lack of prudential regulations and on non-harmonized rules. These led several banks to manage liquidity risk poorly. Indeed, the banks were under the delusion that capital compliance was enough to guarantee stability. Liquidity risk was seriously underestimated. The GFC demonstrated that even well-capitalized banks faced liquidity problems jeopardizing the stability of the bank itself. Hence, the growing awareness that bank stability could no longer be guaranteed by regulation based solely on the adequacy of capital. In terms of baking stability, compliance with stringent capital requirements was necessary, but insufficient. Liquidity risk cannot be averted by a more substantial capital base, i.e. the increase in bank capital does not solve liquidity problems. The crisis showed that a solid liquidity base, reinforced by robust supervisory practices, is equally important.

The GFC also highlighted the tight interdependence of liquidity and solvency and the fact that the interdependence of financial and capital equilibrium had been inadequately monitored. The crisis in liquidity aggravated solvency risk and inadequate capitalization was, in turn, an important factor in liquidity risk.

What emerged from the crisis was the understanding that capital and liquidity are equally important for bank stability, in light of which, in

L. Chiaramonte, *Bank Liquidity and the Global Financial Crisis*,
Palgrave Macmillan Studies in Banking and Financial Institutions,
https://doi.org/10.1007/978-3-319-94400-5_8

2010, the Basel Committee reviewed the Basel II Accord and introduced new prudential regulations in its place, the so-called Basel III Accord. In addition to the qualitative and quantitative improvement in capital requirements (inadequate at the time of the GFC and unable to prevent massive losses), for the first time the new regulations introduced two liquidity ratios: the LCR, a short-term liquidity standard, and the NSFR, related to structural liquidity.

Although more stringent liquidity regulations can reduce the risk of bank runs and the freezing of the interbank market, there has been a vigorous debate on the potentially negative impact of liquidity regulation, which could impact both at the individual bank (microeconomic) and market (macroeconomic) level. The positive or negative impact depends on the strategies of banks to comply with the Basel III liquidity ratios, each of which is likely to have different welfare implications. Alternatively, a bank can increase liquidity ratios by altering its balance sheet size or by modifying the composition of its assets or liabilities.

Many studies look into the effects of capital requirements; relatively few investigate the effects of liquidity requirements. Partly, this is because capital requirements have been in place for a considerable time and over more than one business cycle, while liquidity standards were implemented only after the recent financial crisis.

On the one hand, from a microeconomic point of view, the limited empirical results, albeit mainly focused on the impact of the LCR, does not seem to show a reduction in credit from banks following the introduction of Basel III liquidity requirements. Not only, several authors also find that the liquidity regulation may reduce the fall in bank credit in response to liquidity shocks, resulting in a lower reduction in aggregate output associated with banking crises than otherwise would be the case. Vice versa, the results of the empirical literature on the impact on bank profitability are ambiguous. To date, it is unclear whether net interest income increases or decreases in response to liquidity requirements. Overall, the impact on both two areas: bank lending and profitability need further investigation.

On the other hand, from a macroeconomic point of view, recent studies agree in attributing a positive effect to liquidity standards in reducing bank failures and improving overall banking stability. Indeed, the compliance with the Basel III liquidity ratios seems to reduce the excessive maturity transformation, that was the key source of bank instability during the GFC.

Again at the macroeconomic level, the imposition of the Basel III liquidity ratios has had a limited impact on lending and should not reduce aggregate consumption and investment or GDP.

These results are of particular interest to regulators who, through the new Basel III rules, have sought to ensure financial stability without imposing excessive regulatory costs which would have negative repercussions on bank behaviour and all the economic entities related to them.

Despite these concerns over the impact of alignment with Basel III liquidity standards, a recent overview of the QIS results by the Basel Committee (based on a representative sample of banks in 27 countries over the period 2012–2016) shows that banks are generally already compliant with the LCR and the NSFR, with values well above the minimum 100% threshold set by Basel III Accord, and growing continuously. This is the case particularly for the short-term liquidity ratio. The weighted average values of NSFR, also higher than the minimum threshold, are below those of the LCR, with moderate growth. On the whole, banks in Europe and the Americas tend to have weighted average values of LCR and NSFR that are lower than banks in the 'rest of the world'.

Finally, with reference to the strategies adopted to meet Basel III liquidity ratios, the results of the QIS show that the increase in weighted average LCR is due mainly to a decrease in net outflows. This is true for all three geographical areas. While the increase in NSFR follows the increase in ASF, therefore on the liabilities side, except for Europe where the structural liquidity ratio is driven by the decline in RSF, thus from the assets side of the bank.

In light of this picture, which is on the whole less worrying than the regulators feared, thanks to the introduction of the LCR and NSFR, the overall assessment of the probable impact of the new Basel III liquidity rules on banks and financial markets is not a simple matter and requires further empirical investigation. As things stand, the Basel Committee may in the future issue new documents for the integration and/or amendment of liquidity legislation, as occurred recently (in December 2017) for capital requirements (BCBS 2017). Both the current empirical evidence and the QIS, suggest caution before any definitive conclusions are drawn.

Reference

Basel Committee on Banking Supervision (BCBS). (2017, December). *Basel III: Finalising Post-crisis Reforms*. Basel: Bank for International Settlements (BIS).

Index

L. Chiaramonte, *Bank Liquidity and the Global Financial Crisis*,
Palgrave Macmillan Studies in Banking and Financial Institutions,
https://doi.org/10.1007/978-3-319-94400-5

The manufacturer's authorised representative in the EU is Springer Nature Customer Service Centre GmbH, Europaplatz 3, 69115 Heidelberg, Germany. If you have any concerns regarding our products, please contact ProductSafety@springernature.com

Printed and bound by CPI Group (UK) Ltd, Croydon, CR0 4YY
25/09/2026
02222849-0003